Trollope
Interviews and Recollections

TROLLOPE

Interviews and Recollections

Edited by

R. C. Terry

M

MACMILLAN
PRESS

First published 1987

Published by
THE MACMILLAN PRESS LTD
Houndmills, Basingstoke, Hampshire RG21 2XS
and London
Companies and representatives
throughout the world

Printed in Hong Kong

British Library Cataloguing in Publication Data
Trollope: interviews and recollections
1. Trollope, Anthony – Biography
2. Novelists, English – 19th century –
Biography
I. Terry, R. C.
823′.8   PR5686
ISBN 0–333–36664–6

For Paul and David

I feel that Trollope and I are living here together, for I seem to spend so much of my time with him, especially in the long hours after midnight. We then wander about Barsetshire in a heavyish carriage drawn by two slow horses with long tails and the motors whiz by us, but with Anthony on the box we do reach our destination which they perhaps don't.

(*Letters of J. M. Barrie*, ed. Viola Meynell, 1942)

Contents

List of Plates

List of Abbreviations

The following abbreviations are used in the editorial matter:

ANZ   Anthony Trollope, *Australia and New Zealand*, 2 vols (1873)

Auto.   Anthony Trollope, *An Autobiography* (1883; Oxford: World's Classics, 1961)

Commentary   Michael Sadleir, *Trollope: A Commentary* (1927; rev. edn 1945)

FT   Frances Eleanor Trollope, *Frances Trollope: Her Life and Literary Work from George III to Victoria*, 2 vols (1895)

Letters   *The Letters of Anthony Trollope*, ed. N. John Hall, 2 vols (Stanford, 1983)

WIR   Thomas Adolphus Trollope, *What I Remember*, 2 vols (1887)

Introduction

The pitfalls of writing lives were much in Trollope's mind at the time he was himself the subject of a sketch by T. H. S. Escott. His own short study of Thackeray had appeared in May 1879, he had already completed a life of Lord Palmerston, and his *Life of Cicero* would appear in 1880. 'How hard it is to put into words all the nebulous ideas as to another man's identity', he remarked to Escott.[1] His reservations about biographical studies had been voiced with typical vigour some years earlier. He found Forster's *Life of Charles Dickens* distasteful for its personal disclosures and raged at the mock humility in Macready's *Reminiscences*:

> These books do not make me pleased with humanity. It is disgusting to see the self-consciousness and irritated crying for applause such men as Macready & Dickens have exhibited; – & which dear old Thackeray did exhibit also. It astonishes me not that men should feel it, but that they shew it. I am sure of myself that whenever such a disease has been oppressing me I have been able to tread it out.   (*Letters*, ii, 671)

No one would accuse Trollope of crying for applause. Indeed, his distaste for personal disclosure suggests, like Mr Chadband's sermon to Jo, that in putting him on show – even though what follows is not a biography – we are about to address a very tough subject.

Like others in the series, however, this book is close kin to biography, and its justification may be urged against Trollope's forthright comments above that, in presenting the man in his habit as he lived, at least it seeks safety in numbers, drawing on the testimonies of those who knew him, some as intimate friends, some as casual and not always felicitous acquaintances. It has the advantage, therefore, of cumulative and dissonant views in a variety of voices, agreeable, querulous, flattering or disapproving, as the speakers reveal something of themselves as well as of him. I think Trollope might consider this kind of record worthwhile – he might even concede it the truest sort of biography.

Although less abundantly chronicled than either Dickens or Thackeray, Trollope enjoyed a double life as civil servant and author, travelled extensively throughout the world, pursued a vigorous social round in London clubs, and hunted with a frantic and foolhardy passion. These occupations brought him into contact with many whose testimonies make up this collection. And, despite Trollope's warnings, an editor is enticed into imposing some kind of unity on this portrait which scholar or general reader may conveniently relate to available biographies.[2]

'What sort of person was Anthony Trollope?' The question was asked again by N. John Hall in 1982, a question, he suggested, as difficult to answer as the more important one concerning the nature of his appeal as a novelist. A. L. Rowse, too, in the same volume celebrating the Trollope centenary, puzzled over the novelist, concluding that the paradox lay in his genius: 'Trollope was such an obsessed person, for all his apparent normality.' In a recent book, Andrew Wright included a chapter entitled 'What the Autobiography Says and Leaves Unsaid' arguing that the author's forthrightness concealed much despite the tone of frank confession. Even his letters, Hall said, 'reveal the inner man only indirectly'; he can be found in them, 'but one must work at it'.[3] As Michael Sadleir observed in his pioneering study in 1927, 'Of self-portraiture he was very sparing' (*Commentary*, p. 110). Certainly to know Trollope well, what follows should be read in conjunction with *An Autobiography*, published posthumously in 1883, and that recent treasure-house of anecdotes, the two-volume edition of *The Letters of Anthony Trollope* published in 1983.

Unlike Dickens and Thackeray, Trollope offered that mixed blessing to scholarly posterity, an account of his life. The *Autobiography* bears witness to Trollope's forceful personality: his intense ambition, craving for love and popularity, and passion for doing everything at full stretch – work at the Post Office, literary endeavours of many kinds, hunting and social pursuits down to the most meticulous counting of pages written and sums earned. At the same time he is reticent about many personal matters where we long for enlightenment, and positively misleading where a judgement of his own merits is concerned. For all its clarity the *Autobiography* seems half designed to throw us off the scent, and Victorian distaste for self-display does not entirely

explain the mystery; his most truthful work, it has all the
resonance and ambiguity of great fiction. His opening statement
reads: 'That I, or any man, should tell everything of himself, I
hold to be impossible.... But this I protest; – that nothing that I
say shall be untrue' (*Auto.*, i) and in those splendid final cadences
he reminds the reader of his pledge: 'It will not, I trust, be
supposed by any reader that I have intended in this so-called
autobiography to give a record of my inner life. No man ever did
so truly – and no man ever will' (xx). This last comment contains a
double irony revealing the man and the artist: the man, perceptive
enough about himself to know that the whole truth cannot be told,
and the writer, canny enough to imply that he could say more but
won't. I imagine Trollope at some celestial airport flourishing the
book at customs officials with a breezy 'Nothing to declare' and
vanishing into the night chuckling and yet not fully aware of the
value of what he has brought in his baggage.

At any rate the *Autobiography* is a doubtful asset for such an
undertaking as the present volume since it casts a shadow over
recollection, its powerful story-telling undoubtedly influencing
the way people remembered Trollope. I have elsewhere called it
Trollope's *David Copperfield* but it evokes other fictions too;[4]
indeed, Trollope remarks that looking back on events from so long
an interval (he was 61 when he wrote it) he can write of his parents
'almost as coldly as I have often done some intended pathos in
fiction' (*Auto.*, iii). Nor surprisingly then, the account of his
wretched father engaged in his unending task of compiling an
Encyclopaedia Ecclesiastica and sinking into calomel-induced
torpor reminds us of George Eliot's Mr Casaubon; while the
lonely child facing the loquacious, dazzling Frances Trollope,
returning from her adventures like a being from another world,
sounds like a less savage version of Thackeray's little Rawdon
eyeing his mother on rare occasions when she deigned to notice
him. Or consider the account of his adolescence in dingy London
lodgings when he started at the Post Office, being taken up for
debt (not imprisoned, surely, but 'secured' as Harold Skimpole
was in *Bleak House*): is there not a touch of Coavinses in the
importunate creditor – 'If you only would be punctual'? This is
not to deny Trollope's truth to events, but to suggest again the
inferences of the fictional mode and to emphasise, as Trollope
does, the slippery nature of biographical study. Julian Hawthorne
said we read between the lines of the *Autobiography* and discover

Trollope despite his attempts to *dis*cover himself to us.[5] For all that I do not think the lines too difficult to read between: what we discover, allowing for a customary number of defence mechanisms, quirks and self-delusions, is an eminently sane, generous and likeable man of monumental integrity. Cecilia Meetkerke, a relative, regretted a certain 'misleading reticence' in the *Autobiography* but concluded that the book would live as 'the exact and faithful portrait of the man'. W. Lucas Collins went further: 'Every word', he said, 'reveals to me the man himself'. His life, said Donald Macleod, in spite of incessant toil was an exceedingly happy one. 'He gave the impression', said Viscount Bryce, 'of liking the world he lived in, and being satisfied with his own place in it'.

Yet there are discordant notes in some recollections. Just as his fiction has provoked divergent views, so his person seems to have caused some puzzlement. Bryce said 'one could never quite recognise in him the delineator of Lily Dale'. Even Julian Hawthorne's admirable essay concludes 'he was something of a paradox – an entertaining contradiction'. Michael Sadleir argued the case for a sensitive soul so deeply affected by childhood experiences that he created for himself in adult life a second skin and played in public the roaring boy. George Gissing was to call him the 'big, blusterous, genial brute of a Trollope'.[6] The *Autobiography* catered strongly to this reading of his character with its accounts of cruel privation, desperation brought close to suicide, and craving for love (somewhat disingenuously labelled 'a certain weakness in my own character' (*Auto.*, ix)). Elizabeth Bowen's radio piece in 1946 elaborated the question 'Were there two Trollopes? The anxious outcast, the successful man of the world – was the first, perhaps, never quite absorbed and lost in the second?'[7] Over the years there have been more doubles to account for Trollope's private and public selves, official and unofficial.

Psychological explanations are fortunately not the province of this book, although it seems pertinent to observe that whatever the complexes wrought by childhood misery Trollope must have hidden or quelled them magnificently, since his contemporaries were quite prepared to take him at face value. Not everyone would have agreed with Hawthorne that 'it was impossible to help liking such a man at first sight' but, beyond the initial shock his manner and appearance occasioned, people quickly warmed to him. He had a knack of winning people over, and even quieter souls admired him. By 1852, long before literary success had arrived, Trollope could write to his mother 'I can't fancy anyone being much happier than I am, or having less in the world to complain of. It often strikes me how wonderfully well I have fallen on my feet' (*Letters*, i, 30), and one can surely believe the tone of his letter to George Henry Lewes in 1861: 'As to myself personally, I have daily to wonder at the continued run of domestic & worldly happiness which has been granted me; – to wonder at it as well as to be thankful for it' (*Letters*, i, 145).[8] A. M. Cunynghame, a Post Office colleague, recalled a journey in late 1858 when Trollope suddenly announced 'Cunynghame, I must have a sleep. Wake me in 20 minutes, will you?' A man who can set himself to sleep almost at will (as several testify) is unlikely to be riven with self-doubt or anxiety; rather the reverse. It bespeaks an admirably composed psyche. There is tremendous assurance and health about the character who emerges from the following testimonies as to assert the categorical truth of Trollope's fine adieu in the *Autobiography*: 'I will not say that I have never scorched a finger, – but I carry no ugly wounds' (xx).

The foundation of the 'two Trollopes' myth may be traced in several accounts, as, for example, W. P. Frith's: 'The books, full of gentleness, grace and refinement; the writer of them, bluff, loud, stormy, and contentious.' Lady Rose Fane found him 'detestable – vulgar, noisy & domineering ... and unlike his books as possible'. But then she found Dickens vulgar too.[9] To James Payn he was 'the least literary man of letters I ever met'. People often bring up the contrast between the man and his books. Meeting the novelist at St Andrews where Trollope was staying with his friend and publisher, John Blackwood, the Revd A. K. H. Boyd looked forward to meeting the distinguished author of *The Last Chronicle* which he was then enjoying. To his horror he found him overbearing and exhibitionistic. On the golf course his 'voice was heard all over the Links' and when he made a bad shot he fell down with pretended agony, only to start up again with a real yell because he had fallen on a golf-ball in his pocket. He swore, too. Such callow hero worship, one can only conclude, deserves what it gets; but then the contrast between the sublimity of the work and the coarseness of its creator has always been perplexing, as Peter Schaffer shows in *Amadeus*, his play about Salieri and Mozart. A quite opposite impression from Boyd's of 'one of these never-to-be-forgotten visits' to St Andrews is recorded by John Blackwood's daughter. She describes him on the golf course pretending to faint when he made a bad shot, 'his immense weight causing a sort of earthquake on the sandy ground', riding with her mother on the sands, and joining in the jokes around the dinner table. Among friends Trollope would sometimes unbosom himself and be quite relaxed. John Blackwood recalled the end of a holiday: 'I had a farewell bathe with Anthony yesterday evening, and we parted almost with tears at Loch Coruisk.' Such differing views are some of the accompanying vexations of celebrity, a phenomenon that began in Victorian times. As Yeats was to put it:

> the children's eyes
> In momentary wonder stare upon
> Sixty year old smiling public man
> ('Among School Children')

Certainly Trollope put on something of an act where he was conscious of being on view. In Boston in 1861 Clara Kellogg, the American soprano, found him 'full of himself' and thoroughly 'on the make'.

To see Trollope hiding his private self by making the public self a scapegoat and a safety valve is tempting, therefore, and certainly more attractive than explaining the slight contradiction in his personality as compensation for a massive inferiority complex. As N. John Hall has said, a great deal of irony in Trollope's conversation was apt to be missed, and this gave rise to misunderstandings Trollope rather relished.[10] To acquaintances who went on first impressions, the two Trollopes made a Jekyll and Hyde picture, the nice one beavering away in his study over noble jilts and gentle clergymen, the other a monster who leered at you over the cruet.

Trollope the Terrible – 'he who with the aspect of a wild boar, and with not infrequent resemblance to the manners of the same' as Frederick Greenwood put it[11] – undoubtedly had his gentler side, chiefly to be appreciated in the context of his family and of his wife, Rose, in particular. She is a shadowy figure in these pages but a vital element in the story. There is a good deal of truth in Julian Hawthorne's enigmatic comment, 'But his wife was his books, though not at all literary, and, in fact, declaiming that she wished Anthony was not a writer.' Tantalising glimpses appear here and there of Rose at home with the cows, chickens and domestic joys while Trollope goes banging about the world; Rose travelling with far too many hatboxes and portmanteaux; one observer comments on her exquisitely tiny feet; another, more waspishly, sees a well-dressed woman with her hair *coiffé en cheveux* (hatless) but with a white rose in it that ruined the effect. In addition to such minute casual references, this volume includes a little more of her in the early sections concerning Trollope's family.

Much of Rose's significance may be inferred from comments about hearth and home. Trollope enjoyed the warm fireside which Thackeray lacked, and many reminiscences surround the elegant house at Waltham Cross, Hertfordshire, and later the town house in Montagu Square. There is a vivid glimpse of George Smith staying with Trollope and discovering that on mornings when he did not hunt 'he dragged about a garden roller at what might be called a canter',[12] and there are charming memories of Waltham from Anne Thackeray and others. Trollope, after all, had his calmer moments, none better described than by W. Lucas Collins: 'in the warm summer evenings, the party would adjourn after dinner to the lawn, where wines and fruits were laid out under the fine old cedar tree and many a good story was told while the tobacco smoke went curling up into the soft twilight'.

One thing everyone agrees on: Trollope was *loud* – really loud. Wilkie Collins said he was an incarnate gale of wind; 'he blew off my hat; he turned my umbrella inside out'. James Payn noted that 'his manners were rough, and so to speak, tumultuous'. To Eleanor Smyth, daughter of Sir Rowland Hill, he was Dickens's Mr Boythorn, minus the canary. There was 'the view-halloo in his heartiness' according to Donald Macleod. To another witness, a rather pleasant voice had been spoiled by so much hallooing, although Anne Thackeray called it a 'deep cheerful lispy voice'. Sometimes the noise got on people's nerves: Lady Russell objected to his drowning out at dinner Huxley who was, she thought, far more worth hearing. Thackeray recalled being outside the Garrick Club and hearing Trollope and Reade going at it inside: 'What must they have been at eighteen?' said Thackeray. In the highlands with John Burns, the chairman of Cunard Line, Trollope told stories far into the night, and next day one old gentleman complained to the landlord that the party had grown far too convivial. ' "I am bound to confess that there was much loud talking and laughter," the landlord admitted, "but they had nothing stronger than tea and fresh herrings." "Bless me", rejoined the old gentleman, "if that is so what would they be after dinner?".' After his return from Australia in 1873, Trollope got together with his old friend, W. E. 'Billy' Russell, at the Garrick. According to Shirley Brooks the party grew steadily wilder: 'When they were at cards we heard Anthony's thunder, and then a wild banshee cry from the Irishman, till we threatened them with the police. Then Anthony said we were conventional tyrants, and Russell said in a weeping voice that Ireland was accustomed to be trampled on.' 'His vociferous roughness repelled many,' said Garnett, 'but was the disguise of real tenderness of heart.' As Edmund Yates said, 'it was just his manner, many agreed, but as Mr Mantalini said of Ralph Nickleby it was "a demd uncomfortable private-madhouse kind of manner all the same" '.[13]

The manner was undoubtedly hard to take sometimes; when he was a house-guest, for example, as one postal surveyor recorded: 'Doors slammed, footsteps resounded, and a general whirlwind arose, as he came or returned from his bath, or walked out in the garden.' In buoyant spirits during hunting parties he was louder than ever. One observer captured a particularly vivid scene of the novelist preparing for the day's sport and peering around the bedroom talking to various missing parts of his hunting kit: 'Oh, Mrs Sock, where have you got to? Not under there? No. Perhaps the chest of drawers. Why, I do delcare, there you are hiding near the curtain. I've got you, ha! ha! ha! Now, Mr Top Boot, where is your twin? Can't go hunting alone, you know.'

High spirits came naturally, and Trollope relished the effects. Children were spellbound when he called. 'He came in at the door like a frantic windmill', said one eyewitness. The daughters of his friend and publisher, George Smith, would imitate him up and down the carpet, mimicking the deep voice after watching him from the upstairs balcony. The girls caught one interesting detail – he ruffled his hair *before* entering the drawing-room. Was this a self-aware gesture of the wild man people expected? The appearance was daunting enough. He was about 5 feet 10 inches in height, although many recall him as being 'tall'. To Julian Hawthorne he was 'of middle height'. Hain Friswell said he looked taller than he was. That was because of his bulky frame. It is doubtful that such a man could have moved quietly; he rode heavily and was often dangerously insecure – escaping serious injury by a hair's breadth – as several witnesses verify. He once took a diet to lose weight, and, according to George Eliot, looked better for it. 'He is a strange-looking person', wrote the *Boston Daily Evening Transcript* in June 1868. 'His complexion and general bearing are much like Dickens's. His body is large and well preserved. He dresses like a gentleman and not like a fop, but he squeezes his small well-shaped hand into a very small pair of coloured kids. He "wears a cane", as all Englishmen do.' Trollope snorted when he saw the report: 'I never wear gloves. What fools people are' (*Letters*, I, 437). His beard was worthy of the rhyme by Lear. Speckled with ash from his beloved havanas (he was a devoted cigar smoker and kept racks of them in his study), it was enormous, wild and unruly. During his visit to America in 1861, one fascinated though disapproving young lady confided in her diary her impression of Trollope as 'a great homely, red, stupid-faced Englishman, with a disgusting beard of iron grey'. His eyes, variously described as hazel, grey, or blue going to black, also compelled attention, especially when, through tiny gold-rimmed spectacles, he fixed them upon his interlocutor with disturbing intensity. Charles Tuckerman's recollections (not previously documented) are the result of several meetings both in America and London, and they typify the effect he had on casual acquaintances. They stress his bounce and aggressive cordiality but they hint at his magnetism and good sense:

My brother[14] was sitting in his library in New York, when, in response to his 'Come in', the door flew open, and a stout, hairy-faced, ruddy-complexioned Englishman burst in upon his solitude like a rough shaggy Newfoundland dog about to leap upon him in the exuberance of animal spirits.

'My name is Anthony Trollope!' exclaimed the visitor in a brusque voice, 'and I've brought you a letter of introduction from a mutual friend in England.' ...

He wore spectacles, through which he seemed to inspect men and things with a quiet scrutiny, as if making perpetual memoranda for future use. In conversation he would sometimes ask a question, or make a suggestion respecting people to whom he had been introduced, which indicated a keen perception of the weak spots in their characters; but this was always said in a good-humoured way that left no sting behind it.

From Post Office colleagues come more details to round out the description, one particularly striking: 'His method of attacking work was rather odd, and I have seen him slogging away at papers at a stand-up desk, with his handkerchief stuffed into his mouth, and his hair on end, as though he could barely contain himself.' Here is a man almost delirious with passion for the job in hand. Nothing more clearly shows Trollope's appetite for work. 'Work to him was a necessity and a satisfaction', said his brother in some wonderment (*WIR*, ii, 358). Cuthbert Bede had heard that he was 'good for sixteen hours' in a day, and his recollection shows how quickly Trollope could also recover from a heavy night. He had an 'iron constitution', said Escott.

He brought the same fierce energy to his travelling, rejoicing in being on the move, oblivious to the upheaval and discomforts of mid-Victorian journeys. He was an adventurous man, this quiet chronicler of home counties goings-on. What he did on those fact-finding tours of America, the West Indies, Australia and South Africa, may be found in his travel books, but accounts below reveal this unique element in Trollope. None of the Victorian novelists was his equal in finding out how other people lived and worked. Going down a mineshaft on a bucket contraption suspended on a rope, battling blizzards or intense heat, hunting kangaroo, cavorting in hot springs with Maori damsels – he threw himself into new experiences with such zest we marvel at his appetite for adventure. People abroad took to him just as they had done in the early days in Ireland.

Several instances of Trollope in conversation are given in the collection, including the longest interview on record, his spirited court room testimony at Tralee Court House in 1849. Unlike Dickens he did not converse well and has left no coruscating witticisms. He once claimed his brother, Tom, was the better conversationalist, but he would attack any topic with vehement satisfaction and an energy which was partly a legacy from his mother. It was more a matter of tossing and goring his opponent than exchange. His dinner in September 1861 with American hosts who included Lowell, Hawthorne, Emerson and the Autocrat himself, Oliver Wendell Holmes, is representative. Trollope was an impulsive arguer who spoke his mind, even before it was made up sometimes; the classic, at a meeting of postal colleagues, is 'I differ from you entirely: What was it you said?' G. A. Sala's recollection of the novelist in full cry at Smith's party launching the *Cornhill*

Magazine is eloquent testimony to his tendency to overdo things in his haste to be among the group, and there is a similar touching quality about the anecdote of his performance at one of George Eliot's soirées at The Priory. This is particularly interesting because it voices Trollope's favourite metaphor about his work as sitting at the desk with a piece of cobbler's wax sticking to his seat. One witness recalled that a thrill of horror ran round the assembled company as he accompanied the words with inelegant gestures towards the seat of inspiration. But it is typical of Trollope that having, as he thought, no right to compare his work with George Eliot's, he hastily made amends by pointing out that her more discriminating sensibility worked in an entirely more subtle fashion. Trollope was shrewder than his coarse manner suggested. Listening to the historian, George Bancroft, at a meeting of the New York Historical Society, he turned to his companion when the speaker had made a point eliciting applause and whispered 'Do you suppose he himself believes what he is saying?' Indeed the novelist relished an occasional irony which often went unnoticed: the same companion (Charles Tuckerman) recalled a time when Trollope asked with some asperity why he had not asked to see him instead of leaving a card at the house:

> I told him that as the servant, in reply to my inquiry, said he was in his library, I did not wish to intrude when, probably, he was in the midst of romance-writing, composing, perhaps, a love-letter from one of his heroines. 'What if I was?', he asked, grinning like a hyena behind his hairy visage. 'Romance-writing with me is a mere mechanical pursuit; it is a *business* and I intend to bring up my son in the same occupation.'

Trollope despised petty snobbery or affectations. Mark Twain got it wrong when he accused Trollope in company with the fellow humorist Joaquin Miller, Tom Hughes and the Hon. Frederick Leveson Gower of toadying to the man of rank. Trollope, in fact, made rather a point of playing down honours and title. A postal colleague recalled him slurring over his family history and belittling the Post Office right royally, leaving out the 'General' and writing with a little 'p' and 'o' 'as though it were a village sub-office retailing stamps with tobacco and onions'. He would goad Thackeray's friend, W. F. Synge, to abuse authority, 'You must come if only to abuse Lord Clarendon [Synge's chief at the F.O.]' (*Letters*, 1, 324).

Cecilia Meetkerke (who gives the best account of how Trollope came to dispose of Mrs Proudie) claimed that he once told her he enjoyed contradicting, and she observed that in the genuine joy of the fight he would sometimes forget which was his own side of the question. 'His nature forced him to take the lead in everything', said a contributor to the *Dublin Review*, and this was especially so in conversation. Thomas Hardy claimed he 'just went on, indifferent to attention and to other people'. This is borne out in Trollope's behaviour on the platform for a debate on the Eastern Question in December 1876 when he just would not sit down: when, after bell-ringing and other hints, the Duke of Westminster as chairman tugged at his coat-tails, Trollope turned round and said 'Please leave my coat alone' and went on speaking. But, as W. Lucas Collins said, geniality was his outstanding characteristic and that made him easy of address. G. H. Lewes noted in his diary (4 June 1866) a ferocious argument Trollope had with Alexander Bain: 'Bain startled us by his anti-Christian onslaught and Trollope amused us by his defence.'[15] Outrageous provocation was a favourite gambit. Once, at dinner with John Blackwood, he taunted the publisher with his Toryism and attachment to Disraeli. The banter was obviously good natured, as George Smalley no doubt appreciated when, calling upon the novelist one day towards noon, he was bidden to take breakfast. He had breakfasted earlier, he said. 'What,' Trollope roared, 'do you mean to say you are not man enough to eat two breakfasts?'

Nor were young people intimidated. Walter Herries Pollock was one of several young writers who valued Trollope's friendship and counsel. Pollock observed:

> To younger men his ways and manner had the special charm that, without for a moment losing dignity, he put them on an equality with himself. He happened to be older, and therefore more experienced than they were – I do not think it ever occurred to him that he was more clever or more gifted – and whatever help might come to them from his greater experience was at their service as between comrade and comrade. It was impossible for the shyest young man to be with him without feeling at ease.

Evidence abounds as to Trollope's gregariousness and warmth. Julian Hawthorne believed that 'no man in London society was more generally liked'. Phrases recur about him as 'a good fellow modelled on Silenus'; 'kindly, despotic, irritable and generous'; 'one of the heartiest, most genuine, moral and generous men'; 'a good fellow, a warm friend, a brave soul, a genial companion'. To Henry James he appeared 'gross and repulsive' in face and manner, but 'he was *bon enfant* when you talked with him'. Carlyle took to him at once though he was to abuse him as 'a distylish little pug' for criticising Ruskin. Lever could not call Trollope pleasant but was devoted to him. Even in the hostile comments of Hill, or Yates, or Hain Friswell, there is a note of grudging admiration. Mrs Oliphant's tribute captures nicely the wondering affection Trollope's nature called up: 'The systematic way in which Mr Trollope grinds out his work is very funny', she wrote in May 1876. 'It must have answered, however, for he seems extremely comfortable; keeps a homely brougham, rides in the Park, etc.'[16]

Thackeray's affection is well known although not translated into any detailed notes save the remarks on pp. 65–8 below, but Dickens's response is typically generous and just: 'He is a perfect cordial to me ... the heartiest and best of fellows.' George Eliot along with G. H. Lewes, his earliest literary friend, judged him 'one of the heartiest, most genuine, moral and generous men'. These are the conclusions of the most vigorous descriptions in the collection, by Viscount Bryce, Frederick Locker-Lampson, Julian Hawthorne, E. A. Freeman and Mabel Wotton.

Trollope's representative Englishness is a recurrent theme. It is, of course, the basis of that most famous of comments by Nathaniel Hawthorne about the novels: 'just as English as a beefsteak'. Henry Adams called him 'a rosy-gilled John Bull' and James Russell Lowell referred to a 'big red-faced, rather underbred Englishman of the bald-with-spectacles type'. Kate Field called him an 'admirable specimen of a frank and loyal Englishman': to Amelia Edwards he was also typically English, 'bluff, hearty, straightforward'. But what is the typical Englishman asked George Smalley. There is no such thing except on the stage and then he is a caricature. There were many types, Smalley concluded, and then proceeded to define which one Trollope exemplified:

He had the bluffness which is supposed to be characteristic of the race; the hearty manner, the love of outdoor life; the loyalty and the red face which belong to the country squire. This man of letters seemed to have spent all his life in the country, growing turnips and preserving game.

Charles Kent in 1871 also claimed Anthony Trollope as a thoroughly representative Englishman, 'as typical of the genius of the age in which he lives as the mass of his own imaginary characters'. He continued:

Happily we can speak of him now with that increased frankness with which one talks of a friend who is no longer present, but who has only just taken his departure. [Trollope was on his way to Australia.] What is specially remarkable about Anthony Trollope is this, that both personally and as a writer he combines the most thorough manliness with the keenest regard for, and the fullest recognition of, the frivolities, the fripperies, the chit-chat going on all about him; in so much that this stalwart, athletic huntsman, who is most in his glory, one would think when throned in the saddle and galloping across country, well to the front, delights just as much in jotting down, pen in hand, page after page, the love-prattle of any number of young ladies and gentlemen.[17]

Manly, loyal, honest, frank – it was an image Trollope hardly needed to work at (although the *Autobiography* implies that he did); it fitted to a tee, like the Henry VIII costume many a Victorian worthy donned for fancy-dress balls. It made people comfortable with him when he roared – it was a British lion after all – and it helps explain why he was so popular in society.

This rather Gilbertian persona of the true-born Englishman allowed Trollope to merge with his peers, something he had longed to do since boyhood. 'I have ever had a wish', he said, 'to be liked by those around me, – a wish that during the first half of my life was never gratified' (*Auto.*, ix). Indeed, he photographs like a score of his contemporaries, and friends often make comparisons of him with others – Tom Taylor, Browning, Walter Besant. We also find him described in stereotypes, as though he would pass muster for a seaman, squire, farmer, doctor, professor, family lawyer of the old school and a cross between a country farmer and a whipper-in.

The author himself, as well as his fiction, mirrored the

Victorians as they liked to see themselves – much to Dickens's amusement: free from snobbery, quick to dispose of cant and humbug, generous to the underprivileged, enterprising, industrious, honest, sound in money and judgement, reliable in love and war. As paterfamilias, career civil servant, artist, social being, sportsman and gentleman, Trollope did not disappoint. But although he was thoroughly of, and at one with, his time, he was, as a man, more playfully ironical and, as a writer, more subversive than his own age generally realised.

Trollope's personality is not as complex as that of either Dickens or Thackeray. Beyond the appealing over-simplification of the two Trollopes – 'outwardly a curmudgeon, inwardly the soul of good fellowship' as Walter Sichel put it – there is an undivided wholeness about the man. He fended off the world with hearty bravura, and whatever ghosts of his unhappy childhood returned to haunt him, he could command them away when he chose. Donald Macleod maintained that those who came to know Trollope after he had become famous saw no trace of the sorrow or hardships of his early life described in the *Autobiography*. He did not rank himself with Thackeray or George Eliot but his self-esteem was higher than he let on, and with all his genuine modesty and clear-sightedness there was some vanity. Why not? He had every right to consider himself a superior man; he *had* triumphed over the odds. Why, for instance, did he among the novelists leave an autobiography at all? To set the record straight certainly and do some stocktaking and realign future goals perhaps, but at bottom with pride to show them all 'There, I've done it!' 'Awfully "interesting to himself" he be': Carlyle was feeling waspish when he wrote that, but it contains a grain of truth. More justly, I think, Frederic Harrison, praising the *Autobiography*, speaks of its 'genial egoism', and indeed it gives no grounds for reading self-pity, inverted snobbery or false pride as a sub-text. Roaring or still, vulgar or fastidious, apoplectic or tender, Trollope was in himself all that his fiction proclaimed him to be – honest, direct, sincere, lovable, worthy of that compliment paid to his work as whatsoever spoke of that which was lovely and of good report. Few among his contemporaries achieved such equilibrium. He had an enviably equal mind[18] (the phrase occurs in *Orley Farm*, an ideal introduction to his work), and just as the fiction voices his integrity and the *Autobiography* reveals his honesty, both are consonant with the person as the following accounts present him. Escott has the gist of it when he claims that Trollope the man is as Trollope the artist: 'the popular and successful author is the straightforward and unreserved friend; the courageous, candid, plain-speaking companion'.

This book, like its predecessors in the series, arranges groups of comment or single testimonies in roughly chronological sequence through childhood, school, Post Office service, to the author's literary life, home and leisure pursuits, the recollections of eminent friends in art and letters, some parodies and verse tributes, a lengthy section on his journeys about the world, and accounts of his last years. Critical estimates of Trollope's work have been excluded, with the exception of an excerpt from Henry James's perceptive essay.

Trollope belonged to a family of writers and for this reason the collection uses materials by his brother Thomas Adolphus and his sister-in-law Frances Eleanor Trollope. It is helpful to have their versions (from sources hard to come by for the general reader), partly to correct some of Anthony's own accounts: if as a child he was not quite the Benjamin brother Tom called him neither was he quite the odd man out he offered posterity. T. H. S. Escott, notoriously inaccurate about details, may be tolerated in the context of his feeling for the novelist and his position as the first biographer. Trotting in the novelist's wake he noted items with an immediacy worth recalling. Materials which may be helpful to the student and general reader include 'A Trollope Chronology' and 'Suggestions for Further Reading'.

Sources are given in each headnote and, where necessary, explanatory materials have been bracketed. Questions inevitably raised in the reader's mind – where and when did the event occur? What was the relationship between subjects and diarist or listener? Who is doing the interviewing and recalling? – are, I hope, in some measure, addressed by information either in the text or footnotes. Material has been reproduced from original sources and obvious typographical errors such as a misspelling of a book title have been silently corrected. Other more significant slips have been indicated by the usual editorial conventions. Books are listed by author and title and date, place of publication being London except where stated otherwise. Book titles are italicised. A 'List of Abbreviations' used in the text is included.

In a work such as this the debt to fellow Trollopians is large and I wish to record my thanks to many scholars whose work has led me to track down useful materials. I am particularly grateful to N. John Hall whose expertise has been readily applied to a succession of queries. To P. D. Edwards, also, I must express appreciation for help over Trollope's travels in Australia. For more general interest and advice I wish to thank Helen Heineman, Kathleen Tillotson, Nina Burgis, Arthur Pollard, and previous editors of this series, Norman Page and Philip Collins to whom a debt of long standing is acknowledged. Among colleagues nearer home I am grateful to members of my own department for answers to a variety of queries, and to Elaine Limbrick, Department of French, and Peter Smith, Department of Classics.

For practical assistance by means of inter-library loans, resources, xeroxes and answers to a host of queries the staffs of many libraries have been called upon. Colleagues at the University of Victoria Library have been endlessly patient and helpful. I also wish to thank the following: the British Library, Senate House Library of the University of London, and the Bodleian, University of British Columbia, University of Alberta, Toronto Public Library. I owe a special debt for invaluable editorial assistance to Sarah Harvey who has painstakingly followed up clues and delved into minute points which might otherwise have gone by me. For useful work in the early stages of research I must thank Robin Mawhinney.

In preparation of the text I have had the secretarial help of Susan Meisler, and I am indebted to Colleen Donnelly for her careful transference of my assorted pages, pencilled notes and second thoughts to the order and clarity of the word processor.

Generous facilities and leave granted by my own university have given me time to bring this project to a conclusion.

The editor and publishers wish to thank the following who have kindly given permission for the use of copyright-material:

Princeton University Press, for the extracts from *The Letters of Edward Fitzgerald*, ed. Alfred McKinley Terhune and Annabelle Burdick Terhune, vol. I: *1830–1850*, vol. II: *1851–1866*, vol. III: *1867–1876*, vol. IV: *1877–1883* (Princeton, N. J.: Princeton University Press, 1980); all copyright © 1980 by Princeton University Press;

Stanford University Press, for the extracts from *The Letters of Anthony Trollope*, ed. N. John Hall with the assistance of Nina Burgis, 2 vols (Stanford, Calif.: Stanford University Press, 1983);

Yale University Press, for the extracts from *The George Eliot Letters*, ed. Gordon S. Haight, vol. III: *1859–1861*, vol. IV: *1862–1868*, vol. V: *1869–1873*, vol. VI: *1874–1877*, vol. VIII: *1840–1870*, vol. IX: *1871–1881* (New Haven, Conn.: Yale University Press, 1954–76);

The Regents, University of California Press, for the extracts from 'What I Was Told' by Muriel Trollope, reprinted from *Trollopian*, II (March 1948) pp. 223–35, and from 'They Knew Trollope' by Bradford Booth, reprinted from *Trollopian*, II (September 1947) p. 118;

Every effort has been made to trace all copyright-holders, but if any have been inadvertently overlooked the publishers will be pleased to make the necessary arrangement at the first opportunity.

Victoria   R. C. T.

Notes

1. References to excerpts in the text will be given thus. Other references to frequently cited texts will be bracketed. Quotations in this introduction will be found in the body of the text unless noted. T. H. S. Escott, 'A Novelist of the Day', *Time*, 1 (Aug 1879) 626–32; *Lord Palmerston* (1882).
2. Notably Michael Sadleir, *Trollope: A Commentary* (1927, rev. edn 1945). More recent studies are: James Pope Hennessy, *Anthony Trollope* (Boston, Mass., 1971); C. P. Snow, *Trollope: His Life and Art* (1975). A new biography by N. John Hall is currently in preparation.
3. N. John Hall, 'Trollope the Person' and A. L. Rowse, 'Trollope's *Autobiography*', both in *Trollope Centenary Essays*, ed. John Halperin (1982) pp. 146, 142; Andrew Wright, *Anthony Trollope: Dream and Art* (1983) p. 148.
4. R. C. Terry, *Anthony Trollope: The Artist in Hiding* (1977). The interaction of biography and fiction is currently under scrutiny as in novels such as *Flaubert's Parrot* (1984) by Julian Barnes. Where biography or autobiography

aspires to the condition of the novel is an area of profound interest in Trollope's case. See James R. Kincaid, 'Trollope's Fictional Autobiography', *Nineteenth Century Fiction*, xxxvii, 3 (Dec 1982) 340–9.

5. Julian Hawthorne, *Confessions and Criticisms* (Boston, Mass., 1887) p. 144.

6. George Gissing in *The Private Papers of Henry Ryecroft* (1903, Brighton, 1982) p. 214.

7. Elizabeth Bowen, *Anthony Trollope: A New Judgement* (1946).

8. The prevailing cast of Trollope's mind seems to have remained consistently hopeful and optimistic, which is not to say he was without his moods of despondency. Irritability increased with failing health in later years, and Escott records his confidence to J. E. Millais of 'recurrent moods of indefinable dejections and gloom' (*Anthony Trollope: His Work, Associates and Originals* (1913, repr. New York, 1967) pp. 191–2).

9. Lady Rose Sophia Mary Fane (1834–1921), daughter of the 11th Earl of Westmorland, letter of 17 Jan 1866, Weigall MSS, Kent County Archives (cited *Letters*, i, 321).

10. 'Trollope the Person', *Trollope Centenary Essays*, pp. 166–8.

11. J. W. Robertson Scott, *The Story of the Pall Mall Gazette* (1950) p. 137.

12. Ibid., p. 84.

13. Edmund Yates, *World*, xxxvi (24 Feb 1892) 19.

14. Henry Theodore Tuckerman (1813–71), critic, essayist and poet.

15. *The George Eliot Letters*, ed. G. S. Haight (New Haven, Conn., 1955) iv, 266.

16. *Autobiography and Letters of Mrs Margaret Oliphant*, ed. Mrs Harry Coghill (Leicester, 1974, first publ. 1899) p. 258. This courageous veteran could not help envying Trollope's financial success when she had been just as industrious, but she called him 'a thoroughly sensible genuine man' (p. 4) and in later life said of Charles Reade and Trollope 'they have never had justice done them'; both were admirably 'full of insight and power, the latter especially' (p. 434).

17. 'Anthony Trollope', *Illustrated Review* (15 May 1871) 487–92. As a Dickens loyalist, Kent might well have been less enthusiastic towards Trollope.

18. Doubtless familiar to Trollope from Tennyson but common earlier, as in Herrick's 'Although our suffering meet with no reliefe, / An equall mind is the best source for griefe'.

A Trollope Chronology

1815	Born 24 Apr at 16 Keppel Street, Bloomsbury, London.
1823–34	Educated at Harrow, private school at Sunbury, and Winchester. Family flight to Bruges. Briefly employed as an usher in Brussels.
1834	Joins General Post Office as junior clerk.
1841	Appointed Surveyor's Clerk in Ireland.
1843	Begins first novel, *The Macdermots of Ballycloran*.
1844	Marries Rose Heseltine. Transfer to Southern District of Ireland.
1846	First son born, Henry Merivale Trollope.
1847	Second son born, Frederic James Anthony Trollope.
1851	Postal mission to west of England and Channel Islands. In course of time his recommendations lead to pillar letter boxes being tried out in Jersey, later installed throughout all Great Britain.
1853	Begins *The Warden* (publ. 1855).
1855	Begins *Barchester Towers* (publ. 1857).
1858	Postal mission to Egypt, followed by others in Scotland, England and West Indies (until 1859).
1859	Settles at Waltham Cross, Hertfordshire
1860	*Framley Parsonage* begins in *Cornhill Magazine* (book publ. 1861) which establishes him as novelist.
1861	First postal mission to the United States.
1862	Elected to Garrick Club.
1863	Death of his mother, Frances Trollope
1864	Begins first of the Palliser novels, *Can You Forgive Her?* (book publ. 1864/65). Becomes member of General Committee of Royal Literary Fund. Elected to Athenaeum Club.
1865	Begins contributing to *Pall Mall Gazette*. Joins in founding of *Fortnightly Review*.

1866	Writes *The Last Chronicle of Barset* (book publ. 1867).
1867	*St Paul's Magazine* launched with Trollope as editor.
1868	Second postal mission to United States. Runs for Parliament as member for Beverley, Yorkshire, and is defeated.
1870	Gives up editorship of *St Paul's*.
1871	Visits Australia with Rose to see Fred in New South Wales.
1872	Travels home via Hawaii and United States.
1873	Moves to his London house, 39 Montagu Square.
1875	Travels to Australia for second time, via Ceylon.
1876	Begins last of the Palliser novels, *The Duke's Children* (book publ. 1880). Finishes *An Autobiography* begun previous year and entrusts it to Henry (publ. 1883).
1877	Visits South Africa, sending home travel letters for provincial press.
1878	With friends in yacht *Mastiff* explores Iceland.
1880	Gives up London home and settles at North End, South Harting, Hampshire.
1882	Begins last novel, *The Landleaguers*, unfinished (publ. 1883).
1882	Dies 6 Dec in nursing home at 34 Welbeck Street, London.

Family Memorials

MURIEL TROLLOPE

From 'What I Was Told', *Trollopian*, II (Mar 1948) 223–35. Muriel Rose Trollope (1885–1953) was the daughter of Trollope's elder son, Henry Merivale Trollope (1846–1926). She wrote these random recollections (continued in the final item of this collection) at the prompting of a distinguished Trollopian, Bradford Booth, on the appearance of a hostile book by L. P. and R. P. Stebbins, *The Trollopes: The Chronicle of a Writing Family* (1946). Although she is writing from another generation and relying upon family tales doubtless many times rehearsed she manages to convey essentially what unites many of the recollections that follow: that for all the roughness and bluster in Anthony Trollope's manner great generosity and gentleness lay at the core of his nature. Rightly she begins her reminiscences with emphasis on the family and particularly on Anthony's mother whose indomitable spirit, energy and zest for life were the legacy her son inherited.

I deeply regret that I never knew my grandfather. Both he and his mother were thoroughly English, yet fairly cosmopolitan. Intelligence and learning were the breath of life to Frances Trollope. What girl, brought up in a country vicarage in England over a hundred years ago, where life was so placid and uneventful, usually studied Italian as she did and acquired a more than superficial knowledge of Dante, never an easy poet? When her spouse-to-be enquired of her how she spent her time, her reply was 'Reading Dante and hemming sheets.' (Linen ones in those days!)[1]

She was far better educated than the average woman of her day and, given easy circumstances, she would have been an ideal companion for her pedantic, erratic and unpractical husband. His curious temper may have been caused by his physical constitution. This, of course, his wife, let alone his unfortunate children, could not have known; otherwise they might have suffered less under his rigorous and disagreeable discipline. His wife and her eldest son Tom seem to have borne it the best. Her steadfast nature (at heart she was a philosopher, though at times her philosophy must nearly have deserted her completely) took the slings and arrows of outrageous fortune with far more equanimity than her younger son Anthony was able to do. She had so much to think of and to do, everything lay upon her shoulders; whereas he had only too much time for brooding over his own troubles.[2]

The responsibility for the crackbrained enterprise of the Bazaar was as much her husband's as hers.[3] ... He could not understand why their fortunes were not instantly remade! She had been obliged to leave him, for something had to be done and done at once.

Why her 'naughty book' (as I called her *Domestic Manners of the Americans* when I was in your hospitable country) raised such a storm of indignation I am at a loss to understand.[4] It seemed to me that there was just as much that she liked in America as she disliked. If the Cincinnati folk did not appreciate her, lack of esteem was apparently mutual. Country dwellers, especially in those days, were often uncouth, and theirs was a young State whose inhabitants, perhaps, had not mingled much with well-educated people of the outer world. An American friend of mine told me that her great-uncle, about the same time, I imagine, as when my great-grandmother was there, wrote in his diary: 'I had rather be among my peers in New York than a King among these people.'

The moving story of Frances Trollope's life is too well known for any further account to be necessary. How many of us could develop such innate fortitude? When things went from bad to worse, as my grandfather stated in his *Autobiography*, she was forever cheerful, clear-headed and undaunted.[5] She wrote night after night as she nursed her dying son and husband, so that her remaining dear ones, at least, might have food to eat and a roof over their heads.[6] Truly, she has earned her immortality.

The exquisite portrait of her by Hervieu resembles a large miniature. It is here in my house, and at my death will go to the National Portrait Gallery in London to hang, I hope, in company with Mrs Gaskell and Charlotte Brontë. Some unseeing person labelled her 'sour'. It is the sweetest and most intelligent face. Her eyes are far apart, always a sign of intellect – and of music. She has a lovely mouth, with upturned corners denoting good temper and a sense of humour. She wears an almost transparent muslin cap with large, soft grey-blue bows under its lace-edged frill which harmonise with her grey, far-seeing, reflective eyes. A gentle and refined nature is what one would judge. Yet she suffered from misunderstanding at home as well as in America. A Mrs Lynn Linton dubbed Frances Trollope 'vulgar', though her mother was a Gresley, and they are, or were, one of the oldest families in England.[7] I once saw a model of Drakelow Hall, the home of the Gresleys, in the Victoria and Albert Museum in London. Because Frances Trollope described vulgar people inimitably, she was not of necessity vulgar. She was often impish and full of fun – spicy fun – and probably made her famous retort about putting a pig into a sausage quite unthinkingly and mischievously, never dreaming that, henceforth, to narrow-minded folk she would not be 'quite genteel'.[8] That word describes the age admirably. Conventionality, born of narrow-mindedness, is a besetting passion with some 'good' people.

I have enjoyed her travel books very much. Of her novels, *Father Eustace*, *The Vicar of Wrexhill*, *The Widow Barnaby* and *The Widow Married*, and *Tremordyn Cliff*, are about the best. Her style is transparently simple, but her English is excellent. To this day *Vienna and the Austrians* is of interest. The Cincinnati folk who disapproved of her would have been surprised had they witnessed her reception in Vienna.

The beautiful mosaic brooch of daintiest workmanship that Princess Melanie Metternich presented to 'Madame Trolloppe' is now my proud possession. My great-grandmother loved her daughter-in-law and gave it her before she died. Rose Trollope, in turn, gave it to my mother. It depicts a cherub with iridescent wings, drawing a pearly nautilus shell as a minute chariot on a black ground. It almost reminds one of Queen Mab's chariot in *A Midsummer Night's Dream*. The gold surrounding it is likewise lovely. ...[9]

NOTES

1. The love letters are described in *FT*, i, ii.

2. Thomas Anthony suffered blinding headaches for which he took doses of calomel. His elder son, Thomas Adolphus, blamed this addiction for hastening his death: 'My father's mind was, I think, to a singular degree under the dominion of his body' (*WIR*, i, xiv). Not only from the health point of view is this just; intense emotional drives fought against his mental stability.

3. One attempt to recoup the family fortunes. The bazaar at Cincinnati sold 'pincushions, pepper-boxes and pocket-knives' (*Auto.*, i) in an ornate Graeco-Moorish emporium Harriet Martineau called 'the great deformity of the city'

(*Commentary*, p. 69). The edifice later became dancing academy, hydropathic clinic, and female medical college: 'it was the home of varieties of dreamers and reformers until it housed convalescent Federal soldiers during the Civil War' (*Autobiography, Memories and Experiences of Moncure D. Conway* (1905) I, 230).

4. A wrathful Press descended. James Kirke Paulding, Washington Irving's collaborator in *Salmagundi*, revised his play *The Lion in the West; or a Trip to Washington* for its London performance (Mar 1833) to include a satire on 'Amelia Wollope' (See *The Lion of the West*, ed. James N. Tidwell (California, 1954)). See also Helen Heineman, *Mrs Trollope: The Triumphant Feminine in the Nineteenth Century* (Athens, Ohio, 1979) pp. 94–100.

5. Money troubles plagued the family from 1825 but came to a height in Mar 1834 when the bailiffs descended on Julians Hill (immortalised in *Orley Farm*, 1862). Anthony helped beat the bailiffs by driving his father in the family gig to board a boat for Ostend and then selling the equipage. In the late sixties he showed Frith's daughter 'with many chuckles where there had been a hole in the hedge' through which he had smuggled china and silver (Jane Panton, *Leaves From a Life* (1908) p. 202).

6. Trollope wrote movingly of her heroic struggle (*Auto.*, ii). Henry died in Dec 1834, his father in Oct 1835.

7. Elizabeth Lynn Linton (1822–98): 'She was in no sense a *poseuse*, but just a vulgar, brisk and good-natured kind of well-bred hen wife, fond of a joke and not troubled with squeamishness' (*My Literary Life* (1899) p. 89). Mrs Linton had something in common with her. Indeed, Mrs Trollope was rather formidable. Lever would change seats so as not to face her across the whist table, and there is no mistaking Dickens's tone in a letter from Italy when he says 'I suppose I must do the attentive to Mrs Trollope' (Walter Dexter, *Mr and Mrs Charles Dickens* (1935) p. 218).

8. Asked whether she put acquaintances into her fiction she replied 'I draw from life – but I always pulp my acquaintances before serving them up. You would never recognise a pig in a sausage' (quoted *Commentary*, p. 103). Her son inherited equally ribald ways of deflecting the curious.

9. See the reference p. 21.

Three Wolves Trollope

LORD MALMESBURY

From *Memoirs of an Ex-Minister* (1884) I, 234. James Howard Harris Malmesbury (1807–89) succeeded to the peerage in 1841, served as Lord Derby's Foreign Secretary, 1852, Lord Privy Seal in Derby's ministry, 1866–8, and in Disraeli's, 1874–6. Whatever the origins of the family name the pedigree was ancient: *Burke's Peerage* records a John Trowlope or Trolope of Co. Durham, who acquired the Manor of Morden before 1390. In Trollope's time the title descended to Sir John Trollope (1800–74), later Baron Kesteven of Casewick (1868), with whom the novelist was on friendly terms. The title eventually came to descendants of Trollope's second son, Frederick James Anthony (1847–1910), who settled in Australia. The present baronet, who lives in Sydney, is another Anthony Trollope, the son of Gordon Clavering Trollope. See Revd M. N. Trollope, *A Memoir of the Family of Trollope* (1897); P. D. Edwards, *Anthony Trollope's Son in Australia* (St Lucia, Queensland, 1982).

11 October [1848] ... Sidney Herbert[1] told us a funny story about the origin of the name of Trollope. A son of Mrs Trollope, the authoress, who was with him at Harrow, first told it of his own accord, but used to be made to repeat it by sufficient punchings on the head, as follows: 'Tallyhosier the Norman[2] came over to England with William the Conqueror, and being out hunting one day with his Majesty in the New Forest, happened to kill three wolves, and "*trois*" being the French for "three", "*loup*" for "wolves", he was called, "*troisloup*", which with many changes and corruptions during countless centuries became "Trollope" '![3]

NOTES

1. Sidney Herbert, first Lord Herbert of Lea (1810–61), was at Harrow, 1824–7, served in Peel's Cabinet, 1845, as Colonial Secretary under Palmerston 1855, and as Secretary for War, 1859. He accepted a peerage in 1860.

2. 'Tallyhoiser' in Frederick Locker-Lampson, *My Confidences* (1896) p. 331.

3. Another story went the rounds at Harrow: that young Trollope's pater was an outlaw. 'It is the nature of boys to be cruel', observes Trollope quietly (*Auto.*, i). The surname had afforded risibility for generations. Apart from its traditional meanings since the seventeenth century, it acquired a particular force when Frances Trollope published *Domestic Manners of the Americans* (1832) in which she roundly condemned chewers and spitters in public. Henceforth in the theatre pit between acts a person standing with his back to the stage would elicit the cry 'Trollope! Trollope!' (*The Diaries of John Bright*, ed. R. A. J. Walling (New York, 1930) p. 21). A foot protruding over the gallery would provoke the same taunt, Henry T. Tuckerman observed (Tidwell, *The Lion of the West*, p. 13).

A Very Lively, Pleasant Young Woman

MARY RUSSELL MITFORD AND CHARLES MERIVALE

(1) from Revd A. G. K. L'Estrange, *The Friendships of Mary Russell Mitford* (1882) I, 8–9. Miss Mitford (1787–1855), novelist and dramatist, best known for her tragedies *Rienzi* (1828) and *Charles I* (1834) and her country sketches *Our Village* (1843), met Trollope's mother in 1802 and became a lifelong friend. Frances Trollope assiduously promoted *Rienzi*, persuading Macready to take it to America (L'Estrange, *Life of Mary Russell Mitford* (1870) II, 57–64). She emerges here as an energetic warm body passionately devoted to family and friends; (2) from Anna W. Merivale, *Family Memorials* (1884) pp. 199–200. John Herman Merivale (1779–1844) and his family (numbering eventually 12 children) became intimate with the Trollopes at Harrow; John Lewis Merivale (1815–86) was Anthony's best friend in youth. They hiked together in the Home Counties – 'These were the happiest hours of my then life' (*Auto.*, iii), and later in Co. Leitrim, Ireland, they stumbled on the ruined house which provided the germ of Trollope's first novel, *The Macdermots of Ballycloran* (1847). The Trollopes had many friends at Harrow and nearby Pinner, among them Lady Milman, the Grants, the Drurys (closely linked with Harrow School) and the Pells. About 1830 Albert Pell saw Mrs Opie and Mrs Trollope together, the former 'in the neatest possible cap and shawl, sitting upright and rather silent, Mrs Trollope … not at all prim, neat or silent'.

(1) [Mary Mitford in a letter to her daughter, Mary Russell Mitford, 14 Nov 1802.] I cannot attempt to detail what an agreeable day we had on Friday. The gentlemen dedicated the morning to field sports; the ladies accompanied me round the grounds, and afterwards we took a ride round Lord Rivers' park before we dressed for dinner, when there was an addition to our number of a Mr Milton, his wife and two daughters;[1] the youngest of whom, Miss Fanny Milton, is a very lively, pleasant young woman. I do not mean to infer that Miss [Mary] Milton may not be equally agreeable, but the other took a far greater share in the conversation, and, playing casino a great part of the

evening with Mr S. Lefevre,[2] Mr Monck and your old Mumpsa, [a pet name] it gave me an opportunity of seeing her in a more favourable light than her sister.

(2) [Frances Trollope to an unknown correspondent, a diary entry by Charles Merivale, 2 May 1819.][3] He [Herman Merivale, then about 12] is by far the most wonderful child I ever saw. His enthusiastic love of poetry exceeds that of any person I ever met with, and the correctness of his style equals it. He is familiar with the best Latin, French and Italian poets in the original, and from his darling Dante, in particular, poured forth long quotations, with a spirit and correctness equally astonishing and delightful. ...[4] Several other schoolboys dined with us, and in the evening they played Commerce, in which he joined with perfect good humour. In making the hands of my young neighbours I speedily became defunct, and then he cried 'May I throw up my lives?' – which being permitted, he established himself by me at the fireside, and by degrees he collected round us Dante, Tasso, Ariosto and Spenser, and it was beautiful to see the rapid glance of his young eye from page to page, pausing at his favourite passages, always well chosen, but never hackneyed. These he read aloud (or rather *sotto voce*) with so much grace and so much feeling, that I have seldom, if ever, enjoyed literary conversation more. He is perfectly awake to every species of beauty. Speaking of Dante, he said 'How he kindles at the name of Beatrice!' What will this creature be at five and twenty: I should not omit that he talked of the Greek poets with Trollope, and quoted from them with equal facility and judgement.

NOTES

1. Revd William Milton (1743–1824), Vicar of Heckfield, was given to mechanical experiments. Among his inventions were a device to prevent coaches upsetting, a self-propelled revolving machine, and a dinner plate with a two-inch silver disc in the middle to overcome the irritating scrape of knife on china. His wife, *née* Gresley, bore three children: Mary, Henry and Frances (1779–1863).

2. Shaw Lefevre, MP for Reading (1802–20).

3. Charles Merivale (1808–93), second son of John Herman Merivale, later Dean of Ely and noted historian. Trollope reviewed his *History of the Romans Under the Empire* in *Dublin University Magazine*, xvii (May 1851) and xlviii (July 1856).

4. Few passages show more clearly her fondness for children and home life. Despite her absences, and the emphasis Anthony rightly gives to the grim conditions of his childhood, the Trollope household could be festive; even the austere Thomas Anthony was known to participate in amateur theatricals. For a fictional rendering of Commerce and other party games see the Christmas at Noningsby scene in *Orley Farm* (1862).

A Very Unhappy Man

THOMAS ADOLPHUS TROLLOPE

From *What I Remember* (1887) I, 4–5, 21, 57–60, 61–3, 65, 225–6, 228, 240, 242, 294–6; II, 330–4. Long out-of-print yet valuable memoirs of this garrulous and guileless member of the family. Tom Trollope (1810–92) settled in Florence with his mother in 1844, and his elegant home, Villino Trollope in the Piazza dell'Independenza, became a rendezvous for Anglo-Florentine society. His recollections of early family life and his judgements on his parents usefully complement, even modify in particulars, Anthony's self-dramatising perspective as odd man out in the *Autobiography*, although it must be remembered that the younger son bore the brunt of his father's rages. Tom attended Winchester (1820–8) and Oxford (1830–4), becoming his mother's business manager (1838) after a brief period of teaching. In 1848 he married Theodosia Garrow (1825–65) and they had a daughter, Beatrice ('Bice'), often mentioned in the Trollopes' correspondence. His second wife, Frances Eleanor Ternan (1834?–1913), whom he married in 1866 (Anthony being present as a witness), was the sister of Dickens's mistress. Tom Trollope's literary reputation rests upon studies of Italian subjects such as *A Decade of Italian Women* (1859) and *A History of the Commonwealth of Florence* (1865). His best-known novels were *La Beata* (1861), *Lindisfarn Chase* (1864) and *Giulio Malatesta* (1863). Tom was less of a workaholic than his brother and confessed he liked idleness: 'Anthony had no such turn. Work to him was a necessity and a satisfaction. He used often to say that he envied me the capacity for being idle' (*WIR*, I, 358–9). On good terms with leading literary figures such as Dickens, Geoge Eliot and Browning, he was a much-loved figure, known to all the English residents of Florence as 'dear old Tom Trollope' (Alfred Austin, *Autobiography* (1911) I, 166).

For the present I see myself alone in the back drawing-room of No. 16, Keppel Street, in which room the family breakfast took place – probably to avoid the necessity of lighting another fire in the dining-room below – at 7 a.m., on my knees before the sofa, with my head in my hands and my eyes fixed on the *Eton Latin Grammar* laid on the sofa cushion before me.[1] My parents had not yet come down to breakfast, nor had the tea urn been brought up by the footman. *Nota bene* – My father was a poor man, and his establishment altogether on a modest footing. But it never would have occurred to him or to my mother that they could get on without a man-servant in livery. And though this liveried footman served a family in which two tallow candles with their snuffer dish supplied the whole illumination of the evening, had the livery been an *invented* one instead of that proper to the family, the circumstance would have been an absurdity exciting the ridicule of all the society in which my parents lived. *Tempora mutantur!* Certainly at the present day an equally unpretending household would be burthened by no footman. But on the morning which memory is recalling to me the footman was coming up with the urn, and my parents were coming down to breakfast, probably simultaneously; and the question of the hour was whether I could get the due relationship of relative and antecedent into my little head before the two events arrived.

And that, as I remember it, was the almost unvaried routine for more than a year or two. I think, however, that the walks of which I was speaking when this retrospect presented itself to me must have belonged to a time a little, but not much later; for I had then advanced to the making of Latin verses. We used to begin in those days by making 'nonsense verses'. And many of us ended in the same way! The next step – *Gradus ad Parnassum* – consisted in turning into Latin verse certain English materials provided for the purpose, and so cunningly prepared as to fall easily and almost inevitably into the required form. And these were the studies which, as I specially remember, were the subject of rehearsal during those walks from Lincoln's Inn to Keppel Street.

My father was in the habit of returning from his chambers to a five o'clock dinner – rather a late hour, because he was an industrious and laborious man. Well! we, that is my next brother (not the one whose name became subsequently well known in the world, but my brother Henry, who died early) and myself, used to walk from Keppel Street to Lincoln's Inn, so as to arrive in time to walk back with my father. He was a fast walker; and as we trotted along one on each side of him, the repetition of our morning's poetical achievements did not tend, as I well remember, to facilitate the difficulty of 'keeping our wind'. But what has probably fixed all this in my mind during nearly three quarters of

a century was my father's pat application of one of our lines to the difficulties of those peripatetic poetisings. 'Muse and sound of wheel do not well agree', read the cunningly prepared original, which the alumnus with wonderful sagacity was to turn into, '*Non bene convenient Musa rotaeque sonus*'. 'That', said my father, as he turned sharp round the corner into the comparative quiet of Featherstone Buildings, 'is exactly why I turned out of Holborn!'
...

Before closing this Keppel Street chapter of my existence I may mention one or two circumstances of the family life there which illustrate the social habits of those days. The family dinner-hour was five. There were no dinner napkins to be seen; they were perhaps less needed by clean-shaven chins and lips. Two tallow candles, requiring to be snuffed by snuffers lying in a little plated tray *ad hoc* every now and then, partially illumined the table, but scarcely at all the more distant corners of the room. Nor were any more or better lights used during the evening in the drawing-room. The only alternative would have been wax lights at half-a-crown a pound – an extravagance not to be thought of. Port and sherry were always placed on the shining mahogany table when the cloth was withdrawn, and no other wine. Only on the occasion of having friends to dinner, the port became a magnum of a vintage for which my father's cellar was famous, and possibly Madeira might be added. ...

I was, I think, about eight years old when my parents removed from Keppel Street to Harrow-on-the-Hill.[2] My father's practice, I take it, was becoming less and less satisfactory, and his health equally so. And the move to Harrow was intended as a remedy or palliation for both these evils. M father was a very especially industrious and laborious man. And I have the authority of more than one very competent judge among his professional contemporaries for believing that he was as learned a Chancery lawyer as was to be found among them. How then was his want of success to be accounted for? One of the competent authorities above alluded to accounted for it thus: 'Your father', he said to me many years afterwards, when his troubles and failures had at last ceased to afflict him, 'never came into contact with a blockhead without insisting on irrefutably demonstrating to him that he was such. And the blockhead did not like it! He was a disputatious man; and he was almost invariably – at least on a point of law – right. But the world differed from him in the opinion that being so gave him the right of rolling his antagonist in the dust and executing an intellectual dance of triumph on his prostrate form.' He was very fond of whist, and was, I believe, a good player. But people did not like to play with him. 'Many men', said an old friend once, 'will scold their partners occasionally. But Trollope invariably scolds us all round with the utmost impartiality; and that every deal!'

He was, in a word, a highly respected, but not a popular or well-beloved man. Worst of all, alas! he was not popular in his own home. No one of all the family circle was happy in his presence. Assuredly he was as affectionate and anxiously solicitous a father as any children ever had. I never remember his caning, whipping, beating or striking any one of us.[3] But he used during the detested Latin lessons to sit with his arm over the back of the pupil's chair, so that his hand might be ready to inflict an instantaneous pull of the hair as the *poena* (by no means *pede claudo*) for every blundered concord or false quantity; the result being to the scholar a nervous state of expectancy, not judiciously calculated to increase intellectual receptivity. There was also a strange sort of asceticism about him, which seemed to make enjoyment or any employment of the hours save work, distasteful to him. Lessons for us boys were never over and done with. It was sufficient for my father to see any one of us 'idling', i.e. not occupied with book work, to set us to work quite irrespectively of the previously assigned task of the day having been accomplished. And this we considered to be unjust and unfair.

I have said that the move to Harrow was in some degree caused by a hope that the change might be beneficial to my father's health. He had suffered very distressingly for many years from bilious headache, which gradually increased upon him during the whole of his life. ...

My mother's disposition, on the other hand, was of the most genial, cheerful, happy, *enjoué* nature imaginable. All our happiest hours were spent with her; and to any one of us a tête-à-tête with her was preferable to any other disposal of a holiday hour. But even this under all the circumstances did not tend to the general harmony and happiness of the family circle. For of course the facts and the results of them must have been visible to my father; and though wholly inoperative to produce the smallest change in his ways, must, I cannot doubt, have been painful to him. It was all very sad. My father was essentially a good man. But he was, I fear, a very unhappy one. ...

The move to Harrow was as infelicitous a step in the economic point of view as it was inefficacious as a measure of health. My father took a farm, of some three or four hundred acres, to the best of my recollection, from Lord Northwick. It was a wholly disastrous speculation. It certainly was the case that he paid a rent for it far in excess of its fair value and he always maintained that he had been led to undertake to do so by inaccurate and false representations. I have no knowledge of these representations, but I am absolutely certain that my father was entirely convinced that they were such as he characterised them. But he was educated to be a lawyer, and was a good one. He had never been educated to be a farmer; and was, I take it, despite unwearied activity, and rising up early and late taking rest, a bad one.

To make matters worse moreover he built on that land, of which he held only a long lease, a large and very good house.[4] The position was excellently chosen, the house was well conceived and well built, and the extensive gardens and grounds were well designed and laid out; but the unwisdom of doing all that on land the property of another is but too obvious.

The excuse that my father might have alleged was that he was by no means wholly dependent either on his profession or on his farm, or on the not inconsiderable property which he had inherited from his father or enjoyed in right of his wife. He had an old maternal uncle, Adolphus Meetkerke, who lived on his estate near Royston in Hertfordshire, called Julians. Mr Meetkerke – the descendant of a Dutchman who had come to this country some time in the eighteenth century as diplomatic representative of his country, and had settled here – lived at Julians with an old childless wife – the daughter, I believe, of a General Chapman – and my father was his declared heir.[5]...

One more note from the diaries of those days I will venture to give, because it may be taken as a paraleipomenon to that *Autobiography* of my brother, which the world was kindly pleased to take some interest in:

Went to town yesterday [from Harrow], and among other commissions bought a couple of single-sticks with strong basket handles. Anthony much approves of them, and this morning we had a bout with them. One of the sticks bought yesterday soon broke, and we supplied its place by a tremendous blackthorn. Neither of us left the arena without a fair share of rather severe wales; but Anthony is far my superior in quickness and adroitness, and perhaps in bearing pain too. I fear he is likely to remain so in the first two, but in the third I am determined he shall not. ...

I came down from Oxford to find my mother and my two sisters returned from America, and living in that Harrow Weald farmhouse which my brother Anthony, in his *Autobiography*, has described, I think, too much *en noir*. It had once been a very good house, probably the residence of the owner of the small farm on which it was situated. It certainly was no longer a very good house, but it was not tumbledown, as Anthony calls it, and was indeed a much better house than it would have been if its original destination had been that of merely a farmhouse.[6] But it and 'all that it inherited' was assuredly shabby enough, and had been forlorn enough, as I had known it in my vacations, when inhabited only by my father, my brother Anthony and myself. ...

Here, also, I may record ... an expedition I and my brother Anthony made together, which recurs to my mind in connection with those days. But I think that it must have belonged to the Harrow Weald times before the return of my mother from America, because the extreme impecuniosity, which made the principal feature of it, would not have occurred subsequently. We saw – my brother and I – some advertisement of an extra-magnificent entertainment that was to take place at Vauxhall; something of so gorgeous promise in the way of illuminations and fireworks, and all for the specially reduced entrance fee of one shilling each person, that, chancing to possess just that amount, we determined to profit by so unique an occasion. Any means of conveyance other than legs, ignorant in those days of defeat, was not to be thought of. We had just the necessary two shillings, and no more. So we set off to walk the (at least) fourteen miles from Harrow Weald to Vauxhall, timing ourselves to arrive there about nine in the evening. Anthony danced all night. I took no part in that amusement, but contented myself with looking on and with the truly superb display of fireworks. Then at about 1 a.m. we set off and walked back our fourteen miles home again without having touched bite or sup! Did anybody else ever purchase the delight of an evening at Vauxhall at so high a price? ...

I returned to Bruges, passing one day with the dear Grants at Harrow, and an evening with my brother Anthony in London by the way, and reached the Chateau d'Hondt on 15 October, to find my father very much worse than I had left him. He was in bed, and was attended by the Dr Herbout of whom I have before spoken. But he was too evidently drawing towards his end; and after much suffering breathed his last in the afternoon of 23 October, 1835. On the 25th I followed his body to his grave, close to that of my brother Henry, in the cemetery outside the Catherine Gate of the town.

The duty was a very specially sad one. When I followed my mother to the grave at Florence many years afterwards my thoughts were far from being as painfully sad, though she was, I fear, the better loved parent of the two. She died in a ripe old age after a singularly happy, though not untroubled, life, during many years of which it was permissible to me to believe that I had no small share in ministering to her happiness. It was otherwise in the case of my father. He was, and had been, I take it, for many years, a very unhappy man. All had gone wrong with him; misfortunes were the real and efficient causes of his unhappiness. I do not see what concentration of circumstances could have made him happy. He was in many respects a singular man. Ill health and physical suffering, of course, are great causes of an unhappy life; but all suffering invalids are not unhappy. My father's mind was, I think, to a singular degree under the dominion of his body. The terrible irritability of his temper, which sometimes in his latter years reached a pitch that made one fear his reason was, or would become, unhinged, was undoubtedly due to the shattering of his nervous system, caused by the habitual use of calomel. But it is difficult for one who has never had a similar experience to conceive the degree in which the irritability made the misery of all who were called upon habitually to come into contact with it. I do not think that it would be an exaggeration to say that for many years no person came into my father's presence who did not forthwith desire to escape from it. Of course, this desire was not yielded to by those of his own household, but they were none the less conscious of it. Happiness, mirth, contentment, pleasant conversation, seemed to fly before him as if a malevolent spirit emanated from him. And all the time no human being was more innocent of all malevolence towards his fellow creatures; and he was a man who would fain have been loved, and who knew that he was not loved, but knew neither how to manifest his desire for affection nor how to conciliate it.

NOTES

1. Five children were born here: Thomas Adolphus (1810–92), Henry (1811–34), Arthur William (1812–24), Emily (1813 d. the same day), Anthony (1815–82). Two more daughters, Cecilia Frances (1816–49) and Emily (1818–36) were born at Harrow. Note the liveried servant; Tom's account emphasises the family's social status which Anthony plays down in the *Autobiography*.

2. Frances Eleanor Trollope dates the move as 1817 (*FT*, p. 45) as does Sadleir (*Commentary*, p. 44). N. John Hall cites late in 1815 (*Letters*, i, xxix). See Heineman, *Mrs Trollope*, pp. 19–23.

3. Anthony, however, does not seem to have been so fortunate. He reports being knocked down by a folio Bible (*Auto.*, i).

4. The house was called 'Julians'; the land was leased from Lord Northwick. The *Autobiography* describes the farm as 'the grave of all my father's hopes, ambition and prosperity, the cause of my mother's sufferings, and of those of her children, and perhaps the director of her destiny and ours' (i).

5. Unfortunately, Thomas Anthony's contumacious manner antagonised Meetkerke who subsequently married again and produced an heir, thereby putting an end to the Trollopes' expectations of wealth.

6. A second move had been made to a house called 'Julians Hill' which Millais used as an illustration for Trollope's novel *Orley Farm*. The 'wretched tumble-down farmhouse ... in danger of falling into the neighbouring horse-pond' was the one at Harrow Weald from which Trollope as a day-boarder trudged miserably to Harrow School (*Auto.*, i).

You Will Often Find Him Idle and Plaguing Enough

FRANCES ELEANOR TROLLOPE

From *Frances Trollope: Her Life and Literary Work from George III to Victoria*, 2 vols (1895) i, 94–5, 128–31; ii, 38–9, 161–4, 244–5, 252–6. An act of homage from a devoted daughter-in-law and advocate for her husband, Anthony's brother, but still eloquent testimony to the indomitable woman who not only saved the family from ruin but endowed Anthony with her fighting nature. Much debate ensued after the publication of the *Autobiography* about his feelings towards his mother and hers to him, and both this memoir and T. A. Trollope's reminiscences stressed Frances's concern for all her children. Certainly Tom and Henry, being the eldest sons, were in the forefront of her attention. Her correspondence was chiefly with Tom at Winchester and Oxford and clearly she preferred Tom's company; Anthony took a back seat until he began to prove himself. There is, however, no denying her joy at his appointment in the Post Office, his marriage and consequent success in life. One of her finest letters on this count, written when she was almost eighty (1856), said: 'Tom and I agree in thinking that you exceed in this respect [his industry] any individual that we have ever known or heard of – and I am proud of being your mother – as well for this reason as for sundry others. I rejoice to think that you have considerably more than the third of a century to gallop through yet before reaching the age at which I first felt inclined to cry halta la!' (*Letters*, I, 44). A convincing case for her genuine regard based on many of her other letters has been made by Helen Heineman, *Mrs Trollope*. Today she is best known for her travel book, *The Domestic Manners of the Americans* (1832), and such novels as *The Vicar of Wrexhill* (1837), *The Life and Adventures of Michael Armstrong, the Factory Boy* (1840), and *Jessie Phillips: A Tale of the Present Day* (1843). Much of Frances Trollope's later life was passed with her eldest son 'in the full flood and flow of Florentine society' (*The Letters of Elizabeth Barrett Browning*, ed. Frederic G. Kenyon (1910) I, 476).

Early in the year 1827, Mr and Mrs Trollope's letters constantly express alternate hopefulness and anxiety about getting their son Anthony into Winchester – the father entering, as usual, into minute calculations of the chances of a vacancy, and urging his eldest son to give him every detail as to the boys who may possibly resign before the next election, and so forth. In fact, Anthony was admitted to college in the April of this year. [He was then 12.]

There is before me an affecting letter from Mrs Trollope to her son Tom, dated 11 April 1827, pointing out with great earnestness how essential it is that he should do all in his power to keep his brother up to the mark.[1] 'Your father', she writes, 'must certainly consider himself as very fortunate in getting three boys into College, and yet it will not do us much good, unless we get some dispers of the New College loaves and fishes. As far as Anthony is concerned this must very much depend on you. I dare say you will often find him idle and plaguing enough. But remember, dear Tom, that, in a family like ours, *everything* gained by one is felt personally and individually by all. He is a good-hearted fellow, and clings so to the idea of being Tom's pupil, and sleeping in Tom's chamber, that I think you will find advice and remonstrance better taken by him than by poor Henry. Greatly comforted am I to know that Tony has a praefect brother. I well remember what I used to suffer at the idea of what my "little Tom" was enduring. ...'

Later in the summer [1830] she writes [to Tom]: 'I imagine that when this reaches you, you will be at home for the long vacation. Oh how I long to see you all! – to know how you, my dear Tom, now almost of age, are going on – what your present hopes are and what their foundation. Alas, since last we conversed together my life has been almost one continued scene of suffering.[2] Often have I rejoiced that you were where you could not see it. Yet often would I have given much to have your affection to support me. *Everything* from the time you left us, went wrong, spite of exertions – nay hard labour, on our part that would pain you to hear of. I suspect that poor Henry, in suffering as he did in every way at Cincinnati, thought he had suffered enough, and that he has *altogether* avoided giving the painful details to your father; for by his letters it appears that he is still ignorant of nearly all the events that preceded our departure. For instance, he says that he "cannot imagine why it was necessary for Henry to set off immediately", when the fact was that *every bed had been seized*, and that we – your sisters and myself – were sleeping together in one small bed at Major L.'s [a Cincinnati neighbour] and boarding there, as well as Henry and Hervieu[3] who both lay on the floor in the kitchen, *for the value of my parlour carpet*. And yet your father wonders why Henry did not stay the winter!

'In one letter, in answer to one of mine in which I stated our situation, your father writes, "How is it possible that you are dependent on Hervieu for your living, when I have sent out goods to the amount of £2000?"

'Is it not strange, Tom, that he does not yet know that these goods never brought *one penny* into my hands? The proceeds of those we sold, went to the workmen and servants, and the *rest were seized*. I trust my letters have reached him, and that he now knows this fact, but I would have you recall it to his memory.

'My only hope in quitting Cincinnati was that my old friend Mrs Stone would be able to receive my girls and me until our return home and the manner of it could be settled. I then hoped that some of the brilliant prophecies which poor Hervieu heard for his picture, would be realised. But here again disappointment has followed us.'

The picture was a large oil painting representing the landing of General Lafayette in America. It was exhibited at Philadelphia

and at Washington, and greatly praised. But the exhibition did
not pay its expenses.

'The only thing that has *not* disappointed me is the friendship
of Mrs Stone. Nothing can exceed her kindness, and with her we
have found a home the tranquillity of which has done much
towards the recovery of my health both of mind and body. But
you must expect, my dear Tom, if Heaven indeed permits my
safe return, to see a very old lady! My eyes have greatly failed me
since my illness. I can do nothing without spectacles, and I can
no longer walk as I did. But I am infinitely better than when I
came here [i.e. to Stonington, her friend's house], and still
young enough to enjoy a long, long talk with you as in days of
yore. ...

'Poor Cecilia is literally without shoes, and I mean to sell one
or two small articles tomorrow to procure some for her, and for
Emily. I sit still and write, write, write, – so old shoes last me a
long time. As to other articles of dress, we should any of us as
soon think of buying diamonds! Your dear sisters have had a
pretty sharp lesson in economy. They mend, – and mend, – and
mend. They are, indeed, treasures to me, and their devoted
affection outweighs all my misfortunes. I often comfort myself
with thinking that they would not have loved me so tenderly,
had they not seen me suffer.

'You will think, my dear boy, that I am trying to increase *your*
affection for me by the same means! But I wish not that you
should be ignorant of our life since we parted. It is no one sheet,
however, nor a dozen, that could do justice to it. Be not unhappy
about us nevertheless, dearest. We are really very comfortable
here; you know enough of composition to be aware that nothing
more completely and agreeably occupies the mind; and Hope –
that quits us the last, perhaps, of all our friends – tells me that it
is *possible* my book may succeed. It will have great advantages
from Hervieu's drawings. If it *should* succeed, a second book
would bring money. If I can but get home next spring, I feel as if
I should still find the means of being happy and comfortable.

'My poor dear Anthony will have outgrown our recollection!
Tell him not to outgrow his affection for us. No day passes,
–hardly an hour – without our talking of you all. I hope a letter
from your father is on the way. Tell Henry that my wrist has
lately recovered greatly, and that I trust his ankle will do the
same. The dear girls would fill a volume with phrases of love.

Say all that is affectionate from all to all. God bless you, my dearest Tom. Ever your affectionate mother, F. Trollope.'

[After some years of wandering Mrs Trollope settled in 1843 at the Casa Berti, Florence, with her elder son as her business manager.] In the spring of 1844 the first tidings reached Casa Berti of the engagement of Mrs Trollope's son Anthony, to Miss Rose Heseltine. His marriage took place on the 11th of the following June [1844].[4] How fortunate a union this was for Anthony it is not for me to descant upon. It has been said emphatically by the one person in the world who had a right to say it – by Anthony himself in his autobiography. But I may be allowed to state that it was a source of heartfelt satisfaction to Frances Trollope, who was not long in recognising the excellent influence of the young wife on her son's life in every way.

In May Mrs Trollope and her son went to England, chiefly in order to pay a visit to the Tilleys in Cumberland, and also, doubtless, for the purpose of seeing her new daughter-in-law.[5] Anthony and his bride arrived at Carlton Hill in the course of the summer.

I will give an account of the impression she made on this first meeting, in the words of Mrs Anthony Trollope herself:

'Nothing could have been kinder or more affectionate than the way she received me – kind, good and loving, then and ever afterwards. No one who saw her at this date could suppose she was in her sixty-fourth year, so full was she of energy. There was no one more eager to suggest, and carry out the suggestions, as to mountain excursions, picnics, and so forth. And she was always the life and soul of the party with her cheerful conversation and her wit. She rose very early and made her own tea, the fire having been prepared overnight – (on one occasion I remember her bringing me a cup of tea to my room, because she thought I had caught cold during a wet walk in the mountains) – then sat at her writing-table until the allotted task of so many pages was completed; and was usually on the lawn before the family breakfast-bell rang, having filled her basket with cuttings from the rose bushes for the table and drawing-room decorations.. ...'[6]

[Keeping up her usual brisk schedule of writing and travel Mrs Trollope managed in July 1848 to visit her younger son in County Cork.] Mrs Trollope's visit to Ireland gave her great pleasure.

She had the great comfort of perceiving that, as she writes in one of her letters from Mallow, 'Anthony and his excellent little wife are as happy as possible.' And, moreover, she was interested in what she saw around her.

Mrs Anthony Trollope writes about this visit:

'We took her to Killarney, with which she was enchanted. Lord Kenmare's park especially delighted her. She walked through the gap of Dunlo as easily as if she had been twenty-nine instead of sixty-nine! And was delighted with young Spellan, the bugler. In the evening we had old Spellan the piper introduced with his bagpipes into our sitting-room – at first to her dismay. But soon tears were rolling down her cheeks from the pathos of his music.

'One day we put her on one of Bianconi's cars running to Glengariff, after much protest on her part against the ramshack-le-looking machine. Presently, however, after a few jerks, and a dozen "Niver fear, yer honour!" from Mick the driver, she almost persuaded herself that she would rather travel through Ireland in that way than any other!

'Glengarriff was not a success. She was tired with her journey; the tea was rubbish; the food detestable; the bedrooms pokey; turf fires disagreeable, and so on. And now looking back on it all, I feel that she had grounds for complaint; and I should vote it – nasty. However the next day was better, when we drove through the Bantry demesne.'

One day, during Mrs Trollope's short visit to Mallow, she saw from her bedroom window an aged man breaking stones on the road. She pattered downstairs and bestowed a silver sixpence on the astonished old pauper. Her daughter-in-law says –

'Our old Irish groom,[7] hearing of this, related the occurrence, after his fashion, to the honour and glory of the family. "Sure, her honour gave the ould man a shilling every day for a month." (She was not a week altogether in the town!) And very soon the sum grew into half-a-crown. He told the story until he himself, at any rate, believed it.

'When told of the delightful advance of her one sixpence to half-a-crown a day, she laughed, and said, "Ah, that shows on what slight threads hangs the report of our good deeds – and our evil ones!"'…

[In Mar 1853 Tom's daughter, Beatrice, was born and the following month Anthony and Rose visited the family now living at the Villino Trollope in Florence.] 'The next time I saw my dear old mother-in-law was in Florence [Apr. 1853]. She took me about everywhere, and explained everything to me. And she made me happy by a present of an Italian silk dress. She also gave me a Roman mosaic brooch, which had been a present to her from Princess Metternich during her stay in Vienna. It is a perfect gem.

'At this time she used to have her weekly evening receptions, attended by some of the pleasantest of the English residents in Florence; and she always had her own special whist-table. I thought her the most charming old lady who ever existed. There was nothing conventional about her, and yet she was perfectly free from the vice of affectation; and was worlds asunder from the "New Woman" and the "Emancipated Female" School. I do not think she had a mean thought in her composition.

'She was lavishly generous as regards money; full of impulse; not free from prejudice – but more often in *favour* of people than otherwise – but once in her good books, she was certain to be true to you. She could say a sarcastic word, but never an ill-natured one.'

It was a great joy to Frances Trollope to see her dearly loved youngest son and his wife, for whom she had a warm affection. The arrival of her little grandchild, Beatrice – called, in Tuscan fashion, Bice – had also cheered and brightened the family at the Villino – partly by the sense of peril past, and greatly by the hopes for the future entwined with the baby life. ...[8]

In May 1855, Mrs Trollope with her son Tom met Mr and Mrs Anthony Trollope at Venice. The latter writes –

'In Venice Mrs Trollope had not much scope for her pedestrian powers. But the stairs she climbed, and the walks she took on the sands of the Lido, were wonderful. She was then seventy-five years old.'

But her nervous system can no longer have been what it was. Mrs Anthony Trollope says –

'One day returning from Murano, a thunderstorm burst upon us. The waters became rough, and there was a nasty swell which caused our gondola to rock about more than was pleasant. Her nerves gave way, and she fairly broke down with terror. But in the evening she was quite ready to enjoy the Austrian band in the Piazza San Marco, the coffee and the ices.' ...

Mrs Trollope spent some time in London during the season of 1854. And it was at this period that she first saw Mr Hume – or Home – the Medium, and became a constant attendant at his seances.[9]

Mrs Anthony Trollope is strongly inclined to attribute the break up in her mother-in-law's faculties and general health, which soon afterwards manifested itself, to the prejudicial effects of the excitement she underwent at these seances. Mrs Anthony Trollope writes to me –

'It appears very strange that a woman with so much strong common sense, should have placed faith in these absurdities. But her imagination and romance got the upper hand. The effect of these visits told upon her spirits. In the autumn of this year, she fell into bad health. This was her last visit to England.'[10]

NOTES

1. Tom acted on the advice with alacrity; Anthony noted laconically that at Winchester 'he was, of all my foes, the worst ... he had studied the theories of Draco' (*Auto.*, i).

2. This gives some impression of the privations and anguish of the American tour. Besides the financial disaster of the bazaar, Mrs Trollope suffered a serious illness that almost killed her (*FT*, i, 124).

3. Auguste Jean Jacques Hervieu (fl. 1819–58), French painter of portraits, mythological and literary subjects, who had accompanied Frances Trollope to America in 1827. He painted her portrait (*c.* 1832) now in the National Portrait Gallery, London, and illustrated six of her books. His sketches for *The Domestic Manners of the Americans* (1832) were thought to have contributed to its satiric edge.

4. Rose Trollope (1821?–1917) was the daughter of Edward John Heseltine of Rotherham, Yorkshire, who was manager of the local office of the Sheffield and Rotherham Joint Stock Company. After his resignation on health grounds in 1853, audits showed a deficit of some £4000 which indicated that Mr Heseltine had been defrauding the company for many years. Before the law could catch up with him, however, he fled to France, where he died at Le Havre in 1855. See 'Mr Trollope's Father-in-law', *The Three Banks Review*, 66 (June 1965) 25–38.

5. John Tilley (1813–98) was appointed junior clerk in the Post Office service five years before Anthony who had introduced him to his sister, Cecilia. They married 11 Feb 1839. Tilley rose to be Assistant Secretary (1848) and Secretary (1864). Although they had their official quarrels he and Anthony remained close friends.

6. This and other following passages are important not so much because they illustrate Frances Trollope in later years but because they are part of the all too meagre picture we have of Rose Trollope.

7. Barney Fitzpatrick, according to Muriel Rose Trollope ('What I Was Told', *Trollopian*, ii (Mar 1948) 230), the manservant who was paid £5 a year to wake the author at 5.30 a.m. (*Auto.*, xv). James Pope Hennessy gave the surname as MacIntyre (*Anthony Trollope*, p. 75). Trollope's household, according to the 1861 Census, had no 'Barney' but a 'Bernard Smith' (*Letters*, i, 215).

8. Beatrice Trollope (1853–81). After her mother's death in 1865 she lived with her uncle for a few years at Waltham. Her uncle arranged to have Frances Eleanor Ternan instruct her in music. Back in Florence her fine voice caused some attention. George Eliot said she sang with such expression it was 'a thrilling delight to hear her' (*Letters* (New Haven, Conn., 1954) iii, 419). Augustus Hare notes in his journal of 6 Jan 1879, 'On the last evening [of 1878] I went to Mrs Terry's, where Miss Trollope sang exquisitely "Should auld acquaintance be forgot" in the last minutes of the year' (*In My Solitary Life* (1953) p. 168). Beatrice married Charles Stuart-Wortley on 16 Aug 1880 in Paris. She died the following year after the birth of a daughter.

9. Daniel Dunglas Home (1833–86), the spiritualist sensation of London society in the mid-fifties, immortalised by Browning as 'Mr Sludge, "The Medium" '. Thomas Adolphus was fascinated by his powers; see *WIR*, i 369–71.

10. Her last novel, *Fashionable Life: or Paris and London* (1856) uses seance material. An appropriately vigorous final glimpse of this amazing woman occurs in a story that went the rounds of the Browning circle in Florence: at one seance a table hurtled towards the door and Mrs Trollope cried in great excitement 'Damn it, let it go!' (*Letters of the Brownings to George Barrett*, ed. Paul Landis (Urbana, Ill., 1958) p. 201).

The Most Slovenly and Dirty Boy I Ever Met

SIR WILLIAM GREGORY

From *Sir William Gregory, KCMG: An Autobiography*, ed. Lady Gregory (1894) p. 35. William Henry Gregory (1817–92), elected MP for Dublin, 1842; High Sheriff of Galway, 1848; MP for Galway, 1857–71; Governor of Ceylon, 1871–7. Harrow, he decided was 'a fine and manly place' (*Autobiography*, p. 36). Although they were at school together they only became friends when Trollope, working for the Post Office in Ireland, visited Gregory's home, Coole Park, Galway. Here Trollope made the acquaintance of eminent men in politics, law and Irish literature, notably Charles Lever. Trollope's wretchedness gave rise to the most poignant passages in the *Auto*. (i). He attended Harrow 1822–5; 1831–4; and Winchester 1827–30; with an intervening period, 1826–7, at a private school in

Sunbury. At Harrow Trollope was unfortunate in being one of John Lyon's charity scholars, 'a victim of a bad system and hard circumstances' (Edmund Howson and George Townsend Warner, *Harrow School* (1898) p. 40). Trollope maintained he learned little from his formal schooling, although evidence suggests he did better than he made out; Lord Bessborough claimed that Trollope beat him to a prize he had hoped to win (Howson and Warner, *Harrow School*, p. 72). He also noted that Trollope's talent for English was recognised by Henry Drury (P. H. M. Bryant, *Harrow* (1936) p. 63). *En route* for Australia Trollope stayed with Gregory in Ceylon, 27 Mar to 12 Apr 1875. 'I did not much enjoy my visit there', he wrote to Millais. 'He is a very good fellow, but his house was dull and there was nothing to do or be done. I do not think he enjoys his life there very much himself. A Governor has a great deal of luxury but very little comfort. He can admit no equals, and lives in a sort of petty bastard vice royalty which would kill me' (*Letters*, II, 659).

It was when I was turned down that I became intimate with Anthony Trollope, who sat next to me.[1] He was a big boy, older than the rest of the form, and without exception the most slovenly and dirty boy I ever met. He was not only slovenly in person and in dress, but his work was equally dirty. His exercises were a mass of blots and smudges. These peculiarities created a great prejudice against him, and the poor fellow was generally avoided. It is pitiable to read in his autobiography, just published, how bitter were his feelings at that time, and how he longed for the friendship and companionship of his comrades, but in vain. There was a story afloat, whether true or false I know not, that his father had been outlawed, and every boy believed it was the duty of a loyal subject of the crown to shoot or otherwise destroy 'old Trollope' if possible. Fortunately, he never appeared among us. I had plenty of opportunities of judging of Anthony, and I am bound to say, though my heart smites me sorely for my unkindness, that I did not dislike him. I avoided him, for he was rude and uncouth, but I thought him an honest, brave fellow. He was no sneak. His faults were external; all the rest of him was right enough. But the faults were of that character for which schoolboys would never make allowances, and so poor Trollope was tabooed, and had not, so far as I am aware, a single friend. He might have been a thoroughly bad young fellow, and yet have had plenty of associates. He gave no sign of promise whatsoever, was always in the lowest part of the form, and was regarded by masters and by boys as an incorrigible dunce.[2]

NOTES

1. Under the headmaster of the day, Dr Charles Thomas Longley, Gregory won a school prize, but it was decided that an infringement of rules made him ineligible. Disappointment turned Gregory temporarily into a scapegrace: 'there was not a field within miles of Harrow in which I had not poached by day, or a pond I had not dragged at night. ... I really cared very little what I did or what became of me, so bitter and so enduring was the disappointment' (*Autobiography*, p. 34). Since misery loves company it is surprising he did not make friends with Anthony.

2. Trollope survived under two headmasters, Dr George Butler, whose term of office lasted 1805–29, and Dr Longley (1829–36). According to W. J. Courthope, Trollope was 'inaccessible to the *genius loci* of Harrow' (Howson and Warner, *Harrow School*, p. 193).

A Heart-sick, Friendless Little Chap's Exaggerations

T. H. S. ESCOTT

From Thomas Hay Sweet Escott, *Anthony Trollope* (1913) pp. 15–17. Escott (1850–1924), Trollope's first biographer, is worth attending to for his assiduous picking up of scraps from the author's lips. From 1865 he was closely connected with London daily and weekly journalism, a leading writer for the *Standard* and John Morley's successor as editor of the *Fortnightly Review*. Escott's journalistic output included *England: Its People, Polity and Pursuits* (1879), *Masters of English Journalism* (1911) and *Club Makers and Club Members* (1914). Some accounts of public school life of the period are certainly harsher. Doubtless Trollope escaped the sexual harassment Swinburne underwent at Eton, or John Addington Symonds at Harrow some ten years later. See Phyllis Grosskurth, *John Addington Symonds: A Biography* (1964) pp. 22–41. Possibly alleged base behaviour is at the root of the 'nameless horror' of an accusation Trollope alludes to as occurring at Sunbury after his initial period at Harrow (*Auto.*, i). Whatever the privations and sufferings, Trollope rose above them, like Lord Sherbrooke who wrote of his schooling: 'It was a Spartan time; but in thinking with a shudder of the brutalities of Winchester in 1825, let us not forget that three of its boys rose in after life by sheer force of ability to be Cabinet Ministers. ... Nor can either of the Trollopes be regarded as a broken reed' (A. Patchett Martin, *Life and Letters of the Rt Hon. Robert Lowe, Viscount Sherbrooke, GCB, DCL* (1893) i, 67–8).

Twelve years before Anthony's entrance there had happened events not favourable to the position of day-boys at the school. In 1810 the Harrow parishioners petitioned Chancery for the restriction of the school to local residents, chiefly, of course, shopkeepers. The counsel employed by the school bore a name, Fladgate, which, in connection with the Garrick Club, was to be well known by Anthony Trollope in later years.[1] The whole episode, being much talked about at the time, had the effect of familiarising Trollope, while a boy, with the old school of lawyers, figuring so frequently in his novels. Sir William Grant, as Master of the Rolls, thought the boarders so essential to the school's prestige and prosperity, that he would not sanction any limitation of their number. He risked, however, offending the masters by insisting on fresh guarantees as regards day-boys for the rights of residence. 'The controversy', said Trollope to the present writer, 'had the effect of adding a fresh sting to my position as a day-boy. The masters snubbed me more than ever because I was one of the class which had brought about legal interference with their vested interests. The young aristocrats, who lived sumptuously in the masters' houses, treated me like a pariah.'

At the same time the tenant of Julians Farm supplemented the supervision of the boy's home-lessons with Spartan severity of physical discipline, at least one box on the ear for every false quantity in a Latin line. Nor was there any gilding of the pill with pocket-money, books, or even proper clothes. Harrow had then a larger percentage of exceedingly rich men's sons among its boys than either Eton or Winchester. Anthony's appearance may often have been against him; but the public opinion of the place, if not at first, would in the long run have declared itself against persecuting a boy who was not a fool, who knew the use of his fists, and against whom the worst that could be said was that he came from a poor home. He was, however, as throughout life he remained, morbidly sensitive. 'My mother', he said to me in the year of his death, 'was much from home or too busy to be bothered. My father was not exactly the man to invite confidence. I tried to relieve myself by confiding my boyish sorrows to a diary that I have kept since the age of twelve, which I have just destroyed, and which, on referring to it for my autobiography some time since, I found full of a heart-sick, friendless little chap's exaggerations of his woes.'

In all great schools sets are inevitable and disappointments, heartburnings, and jealousies at real or imaginary exclusions are rife. Trollope, however, showed himself capable of holding his own, both in the schoolroom and in the playground. Judge Baylis,[2] his contemporary, admits that home boarders were often bullied and pursued with stones, but emphatically testifies that Trollope, being big and powerful got off easily; he once, it seems, fought a boy named Lewis for nearly an hour, punishing his adversary so heavily that he had to go home.[3] Of course it was, as at every big English school of the time, a rough and occasionally a brutal life, enlivened with such customs as 'rolling-in', 'tossing', and 'jack-o'-lantern'; this last was put down by Longley, who followed Butler as headmaster during Trollope's time. The education was exclusively Latin and Greek, as it was everywhere else.[4] But at home Anthony Trollope received a thorough grounding in modern languages, especially French and Italian, from his accomplished mother, and was noticed by his contemporary Sidney Herbert as a boy full of general knowledge.

NOTES

1. Francis Fladgate (1799–1892), friend of Thackeray, member of the Garrick committee.
2. Thomas Henry Baylis, QC (1817–1908) served as judge of the Passage Court, Liverpool, from 1876 until retirement in 1882. He was the author of *The Rights, Duties and Relations of Domestic Servants, their Masters and Mistresses* (1857), which ran to six editions. 'I entered the school in 1825 at the age of eight, and left as a monitor at sixteen; I was first a home-boarder, but afterwards went into Oxenham's house [Revd William Oxenham]. While a home-boarder we lived at Greenhill Green, and Anthony Trollope, whom I remember well, used to call for me on his way to the school. I used to sit next to him in the Sixth Form. I think he much exaggerated his Harrow sufferings; they were less than other home-boarders who went young to the school: they were often sadly bullied and pursued with stones on their way home' (Howson and Warner, *Harrow School*, p. 80).
3. The fight was witnessed by Henry Stuart Russell (1819–89), who attended the school from 1831 to 1837. By chance Frederick Trollope ran across him in Sydney and wrote to his father in Jan 1881: 'There is a man in the Lands office, Russell by name, who says that he was your fag at Harrow. I had a long yarn with him and he said that you once had a great fight and at last beat your man' (*Letters*, II, 893–4).
4. Edward Robert, 1st Earl of Lytton, pen-name 'Owen Meredith' (1831–91), son of E. Bulwer-Lytton, attended Harrow from 1846 to 1849 and endured the classical curriculum. Flogging for consulting cribs and other incentives to

learning he felt did not help towards 'an intelligent appreciation of the main characteristics of classical literature' (A. B. Harlan, *Owen Meredith: A Critical Biography of Robert, First Earl of Lytton* (New York, 1946) p. 19). Trollope seems to have taken the disciplined grinding well, pursuing his classical studies for the rest of his life.

A Situation and a Setback

JOHN MURRAY AND LADY LYTTON

(1) from Samuel Smiles, *A Publisher and His Friends: Memoir and Correspondence of the late John Murray* (1891) ii, 384. Murray (1778–1843), founder of the great publishing house, promoted the *Quarterly Review* and the work of Byron; his many publishing enterprises included a series of world famous handbooks; (2) from Louisa Devey, *Life of Rosina, Lady Lytton* (1887) pp. 195–7, 200–1. Frances Trollope made friends with Rosina Bulwer (1802–82) in Paris in 1839, and Thomas Adolphus was burdened with negotiations with publishers on her behalf. When she complained bitterly about being cheated he wrote back 'all hopes of a race of publishers, who shall consult their author's interest instead of their own, must be deferred to those promised days when the lion shall lie down with the lamb' (p. 203). See also *WIR*, i, 83. None of the writing Trollopes entertained any illusions about the business end of the profession.

(1)   Mr Murray was frequently invited to obtain situations for young men in London. It was through his influence with Sir Francis Freeling, with whom he was very intimate, that Mrs Trollope obtained for her son Anthony a clerkship at the Post Office.[1] She writes from Bruges to Mr Murray (20 Jan 1835) expressing her thanks to him and the Freelings, and adds, 'he leaves the office at five, and would like to be employed as corrector of the press, or in some other occupation of the kind'.[2] She deplored the loss of her boy, but says, 'I can never forget that the last weeks of his life here were rendered as comfortable as they could be, by your *premature* payment.'[3]

(2)   [Letter from Frances Trollope to Rosina Bulwer, n.d.] I have no heart to write to you, dear friend, and yet I could not see my son sending off a letter without one word from me. Oh! how your kind warm heart would pity me could you witness the

anxious misery I am enduring! My poor darling lies in a state that defies the views of his physicians as effectually as it puzzles my ignorance.[4] It is asthma from which he chiefly suffers now; but they say this can only be a symptom, and not the disease. He is frightfully reduced in size and strength; sure am I that could you see him, you would not find even a distant resemblance to the being who, exactly three months ago, left us in all the pride of youth, health and strength. Day by day I lose hope, and so, I am quite sure, do his physicians; we have had three consultations, but nothing prescribed relieves him, nor has any light been thrown on the nature of his complaint...[5]

[Letter from Frances Trollope to Rosina Bulwer, 3 July 1840.] My poor Anthony is so very nearly in the same state as when I last wrote that I have not a word to say that can help to give you information of our future movements...

[Thomas Adolphus Trollope in a postscript to the above.] My brother is unquestionably *much* better. We must not, as his sententious Esculapius says, 'cry, "Whoop!" before we are out of the wood'; but I am in great hope that he will now rapidly gain ground, and that our plans will resume their course...

[Letter from Frances and Thomas Adolphus Trollope to Rosina Bulwer, 9 July 1840.] Anthony goes on decidedly improving, but so slowly as to make every morning's enquiry one of fear and trembling. Still I DO hope and believe that we shall be able to leave England early in September; and if so, we shall proceed via Paris direct to Venice by diligence and with diligence (absolute ablative case, if not ablative case absolute), from whence we shall proceed to Naples, seeing as much of the writable about places as we can *en route*. At Naples, where we hope to arrive in November, we propose remaining till it is time to remove to Rome for the Holy Week. After that I know nothing, but think it very likely we shall pass our time at Florence.

NOTES

1. Anthony entered the Post Office as a junior clerk at St Martin's le Grand on 4 Nov 1834. At this time Sir Francis Freeling (1764–1836) was Secretary; his

daughter-in-law, Mrs Clayton Freeling, was a dear friend of Mrs Trollope's. A diary entry of Thomas Adolphus for 28 Oct notes: 'I got a letter from Mr Freeling today, containing an offer to Anthony of a place in the Post Office, and desiring to see me upon it.' Anthony was then in Bruges. See *FT*, ɪ, 224–7. The interview and its aftermath are described in *Auto*. (iii) and produced material for *The Three Clerks* (ch. ii). Regarding the appointment, Frances Trollope said 'I am happier in receiving this news than I thought anything just now could make me' (*FT*, ɪ, 227).

2. Frances Trollope was unquestionably on good terms with John Murray at this period, and it is highly likely that he did put in a good word. However, the interest here lies in the early indication of Anthony's inclinations, encouraged by his mother, towards a literary occupation. This information is omitted from *FT*, ɪ, 226. Heineman cites a further letter in the summer of 1835 in which she urges: 'He is a good scholar and, as I believe, your friend Henry Drury will allow, has very good abilities' (*Mrs Trollope*, p. 130).

3. Refers, of course, to Henry (d. 23 Dec 1834). The payment was for *Belgium and Western Germany in 1833*.

4. Getting a job did little to alter Anthony's bolshy and sullen disposition, and the early years in the Post Office, if we accept his account, were marked by debt, incompetence and dissipations (*Auto.*, iii). See R. H. Super, *Trollope in the Post Office* (Ann Arbor, Mich., 1981) p. 4; Coral Lansbury, *The Reasonable Man: Trollope's Legal Fiction* (Princeton, NJ, 1981) p. 24. Frances Trollope, for a time in Hadley, was anxious about Anthony spending four hours a day travelling to and fro, and moved to Portman Square where Tom and Anthony joined her (Heineman, *Mrs Trollope*, p. 154). In a letter of 26 Sep 1839 she spoke of a trip they both made to Paris, fulfilling her promise to Anthony (Heineman, *Mrs Trollope*, p. 192). But after this pick-me-up her son succumbed to a mysterious illness.

5. In desperation France Trollope turned to her physician, Dr Elliotson, an advocate of hypnosis and mesmeric influence, who brought two cataleptic patients, the Okey sisters, to his bedside. Tom Trollope records that under mesmeric influence they were in the habit of declaring that they 'saw Jack' by the bed of this or that patient in hospital. The patients in question invariably died. 'Now it is within my own knowledge that the Okey girls, especially one of them (Jane, I think her name was), were very frequently in the lodgings occupied by my brother at the time, during the period of his greatest danger, and used constantly to say that they "saw Jack by his side, but only up to his knee", and therefore they thought he would recover – as he did!' (*WIR*, ɪɪ, 370).

The Damned Sassenach

R. J. KELLY, C. BIANCONI AND THOMAS ADOLPHUS TROLLOPE

(1) from R. J. Kelly, 'Trollope in Ireland', *The Irish Book Lover*, xvɪɪɪ, 46 (July, Aug 1931) 110–11. After seven years in the Post Office (1834–41) Trollope's

career was at a dead end, but obtaining a Surveyor's Clerkship in the west of Ireland which no one else seemed to want brought a transformation. He worked hard, rode, married, had two sons and began to write fiction. His Irish hosts took to him, and his self confidence grew. 'It was altogether a very jolly life that I led in Ireland' (*Auto.*, iv); (2) from M. O'C. Bianconi and S. J. Watson, *Bianconi: King of the Irish Roads* (Dublin, 1962) pp. 60, 118–19, 90–1. Charles Bianconi (1786–1875), impressed by the lack of cheap carriage for the poor, developed a coach system which made his fortune. The 'Bians' were four-wheeled cars drawn by three or four horses carrying mail and passengers. By 1843 he had over 1300 horses and 100 vehicles. He was elected Mayor of Clonmel (1844) and held an estate of 1000 acres at Longfield House, near Clonmel. Trollope, intent on improving mail services across the country, was quick to enlist Bianconi's services. In his 'History of the Post Office in Ireland' Trollope wrote that perhaps no one had done more for the benefit of the sister kingdom (*Parl. Papers 1857, IV, 2195, 62: Third Report of the Postmaster General, Appendix J*). See Howard Robinson, *The British Post Office: A History* (1948) p. 227. The Bianconi biography, published in 1878, was chiefly the work of Henry Merivale Trollope (*Letters*, ii, 730); (3) from *WIR*, ii, 258–60; ii, 76–9. Tom visited the transformed public servant at Banagher not long after his appointment as Surveyor's Clerk.

(1) He paid his first visit to Ireland in September, 1843.[1] Irregularities had occurred in the Post Office at Drumsna, Co. Leitrim, then managed by William Allen. Anthony Trollope was ordered to proceed at once to Drumsna to investigate the case. After a weary journey, he arrived late in the afternoon at his destination, and put up at a small public house, the only place of entertainment in the village. His bedroom was approached by a flight of steps, half stairs, half ladder, not far from perpendicular. The room was scantily furnished. It contained two beds close together, a table, a chair and a basin-stand. Weary, after his long journey on the outside of a coach, he retired early, and tried to fasten his door, but found he could not, as it had neither bolt nor lock. When he went to bed it was some time before he slept, as he felt nervous and uncomfortable in this strange place. He kept regretting that he had not waited a day longer till his friend Merivale (the historian) could have accompanied him.[2] At last he fell into an uneasy restless sort of sleep, and did not know how long he had been sleeping, when he woke up and heard a footstep stealthily approaching his bed. Frightened, and but half awake, he sprang from his bed, seized the intruder, and found himself grappling with a powerful man, clad, like himself, only in his shirt, whom he held so tightly by the throat that he could not speak. In their struggle they came to the open door, where his antagonist stumbled and fell down the stairs. Aroused by the noise of the

struggle and the fall, the inmates of the house rushed into the room and struck a light. The moment they had done so, Trollope heard his landlady cry out; 'Oh, boys, that murderin' villain upstairs has killed his raverance!' 'We'll soon settle the damned Sassenach', said the men, rushing to the steps; and but for the intervention of the half-strangled priest, who had now come to himself, Trollope would have no doubt have been lynched without more ado, and we should never have had the pleasure of reading his many interesting novels.[3] The first of these novels was the outcome of this visit to Drumsna. It was called *The Macdermots of Ballycloran*. The scene is laid at Headfort Castle, now in ruins, once the seat of the Jones family, and afterwards of the Johnstones who married into the Jones's. But to return to the scene in the Drumsna village inn. When peace was established, apologies made and accepted, and explanation given, Trollope found that the man he had assaulted was the parish priest, who had been kept out at a late call in this part of his parish, had come into the inn to get a bed. Hearing that an English gentleman was occupying the other bed in the room, and not wishing to disturb him, he went up as noiselessly as possible, undressed, put out his candle and was creeping into bed as softly as he could lest he might awake the stranger. He was amazed when he was seized by the throat and flung down the stairs. Fortunately, he was none the worse of his fall, and he and Trollope became fast friends. Trollope draws a picture of this kindly gentleman, as a priest of the old school educated in France, in *The Macdermots of Ballycloran*. Merivale and Trollope walked out the day after Merivale's arrival to Headfort Castle, and there, on the strength of a true story told him as he came down on the coach from Longford, by McCluskie, the Guard of the Coach, he laid the scene and founded the plot of his first novel.[4]

(2)   It was about this time that Charles's surname received its final adaptation. It proved too difficult for the country people to say 'Bianconi cars', so they simply called them 'Bians' (pronounced 'By-anns') instead. This abbreviation was finally perpetuated by no less an authority than Anthony Trollope who, when asked by Bianconi's daughter whether such a slang term could properly be used in writing her father's biography, replied 'Certainly call the cars "Bians". The name became too well known to be slang.'...

It now became necessary to provide guards to travel on the larger cars not only to protect the mails but to attend to the luggage and parcels traffic. To entertain the passengers *en route*, the guards were issued with key-bugles on which they used to play popular marching songs such as 'The Girl I left behind me'. The most famous of these guards was called McCluskie who was distinguished by his ready wit, by his wide knowledge of literature and by his understanding of human nature. The novelist, Anthony Trollope, once travelled with him, and spent most of the trip extolling the virtues and usefulness of the donkey – only to receive the devastating rejoinder from McCluskie 'Ah well, sir, a fellow feeling makes us wondrous kind.'...

Trollope had no doubt seen Bianconi striding through St Martin's le Grand in London; and, having come to Clonmel in the course of his inspections, he was able to make his acquaintance which quickly ripened into friendship. Indeed, Eliza Bianconi used to say that 'Silverbridge' in *The Last Chronicle of Barset* was so called in memory of his happy visits to Silver Spring, where he would always wake up early to write for an hour or so before going out hunting. Young Charley Bianconi, who always had two of the best horses out at each meet, used to remark condescendingly that Trollope 'went quite well, but his horses were not much good'.

(3)   Having spoken of Anthony's efficiency as an officer of the Post Office, I may, I think, in the case of so well known a man, venture to expend a page in giving the reader an anecdote of his promptness, of which, as dozens of other similar experiences, he says nothing in his *Autobiography*.[5] He had visited the office of a certain postmaster in the south-west of Ireland in the usual course of his duties, had taken stock of the man, and had observed him in the course of his interview carefully lock a large desk in the office. Two days afterwards there came from headquarters an urgent enquiry about a lost letter, the contents of which were of considerable value. The information reached the surveyor late at night, and he at once put the matter into the hands of his subordinate. There was no conveyance to the place where my brother determined his first investigations should be made till the following morning. But it did not suit him to wait for that, so he hired a horse, and, riding hard, knocked up the postmaster whom he had interviewed, as related, a couple of days before, in the small hours. Possibly the demeanour of the man in some degree

influenced his further proceedings. Be this as it may, he walked straight into the office, and said, 'Open that desk!' The key, he was told, had been lost for some time past. Without another word he smashed the desk with one kick, and – there found the stolen letter!

I have heard from him so many good stories of his official experiences, that I feel myself tolerably competent to write a volume of 'Memoirs of a Post Office Surveyor'. But for the present I must content myself with one other of his adventures. He had been sent to South America to arrange some difficulties about postal communication in those parts which our authorities wished to be accomplished in a shorter time than had been previously the practice.[6] There was a certain journey that had to be done by a mounted courier, for which it was insisted that three days were necessary, while my brother was persuaded it could be done in two. He was told that he knew nothing of their roads and their horses, etc. 'Well,' said he, 'I will ask you to do nothing that I, who know nothing of the country, and can only have such a horse as your post can furnish me, cannot do myself. I will ride with your courier, and then I shall be able to judge.' And at daybreak the next morning they started. The brute they gave him to ride was of course selected with a view of making good their case, and the saddle was simply an instrument of torture. He rode through that hot day and kept the courier to his work in a style that rather astonished that official. But at night, when they were to rest for a few hours, Anthony confessed that he was in such a state that he began to think that he should have to throw up the sponge, which would have been dreadful to him. So he ordered two bottles of brandy, poured them into a wash-hand basin, and *sat in it*! His description of the agonising result was graphic! But the next day, he said, he was able to sit in his saddle without pain, and did the journey in the two days, and carried his point.

[Tom and his mother were living at Penrith, Cumberland in 1842. The following year they left for Florence, where they had decided to settle permanently.] My brother, already a very different man from what he had been in London, came from his Irish district to visit us there and I returned with him to Ireland, to his headquarters at Banagher on the Shannon. Neither of this journey need I say much. For to all who know anything of Ireland at the present day – and who does not? worse luck! – anything I might write would seem as *nihil ad rem*, as if I were writing of an island in the Pacific. I remember a very vivid impression that occurred to me on first landing at Kingstown, and accompanied me during the whole of my stay in the island, to the effect, that the striking differences in everything that fell under my observation from what I had left behind me at Holyhead, were fully as great as any that had excited my interest when first landing in France.

One of my first visits was to my brother's chief. He was a master of foxhounds and hunted the country. And I well remember my astonishment, when the door of this gentleman's residence was opened to me by an extremely dirty and slatternly bare-footed and bare-legged girl. I found him to be a very friendly and hospitable good fellow, and his wife and her sister very pleasant women. I found too that my brother stood high in his good graces by virtue of simply having taken the whole work and affairs of the postal district on his own shoulders. The rejected of St Martin's le Grand was already a very valuable and capable officer.

My brother gave me the choice of a run to the Killeries, or to Killarney. We could not manage both. I chose the former, and a most enjoyable trip we had. He could not leave his work to go with me, but was to join me subsequently, I forget where, in the west. Meantime he gave me a letter to a bachelor friend of his at Clifden. This gentleman immediately asked me to dinner, and he and I dined tête-à-tête. Nevertheless, he thought it necessary to apologise for the appearance of a very fine John Dory on the table, saying, that he had been himself to the market to get a turbot for me, but that he had been asked half-a-crown for a not very large one, and really he could not give such absurd prices as that!

Anthony duly joined me as proposed, and we had a grand walk over the mountains above the Killeries. I don't forget and never shall forget – nor did Anthony ever forget; alas! that we shall never more talk over that day again – the truly grand spectacular changes from dark thick enveloping cloud to brilliant sunshine, suddenly revealing all the mountains and the wonderful colouring of the intertwining sea beneath them, and then back to cloud and mist and drifting sleet again. It was a glorious walk. We returned wet to the skin to 'Joyce's Inn', and dined on roast goose and whisky punch, wrapped in our blankets like Roman senators!

One other scene I must recall. The reader will hardly believe that it occurred in Ireland. There was an election of a member for I forget what county or borough, and my brother and I went to the hustings – the only time I ever was at an election in Her Majesty's dominions. What were the party feelings, or the party colours, I utterly forget. It was merely for the fun of the thing that we went there. The fun indeed was fast and furious. The whole scene on the hustings, as well as around them, seemed to me one seething mass of senseless but good-humoured hustling and confusion. Suddenly in the midst of the uproar an ominous cracking was heard, and in the next minute the hustings swayed and came down with a crash, heaping together in a confused mess all the two or three hundreds of human beings who were on the huge platform. Some few were badly hurt. But my brother and I being young and active, and tolerably stout fellows, soon extricated ourselves, regained our legs, and found that we were none the worse. Then we began to look to our neighbours. And the first who came to hand was a priest, a little man, who was lying with two or three fellows on the top of him, horribly frightened and roaring piteously for help. So Anthony took hold of one of his arms and I of the other, and by main force dragged him from under the superincumbent mass of humanity. When we got him on his legs his gratitude was unbounded. 'Tell me your names', he shouted, 'that I'll pray for ye!' We told him laughingly that we were afraid it was no use, for we were heretics. 'Tell me your names', he shouted again, 'that I'll pray for ye all the more!'

NOTES

1. Incorrect. Trollope was appointed Surveyor's Clerk in the Central District of Ireland in July 1841. He arrived in Dublin on 15 Sep *en route* to Banagher. He was transferred to the Southern District in Aug 1844. In 1845 he was stationed at Mallow. In later life he told William Allingham that he had been in every parish in Ireland (*William Allingham: A Diary*, ed. H. Allingham and D. Radford (1907) p. 106).

2. Not the historian Charles Merivale, but Trollope's close friend John Merivale (1815–86), who became a barrister and later a Commissioner in Bankruptcy.

3. This adventure inspired Trollope's short story 'Father Giles of Ballymoy', published in *Lotta Schmidt and Other Stories* (1867). It first appeared in *Argosy*, May 1866. In his story Trollope places the adventure in Ballymoy, Galway. Kelly's location at Drumsna seems erroneous.

4. The same McCluskie mentioned in the Bianconi item which follows. Trollope describes the origins of his first novel in *Auto.*, iv.

5. Tom marvelled at the transformation, saying that once Anthony had become Surveyor's Clerk he rapidly appeared 'one of the most efficient and valuable officers in the Post Office' (*WIR*, I, 257).

6. As part of his tour of the West Indies Trollope ventured into Central but not to South America.

'Fine Imagination' – 'Admirable Cross Examiner'.

JUSTIN McCARTHY AND *KERRY EVENING POST*

(1) from Justin McCarthy, *Reminiscences* (1899) I, 369–73. McCarthy (1830–1912), politician, historian and novelist, began his career on the *Northern Daily Times* in Liverpool, 1854; he became lead writer for the *Daily News*, 1871. His novels included *Dear Lady Disdain* (1875) and *Miss Misanthrope* (1878). His singular comment on the novel of Parliamentary life Trollope could have written fails to comprehend the great insight into politics and the workings of government shown in the Palliser novels; (2) from the *Kerry Evening Post* (28 July 1849): a report of the case heard at the Kerry Summer Assizes under Judge Ball in which Mary O'Reilly was charged with stealing a letter containing a sovereign, the property of the Postmaster General, represented by James Kendrick, Surveyor. The preliminary evidence dealt with Trollope's elaborate plan to catch the thief.

(1)   My first recollections of Anthony Trollope go back a long way indeed. I do not think I can have been twenty years old when I first saw Trollope, and I saw him under somewhat peculiar conditions. He appeared as a witness in a case which was tried before a Judge of Assize at the Court House of Tralee in the County of Kerry; and I happened to be attending the court as correspondent for a Cork newspaper. Trollope was then employed as an inspector under the Irish Post office; and it had fallen to his lot to be commissioned to inquire into some irregularities in the transmission of letters containing money

through certain parts of the country. In those far-off days, when the Post Office order and the postal note had not yet become popular, it was a common practice to send money in the crude form of gold and silver coin from one place to another. Trollope started out upon his quest, and he adopted an ingenious plan. He travelled by the ordinary mail-coach; and before he began his journey he enclosed a marked sovereign to an address at the town which lay farthest along the track which the coach had to travel. After the coach had passed through the first town on his way, Trollope announced himself, at the first place where the coach stopped to change horses, as a Post Office Inspector, and claimed his right to examine the mail-bags. He did so; and found his letter all right with the seal unbroken and the heavy sovereign still weighing it. The missive was accordingly put back into the mail-bag again and the journey was resumed. Thus the Inspector passed from one town to another, until, before his journey had nearly drawn to its close, he went through a village, on emerging from which he had, as usual, recourse to the mail-bag and found that his letter had been opened and carefully resealed, and that no coin was inside. He promptly went back to the village he had left, and called the police into requisition, and the marked sovereign was found to be in possession of the postmistress of the place.

Thereupon a prosecution was instituted. Now, the postmistress was young and rather pretty, and had a good many friends and backers in the neighbourhood; and her supporters provided her with counsel in order that the best case might be made out for her at the Assizes. The leading counsel who was engaged for the defence was Isaac Butt, the great Irish advocate whom I have already mentioned, more than once, in these pages, and who is best known to modern readers as the first leader of a Home Rule Party in the House of Commons.[1] Anthony Trollope was the principal witness for the prosecution, and Butt's whole case depended on the chance of his bewildering Trollope, and causing him, somehow, to bungle or to break down in his evidence. In those days an extent of licence was allowed to cross-examining counsel, which the more rigorous practices of our law courts at present would render wholly impossible. Butt was a splendid cross-examiner, and did everything he could to baffle and bewilder the Post Office Inspector. He produced in court one of Trollope's own novels – one of the very few novels he had published up to that time – and he proceeded to cross-examine

Trollope as to the meaning of certain passages in the book which professed to describe a trial in an Irish court of criminal law. Trollope was asked whether he wrote this passage and that passage and the other, whether he had described the judge on the bench in these particular words, and the garnishing of the bench in these other words; and whether he held by his humorous descriptions as a just and faithful picture of an Irish court; and whether his description of the countenances and manners of the gentlemen in the jury-box was intended to apply only to an imaginary jury, or meant as a deliberate caricature of Irish juries in general. Butt's object was, in part, to bewilder Trollope and make him lose his temper, and so get into a condition of mind which might lead to his blundering in some way when he came to give the material part of his evidence; and in part also to prejudice the jury against him as a cockney slanderer who was endeavouring to cast ridicule on the institutions of the Green Isle. Butt, however, failed completely in his attempt; he could not puzzle Trollope, or bewilder him, or even cause him to lose his temper; nor did Trollope ever fail to give an effective and droll answer to every effective and droll question. The contest became a most amusing trial of skill, readiness, and temper between the clever counsel and the clever witness. ...

At that time I had only just come to know of Anthony Trollope as a novelist; and a great many years passed away before I met him in London, when he was at the very height of his reputation. Many times during our occasional meetings in the literary circles of the capital I have called to mind that odd scene in the Tralee Court House; and have been somewhat amused by the fact that the chief impression that Trollope then made on me was not so much even by his cleverness as by his imperturbable good-humour.[2] Imperturbable good-humour was not, I think, usually regarded by Post Office officials or by literary men as Trollope's especial characteristic. He had the reputation rather of a man with a rugged rasping temper, and a masterful way. We all know – he has told us himself – of the patient, methodical, dogged way in which he worked at his novels; and I have often thought that, on that distant day in the Tralee Court House, he must have noticed the expression of anticipated triumph beaming on Isaac Butt's broad, rugged, good-humoured face; and must have set it out as a task for himself to keep his temper to the very last, and not to give his opponent the slightest chance of a triumphant laugh at his expense. ...

I am still sorry that he was not successful in obtaining a seat in the House of Commons.[3] I am sorry, first, because success would have gratified him, and next, because I have always thought that a chance still remained, even after Disraeli's early books, for a great novel of English Parliamentary life, and that Anthony Trollope was the man who could have written it. Thackeray, too, failed in obtaining a seat in the House of Commons; but I cannot feel any regret that he was kept altogether for other work. We are told that Dickens had no Parliamentary ambition, and would not have entered the House of Commons if a constituency had begged him on its bended knees.[4] But this surely is a mistake. Whatever Dickens may have thought and resolved at a later period of his career, it is quite certain, I take it, that at one season of his popularity he was very anxious for a seat in Parliament. All consideration of that question may now, however, as Egmont says in the tragedy, 'be quietly put aside'. I only hold to my position that Trollope could have written from the inside a good novel of Parliamentary life, and that I am sorry he did not get the chance of writing it.

(2)   Cross-examined by Mr Butt: It was with this 'official' seal he sealed up the sovereign at last Assizes; it was an official; it was not made under the direction of the Post Office authorities, but under that of a friend – an official authority, kept no facsimile of the sovereign when he scratched it in Killarney; did not take another sovereign and mark it in the same way so as to enable him, by comparison to identify the mark; it never occurred to him, nor did he think it would be a better way of identifying it; has not the slightest doubt of the sovereign from this mark; the mark was made with a penknife under the neck on the head (loud laughter).[5]
Mr Butt: On the head under the neck!
Mr. Trollope: I did not say that. You are making more mistakes than I am.
Mr Butt: I ask you was it on the head?
Mr Trollope: I marked it under the neck on the head (great laughter).

Mr Butt: You marked it under the neck on the head! You are acquainted with the English language, writing it occasionally?
Mr Trollope: Occasionally.
Mr Butt: And yet you cannot give an intelligible answer on this head.
Mr Trollope: You had better give it up.
Mr Butt: You marked it on ... what is it?
Mr Trollope: I marked it under the neck on the head (renewed laughter).
Mr Butt: Be so kind as to tell his Lordship what part of the body that is?
Mr Trollope: I think you misunderstand me. I didn't say I marked the sovereign on the head under the neck, but I marked the neck under the head (great laughter). (*To the Court*): Means by the head, on the obverse.
Mr Butt: You would meake it a head or harp?
Mr Trollope: I didn't mean a head and harp. I marked it under the neck on the head (laughter) – under the neck on the obverse part of the coin, that which has the Sovereign's head upon it.
Mr Butt: Show me on another sovereign where under the neck on the head is.
Mr Trollope: Below the whole figure of the Sovereign's head.
To Mr Butt: There was no other scratch on the sovereign when he marked it, equally visible to the one he put on it; would not state on his oath there was no other scratch; would not say there were not a thousand scratches on it; examined the sovereign so as to identify it; cannot tell if there is another scratch on it; cannot tell the length or depth of the scratch; did not put more than one scratch on it; put another on it since last Assizes, after folding it up, and one only; this was not for the purpose of identifying it again, but to enable him to know if it altered while in the hands of the lawyers (laughter).
Mr Butt: Then you did not depend on your knowledge of the scratch?
Mr Trollope: Not after you knew how it was marked; no sovereign could be marked accidentally in that way, in the pockets; the mark was deeper and broader than the sovereign would get from feeling or use; a person fiddling with a knife might make that mark upon it, but there is no other such mark upon it; has identified the sovereign.
Mr Butt: Where did you put the second mark?

Mr Trollope: I cannot explain till I see the second sovereign; put a mark on the letter 'u' in 'Brittaniarum'; put no other mark upon it.

Mr Butt: Now take the ear on the head above the neck of the sovereign which I now give you, and tell me is there any mark on it?

Mr Trollope: I see a mark not so deep as my mark. I undertake to say it is not a quarter so deep.

Mr Butt (to the Court): Does not use magnifying glasses; uses short-sighted glasses. Then they magnify (laughter).

Mr Trollope: No; their effect is to make my sight equal to that of other people.

Mr Butt: Now tell me, as a matter of fact, when you found the sovereign in Miss O'Reilly's purse, whether that last mark was on it or not?

Mr Trollope: I cannot tell.

Mr Butt: When did you put the second mark upon it?

Mr Trollope: In the hotel in this town, after returning from Court; if ten sovereigns were marked in that way, he couldn't pick out the one; brought the police with him to the post office; prisoner was there when he went in; doesn't think any one else was there; is quite sure Mr Mason was in the office before witness spoke a word; there were three or four persons in the shop from which the office is partitioned off; does not remember the window being put down – the office window (the sliding panel) by Miss O'Reilly; does not remember her saying anything when she closed it; saw no one at the window named Loughnane, did not hear her apologising to anyone for closing the window; will not swear this did not happen; did not observe it; might have observed it and forgotten it; Mr Mason said he had no money about him and turned out his waistcoat pockets; he was searched and had no money; Miss O'Reilly took out her purse; she didn't hesitate in doing so; this sovereign and some silver was in the purse; cannot say if there was anything else.

Mr Butt: What made you say, without being asked 'I cannot say if there was anything else in the purse'?

Mr Trollope: Because I was asked the question last Assizes, and could not give an absolute answer; I since heard there was a pound note in it.

Mr Butt: It is not because you afterwards heard there was no pound note in it that you gave that qualified answer?

Mr Trollope: No.

Mr Butt: Will you now swear that Miss O'Reilly did not say 'I got *money* from Mr Mason three days ago'?

Mr Trollope: I cannot.

Mr Butt: Did she then say she got that sovereign from Mr Mason?

Mr Trollope: I'll swear she led me to understand that she got that identical sovereign from him. I cannot tell the words.

Mr Butt: Did you say to the constable give her back that sovereign, it is her own money, or give her back that pound note?

Mr Trollope: I suggested in the presence of Mr Drummond that the constable should give her back any other money as she might want it; she was examined by a woman; the constable didn't ask him for the sovereign; will not swear if he asked him for it that he would not give it to him; cannot tell if he asked him.

Mr Butt: Did the policeman say to you that his was the proper custody?

Mr Trollope: I cannot tell.

Mr Butt: Look at that jury, and tell them, on your oath, you cannot tell.

Mr Trollope: I have no recollection.

Mr Butt: In that hour and a half, you did not – of course by accident – mark the sovereign?

Mr Trollope: I did not. I took the precaution of putting it in a pocket where there was nothing else; the mail was brought by a foot messenger to Ardfert; he was above sixteen.

Mr Butt: What was the name of your Correspondent?

Mr Trollope: Miss Jemina Cotton.

Mr Butt: She had no existence except in your fine imagination?

Mr Trollope: It was purely a fictitious name.

Mr Butt: And Mr Payton?

Mr Trollope: Was equally a fictitious person.

Mr Butt: You seem to deal in fictitious characters?

Mr Trollope: In another way.

Mr Butt: Do you know *The Macdermots of Ballycloran* (laughter).

Mr Trollope: I know of a book of that name.

Mr Butt: Do you remember the barrister of the name of Allwind (laughter)?

Mr Trollope: I do.

Mr Butt: And another name O'Napper.

Mr Trollope: Yes.

Mr Butt: I believe in drawing that character, it was your intention to favour the world with the beau ideal of a good cross-examiner?

Mr Trollope: Yes. I dreamed of you (loud laughter).

Mr Butt: Do you remember the red moreen over the judge's head (laughter).

Mr Trollope: Undoubtedly.

Mr Butt (reading from Mr Trollope's book): You thought that red moreen, if it could only speak, if it had a tongue to tell, what an indifferent account it could give of the conscience of judges, and the veracity of lawyers (loud laughter)? I hope you do not think that now (laughter)?

Mr Trollope: I'm rather strengthened in my opinion (tremendous laughter).

Mr Butt: 'He told them what he had to say should be very brief, and considering a lawyer and a barrister, he kept his word with tolerable fidelity' (loud laughter). You pictured to yourself a model cross-examiner?

Mr Trollope: I dreamed of someone like you in cross-examination (laughter).

Mr Butt: Had you the mark of the money under the neck on the head when you dreamed of me?

Mr Trollope: Not *that* mark exactly.

Mr Butt: Fine imagination.

Mr Trollope: Admirable cross examiner.

NOTES

1. Isaac Butt (1813–79), the distinguished advocate, was a formidable opponent in the courtroom. One of the original founders of *Dublin University Magazine* which he edited, 1834–8, he served in Parliament, 1852–65, before returning to Ireland where he became the champion of Home Rule.

2. Testimonies to Trollope's geniality in the context of his official life are none too numerous but the abrupt and hostile manner was typical of his class and the civil service lingua franca.

3. Trollope ran as Liberal candidate for Beverley in the General Election of 1868. See *Auto.*, xvi; Arthur Pollard, *Trollope's Political Novels* (1968); John Halperin, *Trollope and Politics: A Study of the Pallisers and Others* (1977).

4. Dickens wrote to Tom Trollope, 10 Sep 1868: 'It was proposed to me, under very flattering circumstances indeed, to come in as the third member for Birmingham; I replied in what is now my stereotyped phrase, "that no consideration on earth would induce me to become a candidate for the representation of any place in the House of Commons". Indeed it is a dismal sight,

is that arena altogether. Its irrationality and dishonesty are quite shocking' (*WIR*, ii, 127).

5. Interviews in the modern sense of the term are rare among Victorian novelists. This one-to-one exchange, however, is the longest example we have of Trollopian dialogue and repartee in real life. Trollope's poise and self-control on this occasion tell us a good deal about his maturity and self assurance.

Booted and Spurred

J. G. UREN AND T. H. S. ESCOTT

(1) from J. G. Uren 'My Early Recollections of the Post Office in the West of England', *Blackfriars*, ix (July–Dec 1889) 157–9. Trollope was sent on special postal missions to the west of England and Channel Islands on 1 Aug 1851, which extended into Wales in Mar 1852. In Aug 1853 he moved to Belfast as acting Surveyor, Northern District of Ireland, and in Oct 1854 he became Surveyor of Northern District; (2) from T. H. S. Escott, *Anthony Trollope*, pp. 113–16. Since Escott was born in 1850 he must have been very small indeed when this incident took place, so allowance must be made for a certain imaginative reconstruction, with the benefit, no doubt, of casual remarks dropped by the novelist.

(1) It was at Falmouth I made the acquaintance of the late Mr Anthony Trollope. He had been sent into Cornwall, I think in 1849 or 1850, to 'revise the Rural Posts', a task about as easy for a stranger in those days as to lay out a post road on the Upper Congo. I remember his stalking into the office, booted and spurred, much to the consternation of the maiden lady in charge. He seemed to us then the very incarnation of a martinet, though I have since heard that he really was a kind-hearted man, and that this was the way he had of showing it. At any rate, he frightened the unfortunate rural messenger, whose walk he was about to test, almost out of his wits. The man had £1 of penny stamps – then unperforated – to take to the sub-office at Constantine and, flurried at the presence of so fierce looking a gentleman, he clapped them into his hat! The day was hot, and before they reached their journey's end the stamps had stuck so closely and firmly to poor old Pollard's head, that all the ingenuity they could

muster could not detach them. Mr Trollope roared at the fun, and brought the man back, stamps and all, so that the aid of a barber might be invoked to release him from his predicament.

In the course of his travels Mr Trollope visited Penzance, and, for once in his life, found his match, in the person of the late postmistress, Miss Ellen Catherine Swain. Miss Swain was the heroine of many a battle, both with officials and the public. A most attractive woman, then 'fat, fair and forty', she had a temper which brooked no opposition, and a tongue, if one may say so of a lady, like a rasp file. When Mr Trollope bounced into the office and, with flaming eyes and distended nostrils, announced that he had come 'to survey the Land's End District', Miss Swain fired up like a tigress robbed of her young. Colonel Maberly she knew, and Mr Creswell she knew,[1] but who was this interloper, a cross between a country farmer and a whipper-in, who, without saying 'by your leave', had intruded on her privacy and shocked her sense of propriety? At any rate she would have none of him, and telling him, in no very complimentary terms, that he was 'no gentleman', she straight-away ordered him out of the house. It should be recorded, however, that although Greek met Greek in this way, Mr Trollope made his peace with the peppery West Cornwall postmistress, and they were afterwards capital friends.

I know that Mr Trollope encountered at least one other knight-in-petticoats during his stay in Cornwall. In pursuance of his duty of 'revising the Rural Posts', Mr Trollope visited the little village of Mousehole, on the western shore of Mount's Bay. The sub-office was kept (and in fact is, as the sub-postmistress is alive to tell the tale) by a Miss Elizabeth Trembath – popularly known as Betsy – a quaker lady, whose fame as a gossip-monger, and for general outspokenness, is of more than local notoriety. Dusting a chair with the corner of her apron, and saying to her guest, in broad Cornish, 'Wusta plaas to tak'a saat?' The following conversation ensued:

Mr Trollope: I am an Inspector from the General Post Office, and I wish to make some enquiries about the posts in this neighbourhood.

Miss Trembath: From the General Poast Office arta? I'm bra glad to see he sure 'nuf. Wusta ha' a dish o'tay?

Mr Trollope: I say I wish to make some enquiries. Can you tell me where –

Miss Trembath: Lor' bless the man. Doantee be in such a pore. I can't tellee noathin' if thee'st stand glazing at me like a chucked pig, as thee art now.

Mr Trollope: (losing his temper): Don't thee and thou me my good woman, but answer my questions. I will report you.

Miss Trembath: Good woman am I? Report me wusta? And I be'n so civil toee, too. Thees't better report my tuppence-farden a day.

Readers of Mr Trollope's works will remember that he puts this identical speech into the mouth of Mrs Crump, the postmistress, in the *Small House at Allington*. The original of Mrs Crump is, without doubt, my old friend Miss Trembath, who is still in office, and whose salary, although not now tuppence-farden a day, has scarcely reached the not too liberal sum of fivepence.

(2)   While that process was going forward I first became known to Anthony Trollope. Living, as a child, with my parents at Budleigh Salterton in South Devon, I found one day the morning's lessons interrupted by the announcement that a strange gentleman who seemed in a hurry desired to see my father at once. The visitor, then on his Post Office rounds in the west, and known as the author of *The Warden*, and the visited had not seen each other since the days when they were schoolboys together at Winchester. The stranger, I can just recollect, as I watched him at our midday dinner, seemingly added to his naturally large dimensions by a shaggy overcoat, or it may have been a large, double-breasted pea-jacket, making him look like one of those sea captains about whom in the fifties we used to hear a great deal on the Devonshire coast. Penny postage, with all its intended benefits, was then, it must be remembered, on its trial. Every corner of the western counties had been, or at the time referred to was being, travelled over by Trollope for the purpose of ensuring the regular delivery of letters throughout the kingdom, of enquiring into all complaints, with a view of investigating the circumstances and removing the cause.[2] This official pilgrimage was for two reasons a landmark in Trollope's course, literary and official. It gave him all that he wanted in the way of human varieties for peopling not only the pages of *The Warden* but, in their earlier portions, of the other Barchester books. Secondly, it enabled him to show that the public department he had entered as a youth of nineteen had now no more active, alert and resourceful

servant than himself. He had for some time reported the usefulness of roadside letter boxes in France, and advised their being tried in England. His proposal was experimentally adopted. On his suggestion of the exact spot for the purpose, the first pillar box was erected at St Helier, Jersey, in 1853.[3]

'...Boy, help me on with my coat.' Those were the only words I can recollect Trollope addressing to me on the occasion just described. It was not until the earliest years of my London work, that I heard his voice again. He had then settled in or near London, and had vouchsafed me the beginnings of an acquaintance which a little later was to grow into an intimacy ended only by his death. During the seventies, my occupations took me a great deal about different parts of the United Kingdom. One November day, at Euston Station, he entered the compartment of the train in which I was already seated, on some journey due north. Just recognising me, he began to talk cheerily enough for some little time; then, putting on a huge fur cap, part of which fell down over his shoulders, he suddenly asked: 'Do you ever sleep when you are travelling? I always do'; and forthwith, suiting the action to the word, sank into that kind of snore compared by Carlyle to a Chaldean trumpet in the new moon.[4] Rousing himself up as we entered Grantham, or Preston, Station, he next enquired: 'Do you ever write when you are travelling?' 'No.' 'I always do'. Quick as thought out came the tablet and the pencil, and the process of putting words on paper continued without a break till the point was reached at which, his journey done, he left the carriage.[5]

Several years later, when recalling this meeting, he told me that during this journey he had added a couple of chapters to a serial story.[6] Ever since he had first turned novelist in Ireland, he had found himself too busy with Post Office work to do much in the day, too tired and sleepy for anything like a long spell of labour at night. He recollected having heard Sir Charles Trevelyan speak of the intellectual freshness and capacity for prolonged exertion felt by him when, having gone to bed an hour or so before midnight, he woke up as long after. 'Never', said Sir Charles, 'did my brain seem clearer or stronger, and the work of minute writing easier or better done than when, indisposed to sleep, I went through my papers, often in the quiet which precedes the dawn.' The suggestion was no sooner made than followed. At first Trollope exactly imitated Trevelyan, and, after a short nap, worked for an hour or two, and then composed himself to slumber again. By degrees he made the experiment of taking as much sleep as he could by 5.30 a.m. Then, if he did not wake of his own accord, he was called, in his early days by his old Irish groom, afterwards by another servant. Coffee and bread and butter were brought to him in his dressing-room. Then came the daily task of pen he had set himself. This accomplished, if in London he mounted his horse for never less than a good half-hour's ride in Hyde Park before sitting down to the family breakfast as nearly as possible at eleven. That left him with a comfortable sense of necessary duty fulfilled, and the whole day lay before him for pleasure or business, his chief afternoon amusement being a rubber at the Garrick.

NOTES

1. Colonel William Leader Maberly (1798–1885), Secretary of the Post Office, 1836–54, thoroughly disapproved of the young Trollope, and indeed sent a letter through to the Secretary of the Irish Post Office upon his transfer, informing him that the new man was practically worthless. Trollope notes triumphantly that he lived down the bad report and 'Before a year was over, I had acquired the character of a thoroughly good public servant' (*Auto.*, iv); George Creswell, Surveyor for the Western District of England.

2. The Surveyors were known as the 'eyes of the department' (F. E. Baines 'Jubilation', *Blackfriars*, x (Mar 1890) 24).

3. According to some, Rowland Hill claimed credit for the idea of the pillar letter box as early as 1840, but for a decade nothing happened. A trial in London thoroughfares was made in Mar 1855, but Trollope definitely pinpointed the site for the first pillar box at St Helier, Jersey, in 1851 (not in 1853 as in Howard Robinson, *British Post Office: A History* (1948) pp. 167–8). Jean Young Farrugia noted that it was Trollope's persistence that finally caused their adoption in 1852 (*The Letter Box: A History of Post Office Pillar and Wall Boxes* (1969) p. 122). Miss Jemima Stanbury of Exeter, it will be recalled, objected to 'the iron pillar boxes which had been erected of late for the receipt of letters. ... She had not the faintest belief that any letter put into one of them would ever reach its destination' (*He Knew He Was Right* (1869) ch. viii). See *Letters*, i, 28.

4. Trollope's gift of cap-napping is also described by A. M. Cunynghame (p. 58 below) and by G. A. Sala (p. 68 below).

5. Escott is retelling this anecdote from his appreciation in the *Quarterly Review*, 210 (Jan 1909) 226, when he reports that the novelist was accompanied by a junior Post Office colleague. The details are substantially the same but Escott has cast himself in the more prominent role.

6. The *Quarterly* article above names the story as *Can You Forgive Her?*. This is impossible since it was written in the latter part of 1863.

Such Delicious Feuds

EDMUND YATES, ELEANOR SMYTH AND
F. E. BAINES

If he was a terror to subordinates Trollope was equally a scourge to his superiors, first Colonel Maberly and next his successor as Chief Secretary, Rowland Hill: 'With him I never had any sympathy, nor he with me' (*Auto.*, viii). Recalling his resignation from the Post Office in 1867 Trollope noted gleefully, 'How I loved, when I was contradicted, – as I was very often and no doubt properly – to do instantly as I was bid, and then to prove that what I was doing was fatuous, dishonest, expensive and impracticable! And then there were the feuds, – such delicious feuds!' These three recollections concern Hill (1795–1879), originator of the penny post, given anomalous position of Secretary to the Postmaster-General (1846) while Colonel Maberly continued as Secretary to the Post Office until his retirement in 1854 (*Letters*, i, 35). (1) from *Edmund Yates: His Recollections and Experiences* (1884) i, 392–5. Edmund Hodgson Yates (1831–94), member of a well-known acting family, was a Post Office colleague and popular minor novelist best known for *Broken to Harness* (1864) and *Black Sheep* (1867). A prolific journalist, he was associated with *Temple Bar* from its beginning in 1860 and its editor, 1863–7. He founded the periodicals the *World* in 1874 and *Time* in 1879; (2) from Eleanor Smyth *Sir Rowland Hill: The Story of a Great Reform, Told by His Daughter* (1907) pp. 277–8; a natural attempt to make light of Trollope's implacable opposition to her father. However, Hill had certainly distrusted Trollope although he admired his capability as a negotiator. The records show a consistent routine of sniping and counter attack. In the autumn of 1852, Hill suspected some understanding between Trollope and his brother-in-law, John Tilley, that Tilley would succeed Colonel Maberly as Chief Secretary. Hill was angry when Trollope's Civil Service paper, first a lecture for the Post Office Library and Literary Association appeared in the *Cornhill*, 3 (Feb 1861) 214–28, and asked the Postmaster-General, Lord Stanley, to censure Trollope. Within months of this Trollope was seeking nine months' leave to write a book on America, and Hill complained bitterly only to receive a sharp retort from Lord Stanley praising Trollope's services. This rankled sorely. On 6 Sep 1862, Hill confided to his diary 'Trollope is suspected of neglecting his official duties to attend to his literary labours.'; on 16 Sep he added the opinion that Trollope was less than sincere and honest. Trollope's rather double-edged letter on Hill's retirement professes admiration for Hill's service: 'And there has been a completeness about it which must, I should think, make you thoroughly contented with your career, as far as it has gone.' For more details see *Letters*, I, 35, 138, 152, 194, 255–6; (3) from F. E. Baines, *Forty Years at the Post Office* (1895) I, 134–5.

(1)   It is scarcely possible to imagine a greater contrast to Rowland Hill than Anthony Trollope, physically – save that both were bald and spectacled – and, mentally. One small, pale, and, with the exception of a small scrap of whisker, closely shaven, the other big, broad, fresh-coloured and bushy-bearded; one calm and freezing, the other blunt and boisterous; one cautious and calculating, weighing well every word before utterance, and then only choosing phrases which would convey his opinion, but would give no warmth to its expression, the other scarcely giving himself time to think, but spluttering and roaring out an instantly formed opinion couched in the very strongest of terms. 'I differ from you entirely! What was it you said?' he roared out once to the speaker who preceded him at a discussion of Surveyors.

Trollope was very little known in the London office, whence he had been drafted many years previously, and he certainly was not popular among the subordinates of his district. He was a very kind-hearted man; but with persons in the position of clerks in small offices, letter-carriers, etc., manner has great effect, and Trollope's manner was desperately against him. I do not believe that any man of his time was more heartily, more thoroughly, more unselfishly charitable; and he not merely did not let his left hand know what his right hand did in such matters, but he would savagely rap the knuckles of any hand meddling his affairs.[1] The larger portion of that collection of books of which he speaks with such affection in the *Autobiography* was purchased to relieve the necessities of an old friend's widow, who never had an idea but that she was doing Trollope a kindness in letting him buy them.[2]

Trollope was as 'thorough' in his Post Office work as he was in his literary labours. His declarations of affection for his official employment are frequent in the *Autobiography*; and in a speech which he delivered at a meeting held at St Martin's le Grand in 1858, to establish a Post Office Library and Literary Institution, he said, 'We belong to the Civil Service. That service has not always been spoken of in the terms I firmly believe it deserves. It has been spoken of as below those other posts to which the ambition of Englishmen attaches itself; but my belief is that it should offer as fair an object of ambition as any other service, and that the manner in which the duties are generally performed by most of the departments with which I am acquainted deserves that the men belonging to it should not be placed in a lower position than those in any other service. I myself *love* the Post Office. I have belonged to it ever since I left school. I work with all my heart, and everyone else should do the same; then they will rise with the department, and the Civil Service will rise to the level of any other profession, whether it be the Church, the Bar, the Army, or the Navy.'[3]

His lecture on the 'Civil Service as a Profession', delivered before his colleagues, and afterwards printed in the *Cornhill Magazine*, was to the same effect.[4] Nevertheless, he resigned his situation in the Post Office at the age of fifty-two, when he was in full bodily and mental vigour, thus cutting himself off from any chance of a pension, which is not granted, save in the case of illness or under abolition of office, to any person under sixty. This step was partly the result of pique, as he himself allows, from his having failed to obtain the post of Assistant-Secretary, then vacant, for which he had applied.[5] Such an appointment would have been worse than fatal. The proverbial bull in the china shop would have been a tame and harmless animal compared to Trollope in the Assistant-Secretary's chair.

But the real truth was, his love for the Post Office had long been evaporating, and was nearly gone: there were no more 'delicious feuds', for Rowland Hill had retired, and Frederick was mild and inoffensive, and not worth fighting; and the then Secretary was Mr Tilley, Trollope's own brother-in-law. Moreover, Trollope was a very different man from the unknown clerk to whom the Post Office was all in all: he was, if not in the first, first in the second, flight of novelists of the day; he was – what he had never been in his office – popular in certain circles, notably at the Garrick Club. He would have more leisure for clubs, hunting and whist, and at the same time be earning more money; and he would have opportunities for foreign and colonial travel, and consequent book-making, such as he never would have had again in the department, where his official trips had already been much discussed. He, too, lived for fifteen years after his retirement a more enjoyable life than is given to most of us, and all the happiness in which he right honestly deserved.

It has often been noticed that Trollope had a very poor notion of humour, either in his works or in private life. He once attempted a professedly funny story, *The Struggles of Brown, Jones and Robinson,* but it was a ghastly failure, as he admits; nor was he a good raconteur or conversationalist. He told one story, however, remarkably well, and it always struck me as one of the funniest I ever heard. So I give it, confirmatory as it also is of what I have previously said regarding the eccentricity of some of the members of the Blank family. I happened to be keeping a diary the last time I heard it, and I give the extract:

(Monday, 18 Feb 1878) – Escott gave a dinner tonight at the Thatched House Club, which turned out very pleasantly.[6] Present: Colonel Colley, CB, Lord Lytton's private secretary, home from India on leave for a few weeks; J. A. Froude; Anthony Trollope; Major Arthur Griffiths; Dr Quain; J. C. Parkinson; and myself.... Trollope told a remarkably funny story about a dinner given him by F. Blank. It appears that F. Blank and Trollope, who while in the Post Office together never agreed, had a tremendous row, and at the subsequent *rapprochement* Blank asked Trollope to dine with him at Hampstead at five o'clock.[7] Trollope went; found the dining-room full of ladies, twenty or thirty of them, and himself and Blank the only men present. Dinner was announced, and Trollope went to offer his arm to Mrs Blank, when he was cut short by Blank, who said, 'The ladies have already dined.' He and Trollope accordingly went down together to the dining-room, where, at one end of the table, there was part of a cold leg of mutton, at the other a salad – nothing else on the table. F. Blank told Trollope to sit down opposite the mutton, which he, being very hungry, did. Blank seated himself opposite the salad, and commenced devouring it, taking no mutton. There were no potatoes or any other vegetable, and nothing to drink, absolutely nothing of any kind – no water, beer or wine. When Blank had finished the salad, and Trollope had disposed of two huge helps of mutton, Blank said, 'Shall we join the ladies?' and they went upstairs. In the dining-room they found the ladies seated in a huge circle, with a chair in the middle of it, into which Trollope was inducted. Blank said, 'The ladies will now proceed to interrogate you upon various matters'; which they did.

I saw but little of Trollope during the last years of his life. I believe he disapproved of 'society journalism', and he certainly refused to pose as a 'Celebrity at Home'. 'I allow that your articles are cleverly done, and without the least offence', he wrote, 'also that you have many very distinguished people in your gallery. But I would rather not.'[8] On the other hand, he could have had no serious objection to the *World*, as on two occasions he wrote to me proposing to supply a novel for its columns. I did not think it expedient to comply with his suggestion.

(2)   One of the most prominent among the irreconcilables was the novelist, Anthony Trollope. But as he was a Surveyor, which means a postal bird of passage or official comet of moderate orbit regularly moving on its prescribed course, with only periodic appearances at St Martin's le Grand, he did not frequently come into contact with the heads there. He was an indefatigable worker; and many of his novels were partly written in railway carriages while he was journeying from one post town to another, on official inspection bent. On one occasion he was brought to our house, and a most entertaining and lively talker we found him to be. But somehow our rooms seemed too small for his large vigorous frame, and big, almost stentorian voice. Indeed, he reminded us of Dickens's Mr Boythorn,[9] minus the canary, and gave us the impression that the one slightly built chair on which he rashly seated himself during a great part of the interview, must infallibly end in collapse, and sooner rather than later. After about a couple of hours of our society, he apparently found us uncongenial company; and perhaps we did not take over kindly to him, however keen our enjoyment, then and afterwards, of his novels and his talk. He has left a record in print of the fact that he heartily detested the Hills, who have consoled themselves by remembering that when a man has spent many years in writing romance, the trying of his hand, late in life, at history, is an exceedingly hazardous undertaking. In fact, Trollope's old associates at the Post Office were in the habit of declaring that his *Autobiography* was one of the greatest, and certainly not the least amusing, of his many works of fiction.

But Anthony Trollope had quite another side to his character beside that of novelist and Hill-hater, a side which should not be lost sight of. In 1859 he was sent out to the West Indies on official business; and, although a landsman, he was able to propose a scheme of steamer routes more convenient and more economical than those in existence, 'and, in the opinion of the hydrographer to the Admiralty, superior to them even in a nautical point of view'.[10] Nevertheless, the scheme had to wait long for adoption. Indeed, what scheme for betterment has *not* to wait long?

(3) An amusing anecdote is still current concerning Sir Rowland Hill and Mr Anthony Trollope, the novelist, who for many years was a Surveyor in the Post Office. One day Sir Rowland (then Mr) Hill called the surveyors together to consider a paper of instructions about to be sent out on some important matter. It was probably the draft of the circular to surveyors of nineteen paragraphs which Sir Rowland issued on 25 April 1855 (my official service was then just a week old!), defining their duties and responsibilities. His object, no doubt, was to satisfy himself that the circular covered all the intended ground. When it was read aloud, the impetuous Trollope, properly eager, as a young man, to show that he had a head on his shoulders, challenged not the scope and tenor of the instructions, but the literary composition. That, however, was not Sir Rowland's object in convening the meeting.

'I think, Mr Hill,' Trollope is reported in substance to have said, 'that the language of paragraph so-and-so, literally construed, may be held to mean what you do not intend.' Sir Rowland was hardly the man to be checked by anyone, much less by a younger and (on postal policy, at any rate) less-informed man; so he neatly rejoined, speaking slowly and deliberately, and enunciating the letter 'r' in each word with Midland distinctness: 'You must be aware, Mr Trollope, that a phrase is not always intended to bear a literal construction. For instance, when I write to one of you gentlemen, I end my letter with the words, "I am, Sir, your obedient servant", whereas you know I am nothing of the sort.'

NOTES

1. In view of their rivalry Yates's comments are to his credit, and he is certainly not unfair about Trollope's manner. But see his more waspish references in the *World* (24 Feb 1892) 19.

2. The friend was Robert Bell (1800–67), journalist and friend of Thackeray, who recruited Trollope to the Royal Literary Fund. Trollope was elected to the Garrick Club (Apr 1862), proposed by Bell and seconded by Thackeray. Bell was asked to take on the sub-editing of *St Paul's Magazine* for Trollope in Jan 1867, but died in Apr. When his library was up for auction Trollope stepped in and bought it at a price well above market value. 'We all know the difference in value between buying and selling of books', he said (Escott, *Anthony Trollope*, p. 307).

3. The Post Office Library and Literary Association was a professional club for the clerical staff providing leisure educational activities. It was established in Nov 1858. Trollope was active engaging lecturers including Yates, Lewes, Hughes and George Grossmith. Facilities included a general reading room, a meeting room and a permanent library for reference and circulation.

4. First published in shortened form in *Cornhill Magazine*, III (Feb 1861) 214–28. The full lecture is in *Four Lectures*, ed. Morris L. Parrish (1938).

5. *Auto.*, xv. Trollope's actual letter of resignation has not been traced, but see *Letters* (9 & 14 Oct 1867) I, 392–3, 396. A farewell dinner in his honour was given at the Albion Tavern attended by nearly 100 people and reported by the *Spectator*, XL (2 Nov 1867) 1219. His host on the occasion was the man who got the job he wanted, Frank Ives Scudamore (1823–84). Whatever his rue Trollope bore up manfully, but around the Post Office Yates's view predominated. 'He retired in a pet, in fact', wrote R. W. J. in 'Early Post Office Days', *St Martin's le Grand*, VI (July 1896) 430, adding that it was well for his literary career that he did retire then.

6. Thatched House Club, St James's, a Tory haunt in Swift's day; by 1865 a dining club.

7. Presumably Frederic Hill (1803–1906), brother of Rowland, Assistant Secretary of the Post Office, 1851–75.

8. *Edmund Yates: His Recollections and Experiences*, II, 231. Perhaps Trollope recalled sardonically how he had been invited to take on a dummy editorship of *Temple Bar* in Aug 1861. See p. 152 below.

9. In *Bleak House* (1853).

10. Trollope left England on 16 Nov 1858. His work on new routes for mail and local controls of post offices was highly commended in the Sixth Report of the Postmaster General (*Parl. Papers 1860*, XXIII, 2657, 27–8). The spin-off from his journey was the very successful first travel book, *The West Indies and the Spanish Main* (1859).

Raw Beef Steak and the Giant Refreshed

VARIOUS

The following extracts give several views of Trollope in action as a postal official, energetic beyond belief, frank to the point of brutality, dictatorial, tactless, but certainly dedicated and efficient. Allowance needs to be made for the legend, but he was clearly an outside figure to the more orthodox public servants of his day. (1) from 'A Retired Post Office Official', *St Martin's Le Grand*, XIV (Oct 1904) 453–4. This may have occurred when Trollope was pursuing his postal mission to the West of England and Wales in 1852; (2) from A. M. Cunynghame, *Scottish Leader* (12 Jan 1894) 5. Cunynghame, just retired as Surveyor-General for

Scotland, may be recalling a period in late 1858 when Trollope was occupied
with missions in the north of England and Scotland; (3) from R. S. Smyth, 'The
Provincial Service Fifty Years Ago', *St Martin's Le Grand*, xiii (Oct 1903)
374–6; (4) from Susan E. Gay, *Old Falmouth* (1903) pp. 216–17. Her father,
William Gay (1812–68), was surveyor for the Manchester District and a good
friend; (5) from 'R. W. J.', 'Early Post Office Days', *St Martin's Le Grand*, vi
(July 1896) 293–5. In the 1860s important changes in organisation occurred.
The noble building designed by Sir Robert Smirke was modified with an
enlarged Sorting Office and other changes. London districts were reorganised
into Postmasterships and placed under a Surveyor of the Metropolitan District,
the first being A. M. Cunynghame (above). The post was offered to Trollope on
20 June 1866 (*Letters*, i, 281n).

(1)   Everyone is acquainted with the literary characteristics of
Trollope as indicated in his work (writes a retired Post Office
official); but not one in a thousand of his readers knew him in his
official life. I did; and it was when he was revelling in the fullness
of his athleticism. I was attached to a country office in South
Wales when he strode in one day, fresh from a tramp over the
heather, just as Professor Wilson – Christopher North – was wont
to do in surprising his students.[1] No other description could well
be applied to the gait of Trollope. About the first remark he made
was 'I have walked up from Cardiff' – a distance of 24 miles. 'Any
hotels here; which is the best?' I directed him; and as he marched
out, still at a 6 mile-an-hour-stride, he said, 'back soon, going to
have a raw beef steak'.[2]

He left me pondering over his powerful build, his physical go,
and his reference to the 'underdone'. I mentally saw him going
with a dash into our unsophisticated Welsh hotel, attacking the
steak, and combining it with deep quaffings from a pewter; for it
was evident that he had a thirst on in keeping with the hot and
June-like weather – a thirst that would have been disgusted with
the offer of a glass! I was still pondering when the giant foot-fall
was again heard, and he reappeared. 'Ah!', he exclaimed,
evidently in better form, 'Now, where is the postmaster?' That
gentleman, a man of intellectual force, quiet and philosophical,
came in response to my signal and was told, 'I am Mr Trollope of
the Surveyor's staff'; and then business was entered upon. I can
see now, at the lapse of half a century, the thoughtful grey eyes of
the postmaster twinkle as he 'read his man'.

One of the postmen of a neighbouring village had applied to the
Department for increased pay, and now put in an appearance and
stated his case. Unfortunately, he was not satisfied with putting

his pleas forward in a manner seemly to a petitioner, but foolishly coupled them with the threat that if he couldn't get more money for the job he'd throw it up. I saw at once that this was not the way to obtain even a hearing, much less a favour. 'Look here, my man,' Trollope exclaimed, 'don't think that we cannot manage without you. Throw it up; there will be twenty after your place tomorrow', and then entered into facts and figures.

The postman was glad to beat a retreat, and lived not only to be placed on a better scale, in accordance with the increase asked for in his letter, but to attain a good old age in the service. To the last he never forgot energetic Mr Trollope. The postman episode ended, Trollope turned round to the postmaster, chatting genially and giving his impression of the district and of the people. He was keenly observant of men and manners, and gathered up into his store-house of a mind the novelties of this, to him, new land, which, in one of his novels, he refers to as more isolated and dreary than many. 'In fact', he adds, 'if you wish to put a man decently out of the world, make him an official of Merthy Tydvil or Chief Justice of Patagonia!'

(2)   The interviewer asked: 'Your memories date back to the time of Trollope, I suppose?'

Cunynghame: 'Oh yes; I knew Anthony Trollope well. Many a journey we took together. His most curious quality was a power of going to sleep at any moment for a brief space of time. For instance, I was working with him one day, and he was very tired. At last he said to me, "Cunynghame, I must have a sleep. Wake me in 20 minutes, will you?" "All right", I said, and took out my watch. In a moment he was fast asleep in his chair. At the end of 20 minutes I woke him, and he was as fresh as possible. Another time he was with a friend of mine in Cumberland. They had been inspecting somewhere, and were walking home at midnight. Trollope was dead tired, and when they came to a milestone he sat down and went to sleep upon it! In ten minutes he woke like a giant refreshed. Trollope was an excellent man of business – he wrote splendid reports – and an indefatigable worker. On hunting mornings he used to get up at four o'clock and begin writing at a novel he had on the stocks, always doing a certain number of pages before breakfast. But of course you have read his reminiscences. They make a delightful book, though he had a faculty for embellishing, which prevents their being always accurate. You remember the story about his upsetting a bottle of ink on Colonel Maberly's waistcoat? Sir Arthur Blackwood told me one day, after he had heard Trollope tell the story, that there was no truth in it.[3] The fact was, Trollope had told it so often that he came to believe it himself, just as George IV believed he had been at Waterloo, but he was a delightful companion all the same.'

(3)   I had the honour of serving under Anthony Trollope, then surveyor of the Northern District. He was brusque in manner, certainly, but he had a kind heart. The latter fact I did not at first know, as he was held out to the juniors in the service as a terror, and my early experience of him was not calculated to remove such an impression. It was in 1857, and shortly after the removal of the Post Office to the new building in Queen's Square, that a survey was being made. The public office and postmen's room occupied a wing of the building, but neither had been provided with a clock. It was my duty to record the time at which the postmen returned from their deliveries, and during the survey a question arose as to the correctness of the entries, some of which, indeed, had been found to be inaccurate. Mr Trollope turned sharply to me for an explanation, and I pleaded that I had not had access to a clock. 'But have you not a watch', he said. I replied that I had not. 'Then you must get one at once' – with emphasis on the concluding words. 'Certainly, at once, as you so instruct me, but –' 'But what?', he asked. 'I would prefer to wait till I can pay cash for it.' A growl was the only reply, and he turned away. It is to be remembered that watches were then by no means so numerous or so cheap as they are now, the expenditure of more than a month's salary would have been necessary to procure a reliable one. As I had had the last word I was curious to know what would follow. A day or two afterwards, however, the postmaster told me that Mr Trollope, who had then gone, had applied for a clock, and that I was to be so informed. I thought this very considerate. It caused me to form a more favourable opinion of him, which subsequent experience only tended to increase; and I greatly prize and carefully keep a characteristic letter he sent me some years afterwards. He had been transferred to a District near London in 1860 or 1861 I think,[4] but in 1865 had been asked to come to Belfast to report regarding a proposed revision of salaries and staff. He seemed glad to visit the office again; and, believing I

could count on his friendship, I took the opportunity of discussing my prospects in the service with which, in view of a very tempting offer of other employment I had at the time – the particulars of which I gave him – I was dissatisfied. While refraining from expressing a definite opinion as to what my decision regarding the offer ought to be, he entered into the matter in a very friendly, almost a fatherly way, and concluded by urging that if I decided to remain in the service, it would be only wise for me to put away all feelings of dissatisfaction and discontent. The interview was a long one, and I believed he had said all he wished to say; but his great kindess was further shown by his sending me immediately after his return to England the letter I refer to. It is, of course, a personal one, yet it contains much wisdom, and will not perhaps be considered out of place in a Magazine which represents a Department that is proud to have numbered him amongst its staff, I therefore may be excused for giving it in full.

> Waltham House,
> Waltham Cross
> *June* 21*st*, 1865

My Dear Sir, That which is unsatisfactory to you in the nature of your position and prospects at Belfast, is owing to the fact that you find yourself to be possessed of better qualities for business than you had, when younger, given yourself credit for possessing, and not by any means to the inferiority of pay or rank which you have in the Belfast Post Office. If you will remember what were your expectations when you joined the Office some ten years since, you will find that this is so. Had you at that time been assured of the senior clerkship, with a prospect of an increase to the then rate of senior clerks' pay, you would have thought the place sufficiently alluring. That is now your position, and you are dissatisfied, not because you think that that is bad, but because you think higher of yourself. Such a condition is very common with men of energy, and such men must then decide whether they will begin the world again by placing themselves where a higher career may be open to them (in which there is always a risk), or whether they will accept the moderate and sure advantages which they already possess. It may well be that you can do better for yourself, as you are still young, by finding service elsewhere; but I think you

should endeavour, if you remain where you are, to teach yourself
not to regard the service with dissatisfaction. That you will
always do your work well I am sure, but it will be much for your
own comfort if you can make yourself believe that the service in
which you are has not been bad or hard to you.

Very faithfully yours,
ANTHONY TROLLOPE

(4) To add a few more reminiscences; when any important
alterations took place with regard to mails, a meeting of the
Surveyors used to be convened, probably at Henley-on-Thames,
etc. These meetings were necessary for arranging the proper
connection of mails passing through each postal district, and a
good deal of intricate work and calculation impossible by
correspondence were carried out, enlivened by good dinners, and
an agreeable social time. They created a pleasant fraternal
feeling.[5] Among them at one time was Anthony Trollope, whom I
well remember at our house on occasions. He was a man of
boundless energy, which enabled him to do his official work, write
innumerable books, and travel and ride to hounds, with apparent
ease. No more repose was left in the house when he awoke in the
morning. Doors slammed, footsteps resounded, and a general
whirlwind arose, as he came or returned from his bath, or walked
out in the garden, and from that time until nightfall, he was as
busy as a man could be. He had a scorn of everything in the way of
pretension − even of justice to time-honoured institutions − and
slurred over his family history, and belittled 'the service' right
royally. 'Post Office' (he always omitted the 'General' or
departmental style and title) − he would write with a little 'p and a
little 'o', as though it were a village sub-office, retailing stamps
with tobacco and onions, and I remarked on this one day to his
brother-in-law, Sir John Tilley, who responded by a hearty laugh.
Such a 'John Bull' was independent at all points, and his
publisher's cheques enabled him to live in good style after
retirement from 'Her Majesty's Service'. An establishment like
the Herald's College, or the stately 'powers that be' of official life,
would have been rent in twain by his indifferent down-rightness,
and pomps and vanities generally dispersed like bubbles. Early
saints and antiquities would have fared no better. Such was his
nature which, as I recollect it, was full of fiery and energetic

bluntness. Who would have thought episcopal dignitaries would have been of his kin? Yet as regards imagination, he was unusually gifted, as shown by his best works of fiction, and he would describe a woman's feelings and ideas in regard to a lover better than a woman herself.

(5)   I was detailed for duty there [Western District Office, Vere Street] when the change took place, and I remember Anthony Trollope superintended the arrangements for constituting postal London into so many separate towns. His method of attacking work was rather odd, and I have seen him slogging away at papers at a stand-up desk, with his handkerchief stuffed into his mouth, and his hair on end, as though he could barely contain himself. He struck me as being rather a fierce-looking man, and a remark which he made to a postmaster on one occasion did not appear to me to savour either of courtesy or kindness. This poor fellow, who had probably seen thirty years' service, and who was wedded to the old system of working the districts, was fretting terribly at the prospect of becoming a postmaster and of being left to his own resources, so to speak, when Trollope turned round on him with the remark: 'Why don't you pay an old woman sixpence a week to fret for you?'[6]

NOTES

1. John Wilson (1785–1854), 'Christopher North', acerbic critic and conversationalist, friend of Coleridge and an early champion of Wordsworth's poetry; he had a long association with *Blackwood's Magazine* to which he contributed from 1822 'Noctes Ambrosianae'; elected to Chair of Moral Philosophy at Edinburgh University, 1820.

2. The pedestrian feats of the Trollopes were prodigious. Tom's autobiography cites an occasion when he walked the forty-seven miles between Oxford and Harrow Weald carrying a heavy knapsack (*WIR*, I, 219).

3. *Auto.*, III.

4. Trollope took up duties as Surveyor for the Eastern District on 21 Nov 1859. About this time, too, he settled at Waltham Cross, Hertfordshire.

5. Solidarity among the Surveyors was never more apparent when in 1864 they pushed for an increase in salary. Trollope was one of nine signatories to a formal request put to John Tilley as Secretary (after Rowland Hill's retirement) and himself lobbied the Postmaster-General, Lord Stanley, in a letter of 18 July 1864 remarkable for its blistering reasonableness and impertinent moderation. At his best in a fight with authority, Trollope met the rejection of the Surveyors' claim with: 'It was exactly the way in which Oliver was treated

when he came forward on behalf of the Charity boys to ask for more – and I own that I thought Mr Tilley was very like Bumble in the style of the answer he gave us' (*Letters*, I, 259–60, 279–81).

6. An illuminating observation. Perplexed *himself* in all probability by the changes afoot, but determined to keep face, irritated the more by his older colleague's display, Trollope blurted out the harsh rebuke.

Triton in a Shoal of Minnows

ARTHUR WAUGH

From Arthur Waugh, *A Hundred Years of Publishing, Being the Story of Chapman and Hall Ltd* (1930) pp. 86–8. Trollope in publishers' offices was no less a giant than the figure just described at St Martin's le Grand or at post offices up and down the country. From the time of modest success with *Barchester Towers* (1857) he bargained firmly with publishers, starting with William Longman, to whom he offered *The Three Clerks* on the basis of his fiction being 'a marketable commodity'. Waugh's account should be seen in the context of Trollope's own description of his interview with Edward Chapman to ask £400 for *Dr Thorne* (1858): 'Looking at me as he might have done at a highway robber who had stopped him on Hounslow Heath, he said that he supposed he might as well do as I desired. I considered this to be a sale, and it was a sale. I remember that he held the poker in his hand all the time that I was with him – but in truth, even though he had declined to buy the book, there would have been no danger' (*Auto.*, vi).

And now there comes upon us, bestriding the office like a Colossus, demanding undivided attention ... the novelist of all others most emphatically connected with the firm's history for the next twenty years – the kindly, despotic, irritable and generous dictator of terms, and disposer of times and seasons, Anthony Trollope, of the General Post Office, and of universal popularity and fame. ...

In charge of the trade counter of Chapman & Hall today there is a certain cool, imperturbable veteran, whose official name is Mr E. F. Gibbons, but who has long been known to all visitors as 'Frank'. ... He came to the old house in Piccadilly as a very small boy; he saw the firm turned into a limited company, and transferred to Henrietta Street; and he remembers vividly many of the notable men to whom he served as messenger in his early days. ... But there is one well-known figure that inspired him with terror in boyhood, and still looms irreconcilably upon his mature imagination, the rough, emphatic, clamourous figure of Anthony Trollope, who was for many years so closely and so amiably associated with the fortunes of Chapman & Hall.[1] Of the heads of the firm, and of their business treatment of him, Trollope always spoke and wrote well, and even generously; but he was certainly a terror to the staff, among whom he splashed around like a Triton in a shoal of minnows. Mr Gibbons recalls how he used to tramp into the office, as soon as the doors were open, clad in his pink coat, with a sheaf of proofs in his great side pocket, and how he would bang on the table with his hunting crop, and swear like a sergeant-major because there was no one in authority yet arrived to receive his hectic instructions. There is even a legend that the sudden illness which caused his death was due to a fit of similar impatience. An organ-grinder was playing outside his house, and refused to move at the command of the servant. So Trollope thundered out into the road in person, and the offending musician fled before him. The big man got his way as usual, but the moment's exposure to the inclement weather resulted in a fatal chill.[2]

Now, as it happens, this passing memory is typically characteristic of Anthony Trollope, who was the kindliest of men at heart, yet suffered all his life from what the psychologists of today call 'an inferiority complex'.

He has told in his *Autobiography* the poignant story of his boyhood, when he had to walk through muddy lanes to Harrow School, neglected and underfed, and was abused by his headmaster for the untidiest little rascal upon the Hill. He grew up under the shadow of penury and restraint; he cherished a conviction that all the world was against him; and, when he relieved the monotony of his duties as a Civil Servant in the Post Office by writing novels, it was years before he made anything out of authorship, for he was generally too shy to press enquiries upon his publishers, when once they had assured him that his latest book had followed the others into their catalogue of failures. It was this very shyness, born of discouragement, that made him burst out into recriminations against subordinates. There is no man so self-assertive as he who is uncertain of himself. But the foible was entirely superficial, and beneath the surface Anthony

Trollope was one of the most punctilious among men of honour. He asked no favour of anyone.

NOTES

1. Edward Chapman (1804–80) was co-founder in 1830. Trollope's association with the company lasted from 1858 until 1882. They published 32 of his books, plus reprints and an edition of the *Chronicles of Barsetshire*. In 1869 Trollope bought a partnership in the firm for his son Henry, and when it became a limited company in 1880 Trollope became a director. Correspondence suggests his foray into business management worried him exceedingly. In May 1880 he wrote to G. W. Rusden: 'Nothing more pernicious and damnable ever occurred, or more likely to break a man's heart. Twice a week I have to meet my brother directors & sit five hours a day. That I am half ruined is nothing to the trouble and annoyance and shame of such an employment' (*Letters*, ii, 867). Perhaps the troubles had to do with Frederic Chapman's problems with creditors; he resigned the Garrick on 19 June 1880 (*Letters*, ii, 905).

2. Sadleir suggests a German band (*Commentary*, p. 325). The aftermath was a stroke.

A Trojan of the Name of Trollope

THACKERAY, GEORGE SMITH AND G. A. SALA

In Oct 1859 Trollope wrote to Thackeray offering stories for the *Cornhill Magazine*, George Smith's new periodical under Thackeray's editorship. By no means unknown (he had published nine novels), Trollope had yet to make his mark in London literary society. Thackeray's response delighted Trollope who proudly reprinted his letter (*Auto.*, viii). With Thackeray's letter came the publisher's offer of £1000 for a novel; *Framley Parsonage* was the result. 'From the opening words the novel found instant and enormous popularity' (*Commentary*, p. 199). Trollope was now famous. It was Thackeray who seconded Trollope's nomination for the Garrick Club, Thackeray who now provided him with his social base and friendships in the literary world, Thackeray who was, says Gordon Ray, 'to be loved as well as revered. Henceforth, indeed, Trollope was *vir Thackeraianissimus*' (*Thackeray: The Age of Wisdom, 1847–63* (1958) p. 299). At his death Trollope commented: 'He who knew Thackeray will have a vacancy in his heart's inmost casket, which must remain vacant until he dies' ('W. M.

Thackeray', *Cornhill*, ix (Feb 1864) 134–7; see also *Auto.*, xiii). (1) and (4) from *The Letters and Private Papers of W. M. Thackeray*, ed. Gordon N. Ray (1946) iv, 236, 262–3, 190; (2) from Leonard Huxley, *The House of Smith, Elder* (privately printed, 1923) pp. 104, 106; (3) from George Augustus Sala, *Things I Have Seen and People I Have Known* (1894) i, 30–1; Sala (1828–95), journalist and minor novelist whose talent was encouraged by Dickens and Thackeray; frequent contributor to *Household Words* and other journals, founder of *Temple Bar*, 1860; (5) from George Smith, 'Our Birth and Parentage', *Cornhill Magazine*, 83 (Jan 1901) 4–17. George Smith (1824–1901) directed the house of Smith, Elder from 1846, publishing the works of Charlotte Brontë (one of his triumphs was *Jane Eyre* (1847)), Thackeray, Mrs Gaskell and Ruskin; began the *Pall Mall Gazette* (1865) and the *Dictionary of National Biography* (1882). His scrupulous dealing made him especially beloved of Trollope and he had a way of combining shrewd business sense with infinite tact: engaging Millais to illustrate *Framley Parsonage* was one instance of it that touched Trollope. Smith also had Samuel Laurence paint the portrait of Trollope now in the National Portrait Gallery. See Elizabeth Smith, *George Smith: A Memoir, With Some Pages of Autobiography* (privately printed 1902).

(1)   [Thackeray's graceful 'Roundabout Paper' launching the first issue of *Cornhill*, Jan 1860, pp. 124–8.] Novels have been previously compared to jellies – here are two (one perhaps not entirely saccharine and flavoured with an *amari aliquid* very distasteful to some palates) – two novels under two flags, the one that ancient ensign which was hung before the well-known booth of *Vanity Fair*; the other that fresh and handsome standard which has been hoisted on *Barchester Towers*. Pray, sir or madam, to which dish will you be helped?

[To Mrs Baxter, 24 May 1861.] I think Trollope is much more popular with the *Cornhill Magazine* readers than I am: and doubt whether I am not going down hill considerably in public favour.[1]

[Thackeray confided to Charles Lever at this time.] He was determined to make *Philip* [serialised in *Cornhill* from Jan 1861 to Aug 1862] 'as strong as I can to fetch up the ground wh[ich] I have – not lost, I trust, but only barely kept. I sang purposely small; wishing to keep my strongest for a later day, and give Trollope the honours of *Violono primo*. Now I must go to work with a vengeance' [Huxley, *Smith, Elder*, p. 106].

[To William Webb Follett Synge, May 1862.] I have just met a Trojan of the name of Trollope in the street (your ingenious note of last night kept me awake all night, be hanged to you), and the upshot is that we will do what you want between us. My dear old Synge, come and talk to me on Friday before twelve.[2]

(2) [Trollope tells with pride how George Smith gave a dinner in Jan 1860 to celebrate the success of his new periodical. 'It was a memorable banquet in many ways, but chiefly so to me because on that occasion I first met many men who afterwards became my most intimate associates. It can rarely happen that one such occasion can be the first starting-point of so many friendships' (*Auto.*, viii). Things did not go so well with Thackeray, possibly because Trollope in his own eagerness overstepped the mark. As Sadleir puts it: 'It is certainly possible that Trollope – always a little aggressive in his desire to conquer shyness and, maybe, at this moment excited by his recent triumphs into a more than normal self-assertiveness – bore himself at this first introduction into the inner ring of Thackeray's intimates with a bounce and a noisiness that caused a momentary offence' (*Commentary*, p. 203). George Smith left a record of the occasion.] We lightened our labours in the service of the *Cornhill* by monthly dinners. The principal contributors used to assemble at my table in Gloucester Square every month while we were in London; and these *Cornhill* dinners were very delightful and interesting. Thackeray always attended, though he was often in an indifferent state of health. At one of these dinners Trollope was to meet Thackeray for the first time and was equally looking forward to an introduction to him. Just before dinner I took him up to Thackeray with all the suitable *empressement*. Thackeray curtly said, 'How do?' and, to my wonder and Trollope's anger, turned on his heel! He was suffering at the time from a malady which at that particular moment caused him a sudden spasm of pain; though we, of course, could not know this.[3] I well remember the expression on Trollope's face at that moment, and no one who knew Trollope will doubt that he *could* look furious on an adequate – and sometimes on an inadequate – occasion! He came to me the next morning in a very wrathful mood, and said that had it not been that he was in my house for the first time, he would have walked out of it. He vowed he would never speak to Thackeray again, etc., etc. I did my best to soothe him; and, though rather violent and irritable, he had a fine nature with a substratum of great kindliness, and I believe he left my room in a happier frame of

mind than when he entered it. Afterwards he and Thackeray became close friends.

(3)   [George Augustus Sala was also present at the first *Cornhill* dinner.]...once a month the contributors to and the artists of the *Cornhill* were bidden to a sumptuous banquet, held at a house in Hyde Park Square. I well remember the first *Cornhill* dinner. Thackeray, of course, was in the chair; and on his left hand I think there sat a then well-known baronet, Sir Charles Taylor. On the president's right was good old Field-Marshal Sir John Burgoyne. Then we had Richard Monckton Milnes, soon to be Lord Houghton; Frederick Leighton and John Everett Millais, both young, handsome men, already celebrated and promising to be speedily famous. I think George H. Lewes was there; but I am sure that Robert Browning was. Anthony Trollope was very much to the fore, contradicting everybody; afterwards saying kind things to everybody, and occasionally going to sleep on sofas or chairs; or leaning against sideboards, and even somnolent while standing erect on the hearthrug. I never knew a man who could take so many spells of 'forty winks' at unexpected moments, and then turn up quite wakeful, alert and pugnacious, as the author of *Barchester Towers*, who had nothing of the bear but his skin, but whose ursine envelope was assuredly of the most grisly texture. Sir Edwin Landseer; Sikes, the designer of the *Cornhill* cover; Frederick Walker – the last a very young man with every line in his features glowing with bright artistic genius; and Matthew Higgins, the 'Jacob Omnium' of *The Times*, who was taller even than his fast friend Thackeray, were also among the guests at this memorable birthday banquet.

(4)   [Unluckily for Trollope it was not long before he was embroiled in a quarrel that prolonged the Garrick Club Affair. Once again it was perhaps his runaway tongue in the heady atmosphere of success and new friendships which contributed to his embarrassment; for, as Gordon Ray puts it, Trollope was 'still out of his depth in the cross-currents of literary London' (*Thackeray: The Age of Wisdom, 1847–63*, p. 306). Edmund Yates wrote 'Echoes from the London Clubs' for the *New York Times* (26 May 1860). The *Saturday Review* maliciously took up the story (23 June). Thackeray retaliated with his 'Roundabout Paper': 'On Screens in Dining Rooms' (*Cornhill*, II (Aug 1860) 225–45). It

came out that Trollope had innocently blabbed to Yates, reopening that Pandora's Box of grievances between Garrick 'gentlemen' and 'bohemians'. Yates's mischievous article began by declaring that sales of *Cornhill* were already declining, and went on to describe the dinner parties Smith had been giving.] But there is one very funny story which will bear repetition: SMITH, the proprietor of the *Cornhill*, and the host on these occasions, is a very good man of business, but totally unread; his business has been to sell books, not to read them, and he knows little else. On the first occasion of their dining there, THACKERAY remarked to those around him, 'This is a splendid dinner, such a one as CAVE, the bookseller of St John's Gate, gave to his principal writers when Dr JOHNSON's coat was so shabby that he ate his meal behind the screen'; then calling out to his host, who was at the other end of the table, THACKERAY said, 'Mr SMITH, I hope you've not got JOHNSON there behind that screen?' 'Eh?,' said the bibliopole, astonished, 'behind the screen? JOHNSON? God bless my soul, my dear Mr THACKERAY, there's no person of the name of JOHNSON here, nor anyone behind the screen – what on earth do you mean?' A roar of laughter cut him short; poor Mr SMITH had probably never heard of Dr JOHNSON and his screen dinner.

[Thackeray to George Smith, June 1860, after composing 'On Screens in Dining Rooms', his response to Yates.] I have been lying awake half the night about that paper in a sort of despair; but I think I have found a climax dignified and humorous enough at last, Heaven be praised, and that our friend won't sin again.

(5) [Smith concluded the story.] Shortly after the *Saturday Review* article appeared Trollope walked into my room and said that he had come to confess that *he* had given Yates the information on which his article was founded.[4] He expressed the deepest regret and said: 'I told the story not against you, but against Thackeray.' I am afraid I answered him rather angrily. Trollope, however, took it very meekly, and said: 'I know I have done wrong, and you may say anything you like to me.'

NOTES

1. In his generous fashion Thackeray had given the lead position to *Framley Parsonage*, putting his own *Lovel the Widower* in second place.

2. William Webb Follett Synge (1826–91), friend of Thackeray, diplomat and writer; government official in Costa Rica during Trollope's West Indies tour (see p. 244 below); when Synge was in dire need both Trollope and Thackeray lent him £1000 each. Trollope told the story in *Thackeray* (p. 60) omitting his own generous gesture: 'Pondering over this sad condition of things just revealed to me, I met Thackeray between the two mounted heroes at the Horse Guards, and told him the story. "Do you mean to say that I am to find two thousand pounds", he said angrily, with some expletives. I explained that I had not even suggested the doing of anything – only that we might discuss the matter. Then there came over his face a peculiar smile, and a wink in his eye, and he whispered his suggestion, as though half ashamed of his meanness. "I'll go half", he said, "if anybody will do the rest." And he did go half, at a day or two's notice, though the gentleman was no more than simply a friend.' See *Letters*, I, 247–8.

3. Trollope was not the first to suffer from Thackeray's odd behaviour in company. When called upon to meet the shy celebrity Charlotte Brontë, Thackeray abandoned the assembled company and crept away to his club (Anne Thackeray Ritchie, *Chapters from Some Memoirs* (1894) pp. 63–4, cited Philip Collins, *Thackeray: Interviews and Recollections* (1983) I, 112n).

4. Trollope may have been foolish in the first instance; he certainly ought to have been aware of the powder keg he was sitting on. For accounts of the origins of the Garrick Club Affair see Gordon Ray, *Thackeray: The Age of Wisdom*, pp. 305–8; Edgar Johnson, *Charles Dickens: His Tragedy and Triumph* (1977) pp. 468–72.

At the Villino Trollope

KATE FIELD AND ALFRED AUSTIN

(1) from Lilian Whiting, *Kate Field: A Record* (Boston, Mass., 1899) pp. 123, 183, 395–6, and *New York Tribune* (Dec 1880). Mary Katherine Keemle Field (1838–96), American journalist, actress and lecturer, daughter of the actor–playright Joseph M. Field, and best known for *Pen Photographs of Charles Dickens's Readings* (1871). She cultivated celebrities in England and Europe, including W. S. Landor and the Brownings, first meeting Trollope in Florence in Oct 1860. Trollope speaks fondly of her (*Auto.*, xvii) and Sadleir devoted much space to their relationship (*Commentary*, pp. 210–29, 275–87). His letters to her were skittish and avuncular, but unsparing when it came to her literary efforts. Frequent contributions from, or concerning, Rose kept the relationship suitably decorous. Certainly a degree of frankness and intimacy in his letters argues for deep affection. In a letter of 8 July 1868 he signs off in typical fashion 'with a kiss that shall be semi-paternal – one third brotherly, and as regards the small remainder, as loving as you please' (*Letters*, I, 438). Unfortunately she left very

little by way of remembrance of him; (2) from *Autobiography of Alfred Austin* (1911)
I, 165–6, 179–80, 197; II, 23–4. Alfred Austin (1835–1913) was named Poet
Laureate in 1896; his output of light verse amounted to twenty volumes between
1871 and 1908, plus satires and verse drama. In 1883 be became joint editor of
the *National Review* and sole editor 1887–95. A particular friend of Tom's, Austin
appreciated Anthony Trollope's concern for Beatrice (Tom's daughter), whom
he escorted to England in 1870 when the family were in some perplexity over
giving up their Florence home.

(1) [The friendship blossomed when the Trollopes visited
Florence. Kate writes to her Aunt Corda in the autumn of 1860.]
'Anthony Trollope is a very delightful companion. I see a great
deal of him. He has promised to send me a copy of the *Arabian
Nights* (which I have never read) in which he intends to write
"Kate Field, from the Author", and to write me a four-page letter
on condition that I answer it.'[1]

[In 1868, during his visit to the United States on a postal mission
she often saw him. Her diary notes with tantalising brevity:] (*25
May*) Met Anthony Trollope. Same as ever. Trollope called in
evening; (*27 May*) Met Anthony Trollope again; (*28 May*)
Anthony Trollope called and went with us to the Capitol; (*6 June*)
Mr Trollope came and remained an hour or two. Asked me to
write a story for his *St Paul's* magazine. If I can it will be a feather
in my cap. If I can't – well, we shall see.[2]

[Before he left the United States on 15 July 1868 the Boston *Daily
Evening Transcript* recorded the following description.] He is a
strange-looking person. His head is shaped like a minnie ball,
with the point rounded down a little, like the half of a lemon cut
transversely in two. It is small, almost sharp at the top, and bald,
increasing in size until it reaches his neck. His complexion and
general bearing are much like Dickens's. His body is large and
well preserved. He dresses like a gentleman and not like a fop, but
he squeezes his small well-shaped hand into a very small pair of
coloured kids. He 'wears a cane', as all Englishmen do (16 June
1868, p. 2).[3]

[From some recollections of George Eliot written for the *New York
Tribune*, 22 Dec 1880.] Here [Florence, 1860] when left as a
school-girl to study singing and Italian, I first met George Eliot.
Being in charge of an accomplished Englishwoman, who

numbered among her friends all that were best in literature, art and diplomacy, I enjoyed advantages far beyond my years, and found a second home at Villino Trollope, the residence of Thomas Adolphus Trollope. Will you come with me there and meet George Eliot? It is a Sunday evening, and she is expected with her husband.

Ah, this Villino Trollope is quaintly fascinating with its marble pillars, its grim men in armour, starting like sentinels from the walls, and its curiosities greeting you at every step. The antiquary revels in its majolica, its old bridal chests and carved furniture, its beautiful terracotta of the Virgin and Child by Orgagna, its hundred *oggetti* of the Cinque Cento. The bibliopole grows silently ecstatic as he sinks quietly into a mediaeval chair and feasts his eyes on a model library, bubbling over with five thousand rare books, many wonderfully illuminated and enriched by costly engravings. To those who prefer an earnest talk with the host and hostess on politics, art, religion, or the last new book, there is the cosy study where Puss and Bran, the honest dog, lie side by side on Christian terms, and where the daughter of the house will sing you the Tuscan *canti popolari* like a young nightingale in voice, but with more than youthful expression.[4]

Here is Anthony Trollope, and it is no ordinary pleasure to enjoy simultaneously the philosophic reasoning of Thomas Trollope – looking half Socrates and half Galileo – whom Mrs Browning called 'Aristides the Just', and the almost boyish enthusiasm and impulsive argumentation of Anthony Trollope, who is an admirable specimen of a frank and loyal Englishman.

(2)   ... One of the most valued friendships of my life, that with Thomas Adolphus Trollope, who was just twenty-five years my senior, was formed shortly after my arrival, and we were often and much together, both in his delightful home in the *Piazza dell' Independenza*, and in the long walks we took.[5] Almost every Sunday evening we joined a young circle at the house of an English lady in the town, who well illustrated the saying of Shakespeare that 'small cheer and great welcome make a merry feast'.

Though the author of the well-known *History of the Commonwealth of Florence* was so much older than myself, we seemed to be close friends from the very moment we first grasped each other's hands. Unlike his brother Anthony, who, though likewise a delightful companion, and brimming over with active intelligence, was in no accurate sense of the word intellectual, and as unhelpful and impatient an arguer as I ever met, Thomas Adolphus Trollope rejoiced in threshing out afresh the old metaphysical and theological problems, handling them with a rare dialectical skill; and many a duologue had we on those unendingly interesting themes. ...

But a shadow was cast over one's enjoyment by the death, not unexpected, of Theodosia Trollope, the charming wife of my friend; and, as he and I walked away together from her grave in the English cemetery, where also lies Elizabeth Barrett Browning, he said he felt very lonely, and would I not come and stay with him in his Villa in the *Piazza dell'Independenza*?[6] Thither I betook myself with my sparse baggage that afternoon; and the change was from Spartan austerity to a happy combination of English comfort, Italian art and a garden blooming with roses. I did all I could to distract him, and to concentrate his attention on the final chapters of his *History of the Commonwealth of Florence*.[7] He was still, in the matter of style, somewhat under the scarcely beneficial influence of Carlyle, whose simpler manner in the *Life of Stirling* I have always admired more than in his later and more popular ejaculatory writings. In opinion and tone of thought, Trollope was a traditional Liberal of the more sanguine kind; generous, but hardly practical, it has always seemed to me, because allowing too little for certain permanent forces alike in individual and collective human nature. I mention this, because, many years later, his brother Anthony said to me one day, when staying at Swinford, 'You know how attached I am to you. But there is one thing for which I cannot forgive you. You have made my brother Tom a Conservative.' Nothing could have been less true. Life had done for his brother what he attributed to me. But the end of this little story has yet to be told. Not many years later, Anthony himself became a 'Unionist', and denounced Gladstone and all his works in the energetic language that was habitual in his fervid conversation. ...

Our welcome by [Thomas Adolphus] Trollope [at Florence, Nov 1865] was most cordial; and we found that, like Curio 'with a taste', depicted by Pope in his *Moral Essays*, he had already developed an irresistible tendency to spend more on his new home than he had received for the sale of his old one, a result that his brother Anthony had predicted was sure to happen. ...

On the following day [20 July 1870] Anthony Trollope came from Waltham Abbey to spend a day or two with us; and shortly after his arrival, I received a pressing letter from the Editor of the *Standard* asking if he could persuade me to try to obtain permission to join the headquarters of the King of Prussia, but adding that I should have to rely entirely on my own personal endeavours and private influence, since the Correspondent of the *Standard* at Berlin, on making such an application, had met with a curt refusal. It was not wonderful; for the Editor, most perversely in my opinion, had suddenly inserted articles of a somewhat violent kind against both Prussia and its King.

I read the letter aloud; and Anthony Trollope at once said, 'if you can get permission, you will be a lucky fellow, for there is not a man in Europe who would not like to go to the Seat of War'.

NOTES

1. Trollope did send the book and a jolly letter 'I hope it will do you good mentally & morally' (*Letters*, I, 127). Kate's crusading, particularly for women's rights, may have influenced Trollope's depiction of aggressive American females such as Wallachia Petrie in *He Knew He Was Right* (1869) and the outrageous Dr Olivia Q. Fleabody in *Is He Popenjoy?* (1878).

2. By persistence Kate parlayed her somewhat meagre talent into the spotlight. Although Trollope advised her that Dickens opposed her publishing an account of his readings (*Commentary*, p. 282), not entirely to her credit she published her *Pen Photographs* in revised edition in England in 1871. During the few years she shone as a lecturer in both England and the United States, Louise Chandler Moulton heard her at the New England Women's Club 'with the voice which is music' (Lilian Whiting, *Louise Chandler Moulton, Poet and Friend* (Boston, Mass., 1910) p. 65). See also Lilian Whiting, *Kate Field: A Record*, p. 223.

3. Trollope's reaction in a letter to Kate Field on 8 July 1868 was: 'If I saw the writer I should be apt to go off and let him know that I never wear gloves. What fools people are' (*Letters*, I, 437).

4. Beatrice Trollope. For a comment on her singing see p. 23 above.

5. Austin arrived in Florence in the autumn of 1864.

6. Theodosia Trollope, *née* Garrow (1825–65), a gifted poet, had married Tom in 1848 and together with Frances Trollope they settled thereafter in Florence. Beatrice ('Bice') Trollope (1853–81) was their much cosseted child. At Theodosia's death gossip revived an old story about her paternity (*Letters*, I, 300). A full discussion of the topic is in *Dearest Isa: Robert Browning's Letters to Isabella Blagden*, ed. Edward C. McAleer (Austin, Tex., 1951) pp. 277, 279–81.

7. *A History of the Commonwealth of Florence from the Earliest Independence of the Commune to the Fall of the Republic in 1531*, 4 vols, was published by Chapman & Hall in 1865.

As If Some Giant Had Hewn a Great Lump Out of the Earth

NATHANIEL HAWTHORNE AND OTHERS

Trollope visited America five times, twice on special missions for the GPO. The first and best known visit was to the West Indies when he was asked to 'cleanse the Augean stables of our Post Office system there' (*Auto.*, vii). His journey, lasting from Nov 1858 to July 1859, took him as far afield as Central America, through Costa Rica and Nicaragua and home via Bermuda and New York. He was again in the United States between Sep 1861 and Mar 1862, some of the time with Rose. His next visit, another postal assignment, took place between Apr and July 1868. As part of his first Australia trip he returned home via Honolulu, San Francisco and New York in 1872 and on a second journey to Australia he was again in the United States between Aug and Oct 1875, calling at Hawaii, San Francisco, Boston and New York. He met many leading figures in American letters, including Lowell, Holmes, Emerson, Adams, Agassiz, Longfellow, Hawthorne, Bret Harte, William Dean Howells, James T. Fields, Charles Norton, John Lothrop Motley and Richard Henry Dana, most of whom refer to him cordially, although R. H. Dana's diary note of a breakfast meeting in Jan 1862 pronounced 'intolerable, no manners, but means well & would do a good deal to serve you, but says the most offensive things – not a gentleman' (MS Massachusetts Historical Society, cited *Letters*, I, 170). Oblivious to this impression Trollope sought Dana's advice on constitutional matters for his book, *North America* (1862), and eventually they became good friends. See William Coyle, 'The Friendship of Anthony Trollope and Richard Henry Dana, Jr', *New England Quarterly*, xxv (1952) 255–62. The first excerpt traces Trollope's meeting with Hawthorne. Lowell's recollection is particularly worth having for its example of sustained dialogue with Holmes. The third excerpt, not previously printed, is striking for its mixture of fascination and disapproval. Not all introductions worked out in literary Boston. Clara Louisa Kellogg left a decidedly frosty comment. (1) from James C. Austin, *Fields of the Atlantic Monthly: Letters to an Editor, 1861–70* (California, 1953) pp. 212–15. James T. Fields (1817–81), partner in Ticknor and Fields, editor of the *Atlantic Monthly*, 1861–70. It was said of Fields and his wife, Annie, that literary Boston of the day revolved around them; (2) from H. S. Scudder, *James Russell Lowell: A Biography* (1901) II, 82–4. Lowell (1819–81), distinguished in letters and public affairs, was the first editor of *Atlantic Monthly*, 1857–61; Professor of French and Spanish at Harvard, 1855–86; minister to Spain, 1877–80; minister to England, 1880–85; (3) from Charles K. Tuckerman, *Personal Recollections of Notable People at Home and Abroad* (1895) II, 8–11. Tuckerman (1821–96) became First minister Resident of the United States in Greece (1868–72); he was an authority on Greek and Turkish affairs and wrote *The Greeks of Today* (1872); (4) from Clara Louise Kellogg, *Memoirs of an American Prima Donna* (New York, 1913) p. 48. Mme Strakosch (*née* Clara Louise Kellogg (1842–1916)), celebrated opera singer, made her New York début in *Rigoletto*, 1861; first appearance in London in 1867. In 1874 she organised an opera company in England.

(1)   [Best-known comment on his work, and one which Trollope cherished from a writer 'whose brilliant intellect and warm imagination led him to a kind of work the very opposite of mine' (*Auto.*, viii). See also 'The genius of Nathaniel Hawthorne', *North American Review* (Sep 1879) pp. 203–22. *The American Notebooks by Nathaniel Hawthorne*, ed. Randall Stewart (New Haven, Conn., 1932) xcii dates the letter 11 Feb 1860.]

It is odd enough, moreover, that my own individual taste is for quite another class of works than those which I myself am able to write. If I were to meet with such books as mine by another writer, I don't believe I should be able to get through them. Have you ever read the novels of Anthony Trollope? They precisely suit my taste; solid and substantial, written on the strength of beef and through the inspiration of ale, and just as real as if some giant had hewn a great lump out of the earth and put it under a glass case, with all its inhabitants going about their daily business and not suspecting that they were made a show of. And these books are just as English as a beefsteak – Have they ever been tried in America? It needs an English residence to make them thoroughly comprehensible, but still I should think that human nature would give them success anywhere –

[James T. Fields first tried to set up a meeting in London, writing to Nathaniel Hawthorne, 20 May 1860:] ... Do come up to London. Among others who wish to meet you is Trollope the novelist whom I met at dinner yesterday. I told him you were a reader of his books and he seemed really delighted that you praised his novels. He is a good fellow. With our kindest regards to you all.

[In Sep 1861 Anthony Trollope was visiting America and Fields finally managed to bring about a meeting. Fields wrote to

Hawthorne, 11 Sep 1861:] I send you enclosed a letter brought as an introduction by Anthony Trollope. He is a jolly good fellow & you will like him. Now he is in Newport & will return for a few days only to finish his visit here. On Monday he will dine with us at 3 o'clock at our house. We make the hour 3 that Emerson may get back to Concord. But you must stay with us & return next day if you wish to. Let me know on receipt of this if you will come. I really hope you can, for Trollope is a fine boy and wishes to meet you very much.[1]

[Hawthorne and Trollope met on 16 Sep 1861 when Lowell, Holmes and Emerson were also present. Trollope and Hawthorne got on well. From Boston, Fields wrote to Hawthorne, 18 Sep 1861:] I wish very much to begin your new story (about the house) in our *January* number. Now dip your pen steadily and briskly to that end. When shall I have the first instalment? I shall depend upon seeing the early chapters of yr story 'right away'. Did you get home safely? Trollope fell in love with you at first sight and went off moaning that he could not see you again. He swears you are the handsomest Yankee that ever walked this planet.

(2)   [James Russell Lowell to ?, 20 Sep 1861.][2] I dined the other day with Anthony Trollope, a big, red-faced, rather underbred Englishman of the bald-with-spectacles type. A good roaring positive fellow who deafened me (sitting on his right) till I though of Dante's Cerberus. He says he goes to work on a novel 'just like a shoemaker on a shoe, only taking care to make honest stitches'. Gets up at 5 every day, does all his writing before breakfast, and always writes just so many pages a day. He and Dr Holmes were very entertaining.[3] The Autocrat started one or two hobbies, and charged, paradox in rest – but it was pelting a rhinoceros with seed-pearl.

Dr: You don't know what Madeira is in England?

T: I'm not so sure it's worth knowing.

Dr: Connoisseurship in it with us is a fine art. There are men who will tell you a dozen kinds, as Dr Waagen would know a Carlo Dolci from a Guido.

T: They might be better employed!

Dr: Whatever is worth doing is worth doing well.

T: Ay, but that's begging the whole question. I don't admit it's *worse* doing at all. If they earn their bread by it, it may be *worse* doing (roaring).

Dr: But you may be assured –

T: No, I may'nt be asshorred. I won't be asshored. I don't intend to be asshored (roaring louder)!

And so they went at it. It was very funny. Trollope wouldn't give him any chance. Meanwhile, Emerson and I, who sat between them, crouched down out of range and had some very good talk, with the shot hurtling overhead. I had one little passage at arms with T. apropos of English peaches. T. ended by roaring that England was the only country where such a thing as a peach or a grape was known. I appealed to Hawthorne, who sat opposite. His face mantled and trembled for a moment with some droll fancy, as one sees bubbles rise and send off rings in still water when a turtle stirs at the bottom, and then he said, 'I asked an Englishman once who was praising their peaches to describe to me exactly what he meant by a peach, and he described something very like a cucumber.' I rather liked Trollope.[4]

(3)   I met Anthony Trollope, the novelist, at two dinner-parties in London. I had previously made his acquaintance in New York during his visit to America to write a book upon the country, which when it appeared proved to be as impartial and unprejudiced an account of things as a critic could well make who had brought with him a predisposition to like what he came to see. This was a matter of surprise to many who remembered with what acrimony and coarseness Mrs Trollope, his mother, had scourged us in her book on America many years before. My brother[5] was sitting in his library in New York, when, in response to his 'Come in', the door flew open, and a stout, hairy-faced, ruddy-complexioned Englishman burst in upon his solitude like a rough shaggy Newfoundland dog about to leap upon him in the exuberance of animal spirits. 'My name is Anthony Trollope!' exclaimed the visitor in a brusque voice, 'and I've brought you a letter of introduction from a mutual friend in England.'

In physique, manner and speech he might have been taken for a dragoon in mufti, or a sportsman fresh from an invigorating run in the fields; certainly not for a novelist whose forte lay in depicting the salient traits of English clergymen, the delicate shades of character among English maidens, and in composing those inimitable love-letters which so plentifully bestrew the pages of his lifelike romances. During his visit to New York, Trollope was introduced to many of our literary men, and to such social gatherings as might interest a man of his pursuits. He wore spectacles, through which he seemed to inspect men and things with a quiet scrutiny, as if making perpetual mental memoranda for future use. In conversation he would sometimes ask a question, or make a suggestion respecting people to whom he had been introduced, which indicated a keen perception of the weak spots in their characters; but this was always said in a good-humoured way that left no sting behind it.*

When we met at a dinner in London, Trollope asked me with some asperity why I had not come in, instead of leaving a card at his house, a few days previous. I told him that as the servant, in reply to my enquiry, said he was in his library, I did not wish to intrude when, probably, he was in the midst of romance-writing, composing, perhaps, a love-letter from one of his heroines. 'What if I was?', he asked, grinning like a hyena behind his hairy visage. 'Romance-writing with me is a mere mechanical pursuit; it is a *business*, and I intend to bring up my son to the same occupation.'

I expressed my regret at such an avowal, and said that I should never take up his books with the same relish as before; something would be missing – a tinge of sentiment which connects the idea one forms of the author with the book one is reading. When the ladies left us to our cigars, the conversation fell, somehow or other, upon theology and the belief in a future state. One gentleman remarked that but for the hope of heaven this world would be a meaningless failure. 'That depends', said another, 'upon what the bliss of heaven consists. If we are to be transformed – as we are instructed to believe – into winged angels playing upon harps and singing hallelujahs world without end, I trust that I may be permitted to remain in this mundane existence to the utmost span allotted to the life of man.'

'There is a good deal to be said on both sides of the question,' remarked Trollope, 'but if I thought I should never see dear old Thackeray again, I should be a very unhappy man.'

*Trollope and myself were present when George Bancroft, the historian,[6] delivered an address before the New York Historical Society. Trollope had never before seen Bancroft, and he studied him closely. He made no remark until the speaker made a point which elicited applause, when he whispered in my ear: 'Do you suppose he himself believes what he is saying?'

'Have you read Ouida's last novel?' I asked him, to change the subject of conversation.

'No,' he replied, 'I have never read any of her books. I promised her I would read one of them, and I suppose I shall have to do so – some time or other.'

There was a tinge of affectation, I thought, in this remark, which clashed with that blunt honesty which I had always associated with Trollope's character, and also, perhaps, a spice of literary jealousy. This should not have been so, for no two writers of romance could very well differ in style and treatment more distinctly than do these two. The high-coloured sentimentality of Ouida is as far removed from the everyday realities of Trollope as the magnificent effects of sunset vary from the shadowless light of noonday.

(4)   On one occasion I met Anthony Trollope at the Fields', the English novelist whose works were then more or less in vogue. He had just come from England and was filled with conceit. English people of that time were incredibly insular and uninformed about us, and Mr Trollope knew nothing of America, and did not seem to want to know anything. Certainly, English people when they are not thoroughbred can be very common![7] Trollope was full of him-self and wrote only for what he could get out if it. I never, before or since, met a literary person who was so frankly 'on the make'. The discussion that afternoon was about the recompense of authors, and Trollope said that he had reduced his literary efforts to a working basis and wrote so many words to a page and so many pages to a chapter. He refrained from using the actual word 'money' – the English shrink from the word 'money' – but he managed to convey to his hearers the fact that a considerable consideration was the main incentive to his literary labour, and put the matter more specifically later, to my mother, by telling her that he always *chose the words that would fill up the pages quickest.*

NOTES

1. The Fields became close friends. On 18 May 1868, Annie wrote to Kate Field: 'We had a very pleasant visit from good whole-souled Mr Trollope. A few such men redeemed Nineveh. He always seems the soul of honesty' (from MS Boston Public Library, cited *Letters*, i, 426). See James T. Fields, *Yesterdays With Authors* (Boston, Mass., 1871) p. 63. Annie Fields (1834–1915) established a

literary salon; wrote poetry, a biography of her husband, *James T. Fields: Biographical Notes and Personal Sketches* (Boston, Mass., 1881), and *Authors and Friends* (1897).

2. The addressee was possibly Charles Eliot Norton. See Edward Wagenknecht, *James Russell Lowell: Portrait of a Many-Sided Man* (New York, 1973), p. 93, but it is not in the collected letters.

3. Oliver Wendell Holmes (1809–1904), Parkman Professor of Anatomy and Physiology at Harvard, 1847–82; best known for his contributions to the *Atlantic Monthly*, notably *The Autocrat of the Breakfast Table* (1858). Trollope would have been on his mettle because Holmes was one of the most assured and elegant talkers of Boston Brahmin society. Holmes's son, Oliver Wendell, wounded on the Potomac, was brought back to Boston, a hero; Trollope was among the many callers in late Nov 1861. During visits to England Holmes called on the Trollopes in the summers of 1865 and 1874. See Mark De Wolfe Howe, *Justice Oliver Wendell Holmes* (Cambridge, Mass., 1957), i, 111; ii, 99; Kenneth S. Lynn, *William Dean Howells: An American Life* (New York, 1970) p. 125; Edwin P. Hoyt, *The Improper Bostonian: Dr Oliver Wendell Holmes* (New York, 1979) pp. 205–6.

4. Less impressed a few years later was William Dean Howells (1837–1920), distinguished author, editor of *Atlantic Monthly*, 1871–81. He had been invited to stay with Trollope at Waltham in the summer of 1865 but found his host 'scarcely spoke to him while he was there; and he offered him none of the hoped for help, or advice, as to English publishers, that the young American was too proud to mention' (*Life in Letters of William Dean Howells*, ed. Mildred Howells (New York, 1928) i, 93). Later Howells came up with a variant of the Hawthorne metaphor: 'Anthony Trollope with his immense quiet, ruminant reality, ox-like cropping the field of English life and converting its succulent juices into the nourishing beef of his fiction' (Oscar W. Firkins, *William Dean Howells* (Cambridge, Mass., 1924) p. 286). Some of the bovine imagery likewise attaches to Henry Adams's description of Trollope at tea with Mrs Proctor (widow of Barry Cornwall, the poet) in July 1879 as 'a rosy-gilled John Bull' (*The Letters of Mrs Henry Adams*, ed. Ward Thoron (Boston, Mass., 1936) p. 157).

5. Henry Theodore Tuckerman (1813–71), Boston-born author who lived in New York after 1845 and established himself as critic and essayist. He wrote *America and Her Commentators* (1864) in which he took Trollope mildly to task for some of his commentary in *North America* (1862).

6. George Bancroft (1800–91), author of *A History of the United States*, 7 vols (1851–61). Trollope wished to purchase the set (*Letters*, i, 207).

7. Her dismay was obviously shared by Fanny Seward, daughter of William Henry Seward (1801–72), statesman; Secretary of State, 1861–1870. Fanny was only 17 at the time of the meeting on 27 Dec 1861, and recorded in her diary her impression of 'a great homely, red, stupid-faced Englishman, with a disgusting beard of iron grey'. Since the dangerous international repercussions of the Slidell and Mason affair had been the topic of conversation, doubtless Trollope was louder than usual. See *Auto.*, ix and *Letters*, i, 165.

A Comfort For Any Editor

DONALD MACLEOD

From 'Anthony Trollope', *Good Words*, xxv (1884) 248–52. Revd Dr Donald Macleod (1831–1916), author of *A Memoir of Norman Macleod* (1876), succeeded his brother as editor of *Good Words* in 1872; Revd Dr Norman Macleod (1812–72), Chaplain to Queen Victoria, 1857–72; editor of *Good Words*, 1860–72. Trollope's scrupulous regard for deadlines was a cardinal point in his literary practice and consonant with his attention to daily quotas and word counts. His relation with the Macleods provides a typical example of his integrity in business dealings. In 1862 Norman Macleod decided it was time to run a novel from such an influential and seemingly 'safe' novelist (the readership of his periodical was solidly religious). Thus in Mar or Apr 1862 he wrote: 'Seriously, you and Kingsley are the only men whom I should like to have a story from. ... I think you could let out the *best* side of your soul in *Good Words* – better far than ever in *Cornhill*' (*Letters*, I, 177–8). Trollope obliged with *Rachel Ray*, whose worldly tone caused Macleod second thoughts, particularly since his magazine was under attack from the strict evangelical journal the *Record*. The letter from Macleod breaking the contract, quoted in the excerpt below, was 'full of wailing and repentance', as Trollope called it (*Auto.*, x). Trollope asked for and got £500 from the publisher, Alexander Strahan. The whole story is told in *Commentary*, pp. 233–43.

In common with all who knew him only after he had achieved distinction, we were surprised by the picture he draws of the hardships of his early life. For no trace of sorrow, no memory of disappointment, could be detected in that bluff and cheery presence. He seemed to revel in the fresh air of a healthy, happy and useful existence. The loud manly voice, the *banging* emphasis and straightness of leap with which he plunged into any matter of discussion, had something in them of his favourite amusement of hunting. He addressed you as a man trotting alongside, and in the teeth of a strong breeze, might address you. There was the ring of the 'view-halloo' in his heartiness. His countenance beamed with thorough honesty and kindness. And yet he describes the first twenty-six years of his life as 'years of suffering, disgrace and inward remorse'. We are disposed to make large allowance, in these statements, for the influence of a sensitive temperament. His 'craving for affection' probably made him exaggerate the slights to which he was exposed. A coarser nature would have forgotten many of the incidents that left deep scars on his kindly spirit. ...

It was indeed a comfort for any editor to have Trollope as a writer, for there was never any anxiety as to 'copy' being forthcoming at the appointed time. We remember the surprise we experienced when, on the occasion of our first arranging with him for a story, he asked, 'How many words do you wish?' 'On what day do you wish copy?' was the next question. A jotting was then taken of the agreement, and it was observed by him to the letter.[1] Such methods cannot but appear inconsistent with any preconceived notions of inspiration, and as being too mechanical for the accomplishment of the best work. Yet we believe it had no such trammelling influence on Trollope, whose temperament was such that he could reach his highest power whether he was flying in an express train or being pitched about in a steamer in a gale. With unflinching regularity and decision he could concentrate his mind on his allotted task – sometimes even timing himself with his watch for the production of so many words in so many minutes. We question, however, whether the consciousness of having to fill so many pages, while quite consistent with the maintenance of a certain literary proportion, did not sometimes lead to undue 'padding'. If he worked hard, he very properly expected to be paid for his work. He had no false sentimentalism as to money in connection with art. ...

His life, in spite of its incessant toil, was an exceedingly happy one, and he recognised its happiness to the full. His duties afforded him the opportunity of travelling extensively. Egypt, the West Indies, America, Australia, South Africa, became familiar ground to him. When at home he had his four hunters ever ready to carry him to the covert side, and (what was more difficult) to carry a rider across country who was so short-sighted that he could never form a judgement of fence or ditch, and who boldly rode straight at everything. From his habit of rising every morning at 5.30 a.m., he was able to have his literary work over in good time, and the day free for any other duty or amusement. Loving his own fireside, he yet enjoyed going into society, and seldom in his later life did he miss, when in town, the afternoon visit to the Garrick, and the afternoon rubber at whist there. Never making any very loud professions of religion, and regarding all that was innocent in life as open to his free enjoyment, all his friends knew him to be a reverent and sincere Christian.

From the affection and admiration with which we regard him, it is painful for us to draw attention to one passage in his *Autobiography* in which his memory has evidently betrayed him, and in which he writes in a tone which, for many reasons well known to us, has filled us with surprise.[2] ...

When we remember the trueness of the friendship which existed between Mr Trollope and Dr Norman Macleod, and which was not even disturbed by the incident of *Rachel Ray*, we are at a loss to account for the irritation which this passage betrays.[3] ...

But Mr Trollope ought to have had no difficulty in divining the reasons for *Rachel Ray* not being accepted, because he had these reasons given at length by Norman Macleod in a letter which we published in the memoir of our brother, and part of which we here reproduce, not only to show that there is very little trace of 'wailing and repentance', but also to give our readers an insight into the principles upon which the former and present editors have tried to select fiction – that most difficult of all elements in a periodical with the aims which *Good Words* has always put before it.[4]

[In a jocose vein Macleod suggested that his periodical was broad-minded yet considerate of the feelings of reasonable Evangelicals.] 'Well, then, was I wrong in assuming that you were an honest believer in revealed Christian truth? I was not. Was I wrong in believing and hoping that there were many truly Christian aspects of life, as well as the canting and humbug ones, with which you heartily sympathised, and which you were able and disposed to delineate? I was not.

'Perhaps I had no ground for hoping that you would give me a different kind of story from those you had hitherto published. If so, forgive me this wrong. Possibly the wish was father to the thought. But the thought did not imply that any of your former novels had been false either to your own world within or to the big world without – false to truth or to nature. It assumed only that you could with your whole heart produce another novel which, instead of showing up what was weak, false, disgusting in professing Christians, might also bring out, as has never yet been done, what Christianity as a living power derived from faith in a living Saviour, and working in and through living men and women, does, has done, and will do, what no other known power can accomplish in the world, for the good of the individual or mankind. ... Why, when one reads of the good men in most novels, it can hardly be discovered where they got their goodness; but let a parson, a deacon, a church member be introduced and at once we guess where they have had their badness from – they were professing Christians. Now all this, and much more, was the substance of my sermon to you.

'Now, my good Trollope, you have been, in my humble opinion, guilty of committing this fault, or, as you might say, praiseworthy in doing this good, in your story. You hit right and left; give a *wipe* here, a sneer there, and thrust a nasty *prong* into another place; cast a gloom over Dorcas societies, and a glory over balls lasting till four in the morning.[5] In short, it is the old story. The shadow over the Church is broad and deep, and over every other spot sunshine reigns. That is the general impression which the story gives, so far as it goes. There is nothing, of course, bad or vicious in it – that could not be from you – but quite enough, and that without any necessity from your head or heart, to keep *Good Words* and its Editor in boiling water until either or both were boiled to death. ...'

We will close this brief sketch of the good Anthony Trollope with a story lately given me, which is both amusing and will serve to show how hearty was the friendship which existed between him and Norman Macleod, long after *Rachel Ray's* rejection had been forgotten. They were both with Mr John Burns (the well-known chairman of the Cunard Line) at a little Highland inn, when, after supper, stories were told, and the laughter became loud and long, lasting far into the night. In the morning an old gentleman, who slept in a bedroom above where they were, complained to the landlord of the manner in which his night's rest had been disturbed, and presumed to express his astonishment that such men should have taken more than was good for them. 'Well,' replied the landlord, 'I am bound to confess there was much loud talking and laughter; but they had nothing stronger than *tea and fresh herrings*.' 'Bless me,' rejoined the old gentleman, 'if that is so, *what would they be after dinner!*'[6]

NOTES

1. The first story for *Good Words* was 'The Widow's Mite' (1863). The Macleods also published 'The Two Generals' (1863), 'Malachi's Cove' (1864), 'The Last Austrian who left Venice' (1867), 'The Golden Lion of Granpere' (1872), 'Why Frau Frohmann Raised Her Prices' (1877), 'Young Women at the London Telegraph Office' (1877), 'The Telegraph Girl' (1877), 'Alice Dugdale' (1878), 'In the Hunting Field' (1879), 'A Walk in a Wood' (1879), 'Kept in the Dark' (1882) and 'The Two Heroines of Plumplington' (1882).

2. Macleod here alludes to the passage at arms concerning *Rachel Ray*, in which Trollope, a trifle smugly, recalled that he had warned the editor: 'As worldly and – if any one thought me wicked – as wicked as I had heretofore been I must still be should I write for *Good Words*.' But he would have a novel and he had to pay up – 'that money I exacted, feeling that the fault had in truth been with the editor' (*Auto.*, x).

3. Trollope loyally supported Macleod at a dinner marking the Scottish Hospital's 201st anniversary on 30 Nov 1865 when Macleod ran into some heckling. On 15 Jan 1866 Trollope wrote 'The Fourth Commandment' in the *Fortnightly Review* commending Macleod's criticism of Scottish sabbatarians. See *Letters*, i, 318, 327.

4. To be fair to Macleod he was under fire from extreme evangelicals objecting to laxity in *Good Words*; even so his letter sounds a note of jocularity worthy of Mr Chadband. Norman Macleod and Burns led 'The Gaiter Club', formed for hikes in Scotland, and Trollope turned out with them on occasion. See Edwin Hodder, *Sir G. Burns: Both His Times and Friends* (1890) pp. 333–5.

5. The Reverend Samuel Prong, the Vicar of Baslehurst in *Rachel Ray*, is the sanctimonious cleric Trollope so often satirises.

6. A similar anecdote was attributed to Thackeray who was in the street outside the Garrick Club when the voices of Reade and Trollope could be heard from inside. They were then about fifty. 'What must they have been at eighteen?' was Thackeray's comment (J. W. Robertson Scott, *The Story of the Pall Mall Gazette* (1950) p. 84).

Waltham House

ANNE THACKERAY, HENRY BRACKENBURY AND SIR FREDERICK AND LADY POLLOCK

Home life meant a great deal to the Trollopes especially after the move to Waltham Cross, Hertfordshire, in Dec 1859. After several migrations Trollope was pleased to settle close to London (about 12 miles) and near good hunting, and he stayed there until 1871 when, after his trip to Australia, he moved to

Montagu Square, London. The 'somewhat too grandly called Waltham House' (*Auto.*, viii) none-the-less had an establishment of five servants including Barney, the groom, who called Trollope to his labours (*Letters*, I, 215n). Having missed the rootedness of childhood Trollope placed great importance on the normal household routines and the weekend in the garden; Smith describes him when not working charging round with a heavy roller (Robertson Scott, *The Story of the Pall Mall Gazette*, p. 84). Away in the United States in 1862 he spoke of the 'children & cows & horses and dogs and pigs – and all the stern necessities of an English home' (*Letters*, I, 161). Longing for home – centred on Rose – increased; on the taxing South Africa journey in 1877 his journal noted: 'Never so home-sick in my life' (*Letters*, II, 740), and wistfully from Ireland in 1882: 'How is the garden, and the cocks & hens, & especially the asparagus bed?' (*Letters*, II, 966). The Trollopes enjoyed entertaining chosen friends on the small scale; he made a far better host than guest. One party that went astray because of a clash with the Derby (May 1863) began well enough with a jaunty invitation. To Morgan O'Connell, friend of Thackeray and Bianconi's son-in-law, he wrote on 10 May 1863: 'There will be some people with us – but the eating will be poor. Our cook has got drunk, –perpetually drunk. If there be nothing to eat we can do the same' (*Letters*, I, 215). Unfortunately the Derby was a rival attraction and several guests defaulted. To Millais he wrote: 'We had a very melancholy day – which wd have been less melancholy had you all come. But it could not be helped. My wife was awfully disgusted as women always are when nobody comes to eat their pastries and sweetmeats. As for me I hope you lost your money at the Derby' (*Letters*, I, 215–16). Two of the more successful gatherings are cited below. (1) from *The Letters of Anne Thackeray Ritchie*, ed. Hester Ritchie (1924) pp. 125, 233–4. A typically deft little portrait of the off-duty novelist and the charms of Waltham. Anne Isabella Thackeray (1837–1919), Thackeray's elder daughter, best known for such novels as *The Story of Elizabeth* (1862), *The Village on the Cliff* (1867) and *Old Kensington* (1873). See Winifred Gerin, *Anne Thackeray Ritchie* (1981); (2) from Henry Brackenbury, *Some Memories of My Spare Time* (1909) pp. 48–53. Henry Brackenbury (1837–1914), writer on military topics; contributor to *St Paul's Magazine*; Professor of Military History at Woolwich, 1868; knighted in 1896; (3) from *Personal Remembrances of Sir Frederick Pollock* (1887) II, 149–51. William Frederick Pollock (1815–88), barrister, Queen's Remembrancer, 1874–86; served with Trollope on the Royal Literary Fund; (4) from *Correspondence of Henry Taylor*, ed. Edward Dowden (1888) pp. 296–8. Sir Henry Taylor (1800–86), poet and civil servant, Colonial Office, 1824–72, best known for his verse drama *Philip Van Artevelde* (1834). Juliet Creed Pollock (d. 1899), wife of Sir Frederick Pollock, regular contributor to *St Paul's Magazine*. Her article 'The Imaginative Literature of America', *Contemporary Review*, XXII (Aug 1873) 347–71, criticising mercantile attitudes, brought a typically Trollopian riposte: 'The best price will get the best article. ... *Il faut vivre*. But with those of us who are highminded there is an overriding object, one more first even than the first, – that of doing our duty; which comprehends such excellence in his work as the workman may attain, though it be attained at the expense of profit' (*Letters*, II, 596–7).

(1)   Journal 1865. Early in the year to Waltham Cross to stay at the Trollopes. It was a sweet old prim chill house wrapped in snow.

The Merivales were staying there too.[1] I remember so well saying to Rose Merivale how *terrible* this pain of parting was, and would it ever cease? She said, 'Life is over so quickly, so very quickly', and now I feel how true that is.

I can also remember in the bitter cold dark morning hearing Mr Trollope called at four o'clock.[2] He told me he gave his man half-a-crown every time he (Mr Trollope) *didn't* get up! 'The labourer is worthy of his hire', said Mr Trollope in his deep cheerful lispy voice.

[From recollections of Sir John Millais by Anne Thackeray Ritchie.] I once saw an artist at work in a little wood near Knole on a certain day in July, when we all started on a happy expedition Mrs Millais invited me to join. Her sister was there, and the Trollopes, and Mr Charles Clifford. We had found sunshine everywhere, and a drag at Sevenoaks, and as we walked through the woods, we came upon this painter at work under the trees. Our host stopped for a moment. 'Why,' said he to the painter, 'you have not got your lights right. Look, *this* is what you want.' And he took the brush out of the painter's hand, and made a line or two on the picture, and then nodded to him and walked away.

Mr Trollope laughed, and said, 'The man looks bewildered; he ought to know it is Millais', and he ran back and told him.[3] Then someone else laughed, and said, 'He ought to know it is Trollope.' So a second message was conveyed to the unfortunate painter, and greatly amused we all walked on through the woods to where the carriage was waiting.

[A postscript added by Anne Thackeray's daughter.] My Mother does not reveal that it was she herself who conveyed the second message – and that another member of the party then ran back, saying: 'Now he must be told that that was Miss Thackeray.'

(2)   In the autumn of 1867, Mr Anthony Trollope started *St Paul's Magazine*, and I offered him a paper on 'The Military Armaments of the Five Great Powers', which appeared in one of his earliest numbers, followed shortly afterwards by a paper on 'Parliament and Army Reform', and other articles. There is not much of interest in the few letters from Mr Trollope which I possess. In one of them he writes, 'Do not be too severe on governments. Having known something of government work for

very many years, my conviction is that as a rule our public men do their work as well as their very peculiar circumstances in subjection to a representative government allow them to do. I do not think our public men are niggards, or are disposed to be mean by disposition.'[4]

At the end of February or beginning of March 1868 I paid him a weekend visit at Waltham Cross. Mrs Trollope, whose beautiful feet made a great impression on me, was there, and the only other guest was Mr John Blackwood, the publisher and editor of *Blackwood's Magazine*, with whom in after years I formed a very pleasant friendship. I am not sure whether Mr Trollope was at that time still in the service of the Post Office, but I remember his telling me that he had decided not to leave the public service till he had made from his writing and invested sufficient capital to give him an income equal to what he would lose by retiring from the public service.[5] He was a great smoker. One wall of his library where he worked was entirely hidden by small cupboards or bins, each with a separate glass door, and filled with cigars, stacked across each other 'headers and stretchers' like timber, so as to allow free circulation of air. On wet days the doors were all kept closed, in dry weather they were open. He told me that each year he got a large consignment of cigars from Havana. There was a pointed stud stuck into the wood above the door of the bin in use, and as soon as this bin was empty the stud was moved to the next bin, and the empty one was filled from the chest. This had gone on for years, the cigars longest in stock being always those smoked.[6]

He had a long thick beard, which it was difficult to keep one's eyes off, as it had a singular attraction for fragments of cigar-ash.

He told me that he began to write at five o'clock every morning, and wrote a certain number of hours till it was time to dress, never touching his literary work after breakfast. I remember telling him that I always worked at night, and his saying, 'Well, I give the freshest hours of the day to my work; you give the fag end of the day to yours.' I have often thought over this, but my experience has always been that the early morning is the best time for study and taking in ideas, night the best time for giving out thoughts.

I said that I envied him the gift of imagination, which enabled him to create characters. He said, 'Imagination! my dear fellow, not a bit of it; it is cobbler's wax.' Seeing that I was rather puzzled, he said that the secret of success was to put a lump of cobbler's wax on your chair, sit on it and stick to it till you had succeeded. He told me he had written for years before he got paid.

My paper on Parliament and Army Reform in *St Paul's Magazine* brought me into touch with Sir Charles Trevelyan and his son, now the Rt Hon. Sir G. O. Trevelyan. The latter wrote to Trollope that he and his father were so much interested in the paper that he took the liberty of asking the name of the writer. The letter lies before me, endorsed 'Is there any object to "giving you up" to Competition wallah and father? Anthony Trollope.'[7]

(3)   [The Pollocks stayed at Waltham House on 21 Apr 1866.] To dine and sleep at Anthony Trollope's at Waltham. Here he lived for some years in an old-fashioned red-brick house of about William the Third's time, with a good staircase and some large rooms in it, and standing in equally old-fashioned grounds, which served as the suggestion for the scene of my first dialogue in *Fraser's Magazine* on the portraits at South Kensington. There was a *corps de logis* and two wings, one of which held the stables in which Trollope's hunters were lodged, and the other was converted into an office for the Post Office clerks who were under him in his work of superintending the cross-post arrangements of the eastern counties. The Arthur Russells were in the house at the same time with us, and there was a dinner-party of neighbours, during which Trollope mentioned his habit of regularly writing a certain fixed amount of the novel in progress during two or three hours of the early morning, and he named the number of foolscap sheets of paper which he filled every day. I at once, to his astonishment, said, 'Then you must write so many hundred words daily.' – 'How can you tell that?' he cried, for I was very nearly right in my guess. I did not trouble the company at the moment with the mystery of law stationers' folios of seventy-two words – with which I had to be familiar in taxing legal costs – but explained to Trollope afterwards how easy it was for me, knowing his handwriting, to make a rough computation of the number of words he would place on a sheet of paper of known size. His manner of writing a novel was thoroughly methodical. Before commencing it he would settle its length, and assign so many days to writing it, at so many words a day. Every morning the appointed portion for the day would be duly put on paper, and the day marked out, in a section of the calendar prepared for the

purpose, as the days are by schoolboys to show how nearly their holidays are approaching. Without fail or mistake the novel was always finished in this way upon the exact date previously fixed for its completion. Trollope's writing for the press was very distinct and regular, and entirely free from alterations or additions, etc. It seemed to have flowed from his pen like clear liquor from a tap. When he went, I think for the first time, to Australia he asked me to correct the proofs of one of his shorter tales – *The Golden Lion of Granpere* – but there was really nothing for me to do. ...

[The Trollopes were guests of the Pollocks at Montagu Square on 15 Jan 1867. They were to become neighbours.] Anthony Trollope's to dine and sleep. At dinner W. Rathbone Greg, Froude, Charles Herries. Next morning when Trollope came down to breakfast, after having been writing the novel then on hand, as usual, he rather astonished us by saying, 'I have just been making my twenty-seventh proposal of marriage.'

(4) [Mrs Pollock[8] to Henry Taylor, 1 July 1869.] If you can catch only one hair out of the tail of a minute, hold it out to me till I catch one end of it; so wide the gap is, that I hardly know whereabouts I stood when I last exchanged words with you, but I rather think it was just before our visit to the Anthony Trollopes, which visit went off very satisfactorily. A. Trollope is pleased about your colonial order,[9] and his plain understanding cannot conceive the fastidiousness which thinks a form of distinction not worth having because it is sometimes ill bestowed. 'Let the man of high desert be satisfied that his desert is acknowledged,' he says, 'and not be scrupulous in weighing the exact degrees. Things cannot be so finely balanced in a rough world.'

He is a man of direct sympathies, strong in a straightforward direction, but to whom many devious, delicate turns and subtle ways of thought and feeling are not intelligible. We had fine weather, and our time was passed chiefly in the garden – a handsome stiff garden of the Queen Anne style, with a square pond at one end of it and a smooth grass lawn at the other. We walked round and round this garden many times, Anthony Trollope smoking and talking all the way. Among other anecdotes he told me a curious one of his early life in Ireland when he was staying at Killarney.

A priest, into whose company he had fallen by chance, and whose name he did not know, was exhibiting to him the beauties of the lake, and Anthony Trollope, who was at that time fresh from the reading of the novel of *The Collegians*, said, 'Ah, somewhere hereabouts poor Eily O'Connor was drowned; 'tis close upon this spot it must have been that the villain Hardress did that foulest of murders. What a scene! what passion, what character, what skill I find in that novel! What a frightful history it tells!' The priest remaining silent, Anthony Trollope thought that perhaps he did not know the story, and went on eagerly: 'Don't you know it? Isn't it a first-rate book? Isn't Eily O'Connor enchanting? Wasn't Hardress – '

'Hardress?', said the priest, turning suddenly round, facing Anthony Trollope, and laying his hands on his shoulders – 'Hardress was my first cousin, and I stood on the steps of the scaffold when he was hung.'

This was a painful moment for Anthony Trollope. However, the priest made no defence of his cousin, and only gave him some more hideous details concerning the crime: he told how *not* Danny Marr, but Hardress himself, held the unhappy woman's head down in the water till she was dead.

It is well that Griffin altered this fact, which for a poetical work of fiction would have been too revolting.[10]

NOTES

1. Old friends from Trollope's early days. John Lewis Merivale (1815–86), youngest son of John Herman Merivale, had known Anthony since schooldays. He was a barrister and later a Commissioner in Bankruptcy. Merivale put Trollope in touch with William Longman who published his first real success, *The Warden* (1855).

2. Other accounts suggest an hour or so later was more usual.

3. John Everett Millais (1829–96), Trollope's friend and favourite illustrator, created baronet in 1885. His drawings appeared in four of Trollope's novels: *Framley Parsonage* (1861), *The Small House at Allington* (1864), *Orley Farm* (1862) and *Phineas Finn* (1869); he also drew the frontispiece for *Kept in the Dark* (1882).

4. Undated letter, 1868 (*Letters*, I, 417).

5. To an unnamed correspondent: 'I shall be a free man on 31 October 1867 as far as the Post Office goes.' He was next year to make his mission to the United States for the Post Office, Apr–July 1868. By retiring eight years before his sixtieth birthday he forfeited his pension of about £500 (*Letters*, II, 392–3).

6. Trollope was fond of distributing cigars among his friends; he wrote to George Eliot in Aug 1866: 'My kindest regards to the Master [Lewes]. If he

wants any of the new batch of 8000 cigars which I have just got over from Cuba let him tell me at once how many' (*Letters*, i, 346–7). Lewes contributed 'The Dangers and Delights of Tobacco' to *St Paul's*, ii (Nov 1868) 172–84. See also p. 178 below.

7. Brackenbury's articles in *St Paul's* were: 'Military Armaments of the Five Great Powers' (i, Nov 1867), 'Our Army' (i, Feb 1868), 'Parliament and Army Reform' (ii, Jul 1868), and 'Influence of Modern Improvements upon Strategy (iii, Mar 1869). 'Competition wallah' was George Otto Trevelyan (1838–1928), whose letters to *Macmillan's Magazine* appeared in 12 parts, 8 May 1863 to 10 May 1864, under that pseudonym. His father, Sir Charles Edward Trevelyan (1807–86), was satirised by Trollope for his introduction of competitive examination in the Civil Service, and appeared as Sir Gregory Hardlines in *The Three Clerks* (1858). '"We always call him Sir Gregory", Lady Trevelyan said to me afterwards, when I come to know her and her husband' (*Auto.*, vi).

8. Her contributions to *St Paul's Magazine* were 'Fashion in Poetry' (Mar 1868), 'M. Victor Hugo's England' (July 1867) and 'Jane Austen' (Mar 1870). Her son Walter Herries Pollock wrote the fine appreciation in *Harper's New Monthly Magazine* (May 1883, see pp. 194–8).

9. The Knighthood of St Michael and St George, 1869. Trollope praised Taylor's manliness and perspicuity in a review of his *Poetical Works* in *Fortnightly Review*, i (1 June 1865) 129–46.

10. Gerald Griffin, *The Collegians* (1847). The story was also used by Dion Boucicault for his popular melodrama *The Colleen Bawn* (1860).

Golf at Strathtyrum

A. K. H. BOYD AND MRS GERALD PORTER

(1) from A. K. H. Boyd, *Twenty Five Years of St Andrews* (1892) i, 99–101. Andrew Kennedy Hutchison Boyd (1825–99), ordained parish minister of Newton-on-Ayr, Scotland, in 1851 became one of the best known Presbyterian divines of his day, settling at St Andrews in 1865. In May 1890 he became moderator of the general assembly. Noted for his shrewd, humorous conversation, he published many light works such as *The Recreations of a Country Parson*, three series, 1859, 1861 and 1878. He seems to have met Trollope in more acerbic mood and his somewhat prissy account proves the point that Trollope rather enjoyed playing to the crowd; (2) from Mrs Gerald Porter, *Annals of a Publishing House* (1898) iii, 197–8. Loyal account of the rise of the Blackwood firm by John Blackwood's daughter, Mary. Trollope's closest friend among publishers was John Blackwood; Trollope gave him the copyright of *The Commentaries of Caesar* (1870). Their correspondence is of great interest since Blackwood read Trollope's manuscripts and was not behindhand in offering suggestions (*Letters*,

I, xvi–xvii). John Blackwood (1818–79) succeeded his father, William Black-wood (1776–1834), as head of the publishing house in 1852. The excerpt is a good example of Trollope's conversational trademark, the deliberate gambit to elicit a response or shock his listeners.

(1)   Later in the season, Anthony Trollope and his wife paid their first visit to this place. They stayed at Strathtyrum with John Blackwood.[1] Trollope tried to play golf. It is a silent game, by long tradition: but Trollope's voice was heard all over the Links. One day, having made a somewhat worse stroke than usual, he fainted with grief, and fell down upon the green. He had not adverted to the fact that he had a golf ball in his pocket: and falling upon that ball, he started up with a yell of agony, quite unfeigned. On 19 August a large party dined at Strathtyrum to meet him: among them Chambers and Tulloch.[2] The charming *Last Chronicle of Barset*, surely as sunshiny a picture of English country life as ever was written, was then delighting us all.[3] While preparing for dinner, I had stuck up the work where I could read it: and I glanced at several of the most beautiful passages, and at one or two of the most powerful. Filled with the enthusiasm of one who had very rarely met a popular author, I entered Strathtyrum that day. The sight of the great novelist was a blow. He was singularly unkempt, and his clothes were wrinkled and ill-made. His manner was a further blow. We listened for the melodious accents which were due from those lips: but they did not come. Indeed, he was the only man I had heard swear in decent society for uncounted years. The swearing, which was repeated, was the most disagreeable of all: the actual asseverating, by the Holiest Name, of some trumpery statement. How could that man have written the well-remembered sentences which had charmed one through these years? Then, by way of making himself pleasant in a gathering of Scotsmen, he proceeded (the ladies being gone and we all gathered to hear him) to vilipend our beloved Sir Walter. One was much interested in hearing what one of the most popular recent novelists thought of the founder of the modern school of fiction. Mr Trollope said that if any of Sir Walter's novels were offered to any London publisher of the present day, it would be at once rejected. We listened, humbly. Then it was asked whether this was because time had gone and Sir Walter grown old-fashioned. 'Not a bit: it is just because they are so dull.' He went on to say that the only heroine in the Waverley series with whom

one could really sympathise, was Jeanie Deans. The tone was most depreciatory, all through. Possibly it was wilfulness on the part of the critic, or a desire to give his auditors a slap in the face; for I have in after time read a page of Trollope's on which Scott was praised highly.[4] It is sometimes very difficult to know what is a man's real and abiding opinion.[5]

(2)   Mr and Mrs Anthony Trollope's was one of these never-to-be-forgotten visits.[6] The echo of Mr Trollope's laugh seems to come back to me as I strive to recall his genial presence, and the incidents of the visit: the walks, the games of golf he insisted on playing on the Ladies' Links, pretending to faint when he made a bad shot, his immense weight causing a sort of earthquake on the sandy ground; his riding off with my mother for a scamper on the sands, his host and Mrs Trollope watching them set out from the doorsteps; the dinner-parties in their honour, where the writer used to appear herself with the dessert, and come in too for a share of the fun and jokes that were flying about.[7] Mr Trollope's big voice drowned everyone else, as he chaffed my father down the length of the dinner-table. He had jested over golf, what would he not do next? He used to make daring assaults upon the most cherished articles of the Blackwood faith. Blind unswerving devotion to the Sovereign was one of his favourite points of attack. 'Now, Blackwood, how could the death of the Sovereign possibly affect *you*?', he would say. 'If you heard of it tomorrow morning you know perfectly well you would eat just as good a breakfast – you would not even deny yourself that second kidney.' It was in vain to protest that in face of such a calamity the very thought of broiled kidneys was distasteful. Mr Trollope bore everything before him, and prepared for another attack. The Conservative party and Dizzy was a tempting subject for a tilt. 'You *know*, Blackwood, you think exactly about Dizzy as I do; you *know* you would be very glad to hear he had been had up for – for shoplifting.' *Tableau*! all holding up their hands, and Mr Trollope delighted with the sensation he had produced.[8]

After the Trollopes' visit my father and mother agreed to go to Skye with them.

John Blackwood to Miss Mozley, STRATHTYRUM, 25 Aug 1868
We had a visit last week from Anthony Trollope and his wife. They are both very pleasant, and have induced us to promise to meet them at Inverness on Friday and go to Skye. From the look

of the weather I begin to repent of my promise. He is great fun, and I daresay we shall enjoy the expedition, though rain and wind may spoil the scenery.

Bathing had formed part of the holiday, and he writes to William Blackwood [John Blackwood's brother (1810–61)]: 'I had a farewell bathe with Anthony yesterday evening, and we parted almost with tears at Loch Coruisk.'

NOTES

1. Blackwood's country house about a mile from St Andrews where every summer many figures in the world of art and letters congregated.

2. Robert Chambers (1802–71) founded with his brother, William, the publishing house of W. and R. Chambers, Edinburgh (1832); established *Chambers' Journal*, 1832; wrote widely on Scottish history, biography and literature. John Tulloch (1823–86), principal of St Andrews from 1854, Chaplain to Queen Victoria, dean of the Chapel Royal, London, 1882. A broad-minded theologian he wrote *Rational Theology and Christian Philosophy in England in the Seventeenth Century*. He briefly edited *Fraser's Magazine*, 1879–81.

3. *The Last Chronicle* was issued in weekly numbers from 1 Dec 1866 to 6 July 1867 and thereafter published in book form, vol. I, Mar 1867; vol. II, July 1867.

4. Frequent references to Scott occur in the *Auto.*, the best known his praise of *Ivanhoe* which, on a second reading, he decided surpassed *Pride and Prejudice* (iii). Literary criticism was not Trollope's forte.

5. Ostensibly to counter this comment, at Sala's request Yates had another go at his old rival claiming that 'a man with worse or more offensive manners than Trollope I have rarely met. He was coarse, boorish, rough, noisy, overbearing, insolent; he adopted the Johnsonian tactics of trying to outroar his adversary in argument; he spluttered and shouted, and glared through his spectacles, and waved his arms about, a sight for gods and men'. He did not though, as Boyd suggested, swear like a trooper, the *World*, XXXVI (24 February 1892) 19.

6. The Trollopes were guests at Strathtyrum on several occasions. This visit was in mid-Aug 1868, certainly until 22 Aug.

7. Blackwood's wife Julia (the daughter of the Revd Joseph Blandford) married John Blackwood in 1854. Trollope was very fond of her (*Letters*, I, 495–6), and vowed once, 'When Mrs Blackwood is in town I will take her whist into my own keeping' (*Letters*, II, 751).

8. A well-observed point: Trollope liked to win an argument, but most of the time he enjoyed the game itself, the thrill of the chase absorbed him and carried him away. To those who did not know him well this looked like inordinate vanity and boorishness.

Authors Never Forget

LAURA HAIN FRISWELL AND OTHERS

Among young women, away from club and covert, Trollope displayed an elaborate old-fashioned courtliness combined with an elephantine skittishness which evidently went down well. That he liked women around was evident from the Waltham days when for a spell in 1865 his brother's daughter Beatrice came to stay. His orphaned niece, Florence Bland, joined his household permanently in 1863 and in later years served as the secretary-helper to whom he dictated several novels (see pp. 228–9 below). With the wives of friends as with younger single women he seems, especially in letters, to have been able to release a part of himself otherwise buttoned up, and he went out of his way to advise, admonish and decorously flirt on paper. Besides Kate Field, among his lady correspondents were Cecilia Meetkerke, Mary Holmes and Anna Steele. One, possibly Dorothea Sankey, received the following: 'My affectionate & most excellent wife is as you are aware still living – and I am proud to say her health is good. Nevertheless it is always well to take time by the forelock and be prepared for all events. Should anything happen to her, will you supply her place, – as soon as the proper period for decent mourning is over?' (*Letters*, I, 144). Rose falling about with laughter over her husband's wit is hard to imagine from this example. (1) from Laura Hain Friswell, *In the Sixties and Seventies* (1905) pp. 169–70. Laura Hain Friswell (afterwards Myall), the daughter of James Hain Friswell (see pp. 121–3 below), writer of children's stories and a book on the actor H. B. Irving; (2) from Bradford Booth, *Trollopian*, II (1947–48) 118; *Anthony Trollope* (1958), pp. 12–13; (3) from O. A. Sherrard, *Two Victorian Girls with extracts from the Hall Diaries*, ed. A. R. Mills (1966) p. 277; (4) from *The Notebooks of a Spinster Lady, 1878–1903* (1919) pp. 74–5.

(1) The speeches over, the ladies retired to the drawing-room, where tea and coffee were served, and the gentlemen came in.[1] I sat with my mother and Miss Stevens on a lounge in the middle of the room, and we were soon surrounded. Wilkie Collins, Ansdell, Marcus Stone, Sir William Fergusson, Blanchard Jerrold, Matthew Arnold, Serjeant Ballantyne, Landseer and I know not who came up. I remember a very pleasant old gentleman came, and bowing with old-fashioned politeness said: 'Can I get you anything, dear ladies?'

He addressed himself to us all, and on my mother thanking him and declining, he sat down by me and talked about the dinner and the speeches, and I was so excited I forgot to be nervous, and gave him *my* ideas, which seemed to amuse him vastly. As to the hero of the evening, he was surrounded by ladies and gentlemen and seemed to be doing nothing but shake hands. At last he came up to us with his son and stood talking a few moments.

'You are the girl', he said, 'who reads *The Old Curiosity Shop*?'

I signified that I was, and he replied: 'What about Little Nell now? You've grown so much I hardly knew you', and then he smiled, shook hands, and left us.

When I sat down again the old gentleman asked me if I was fond of *The Old Curiosity Shop*, and I told him I was, and how much I admired Little Nell. His opinion was, I found, very much like my father's, and not at all complimentary to my heroine; but he was exceedingly complimentary to me, and when I said I wondered Mr Dickens remembered me, he replied 'he did not wonder at it at all; authors never forget those who admire their works'. And then my father came up, and after some conversation with my nice old gentleman we moved away, and my father told me I had been talking so long to Mr Anthony Trollope. I thought of what he had said about 'authors never forgetting those who admire their works', and I wished I had read some of his, and could have talked of them; but I had never read a line, though you may be sure I soon remedied that, but I never met Anthony Trollope again.

(2)   A few days later I was pleasantly surprised, in meeting Mrs Reginald Smith, to learn that she too remembers Trollope. Mrs Smith, now in her eighty-fifth year, is the daughter of Trollope's onetime publisher, George Smith, proprietor of the *Cornhill Magazine*. She recalls vividly how she and her sister watched from the balcony and counted guests as they arrived at her father's famous weekly open house at Hampstead so that the butler might know how many places to lay for dinner. The girls always waited expectantly for Mr Trollope, who had such a delightful habit of ruffling his hair before entering the drawing room. He was an extremely genial person with boisterous spirits and a loud voice, for imitating which the Smith girls frequently incurred the paternal wrath. ...

The charge of bad manners cannot so easily be broken down. Trollope was often irritable, frequently contentious and always loud. Family legends have established the fact of his irritability, but it is not easy to see in what category of frustration or maladjustment he should be placed. A faithful study of his letters reveals no unfulfilled ambition, no withered friendship, no cankered idealism. He resented the tardiness of his promotion at the Post Office, but there was no perceptible change in his character after his resignation. ... Whatever the subject, whatever the company, Trollope made himself heard. ... If Trollope could not win his case by sound argument, he sometimes resorted to shouting his opponent down. He might have been more generally popular had he played his instrument pianissimo, but he chose to pull out all the stops and greet Everyman with a hearty blast of forthright but not always well-considered opinion. The extra run up and down the keyboard which he could not resist usually produced a bit of dissonant hyperbole.

(3) *28 December* [1860] ... read scenes from *Barchester Towers* aloud. I think Trollope is closer to describing women, in drawing their minds and the wanderings of their feelings, than any writer of modern days. The more I read him the more I feel this. He must be a most acute observer, and in spite of his mother must have had ladies about him at whose hearts he has been able to get at all times.

13 November 1883. *Staying at Witley.* – During a conversation about novelists, Trollope was mentioned, and the wonderful sort of intuition by which he evolved out of his inner consciousness scenes he never could have witnessed. I remember myself having said to him one day: 'I understand, Mr Trollope, your knowing what a young gentleman and a young lady say to each other when they are alone together; but how can you possibly know the way that two young ladies talk to each other while brushing their hair?' Mr Trollope only laughed and said: 'It's not by listening at the keyhole, I assure you!'

NOTE

1. The occasion was the farewell banquet for Charles Dickens at the Freemasons' Hall, London, on 2 Nov 1867 before he left for his reading tour in America. Lord Lytton was in the chair and Trollope responded gracefully to the

toast to literature, taking his opportunity of toasting Dickens as 'a great chieftain' and roasting Carlyle for his attacks on fiction. See Charles Kent, *The Dickens Dinner* (1867) pp. 23–5. William Charles Mark Kent (1823–1902), minor poet, journalist, owner–editor of the *Sun* (1850–71), wrote of Trollope in the *Illustrated Review* (15 May 1871) pp. 487–92: 'the bearded leonine face of the man, with its bold front look, is but a mask before a nature intensely sympathetic' (cited *Letters*, II, 547).

His Characters Were to Him Absolutely Real

AMELIA EDWARDS AND MRS OLIPHANT

(1) from Amelia Edwards, 'The Art of the Novelist', *Contemporary Review*, LXVI (Aug 1894) 225–42. Amelia Ann Blanford Edwards (1831–92), popular authoress and Egyptologist. Trollope thought well of her novel *Debenham's Vow* (1870) and told her so (*Letters*, I, 489); (2) from Mrs Margaret Oliphant, 'Anthony Trollope', *Good Words*, XXIV (1883) 142–4. Mrs Margaret Oliphant Wilson Oliphant (1828–97), popular Scottish novelist, best known for her *Chronicles of Carlingford* (1863–76). In a prodigiously heroic life (not unlike that of Frances Trollope) she wrote almost a hundred novels, plus biographies of Edward Irving, Principal Tulloch, Montalembert and Lawrence Oliphant, and over 200 essays and articles for *Blackwood's Magazine*. See R. C. Terry, *Victorian Popular Fiction 1860–80* (1983) pp. 68–101. Only one letter to Trollope survives in which she refers kindly to *Phineas Finn* and *He Knew He Was Right*: 'You would be amused if you could hear the hot discussions that go on in this quiet corner of the globe [Windsor] concerning the behaviour of Mr Louis Trevelyan' (*Letters*, I, 470).

(1)   These last three [Dickens, Thackeray and Trollope] are essentially representative writers of what I should like to call the historical novel of contemporary English life. They wrote at the same time. They had an absolutely parallel experience. The same clubs, the same drawing-rooms, the same parks, streets and places of public amusement were familiar to all three. And yet with what different eyes they viewed the social structure of their time!

Dickens was essentially a caricaturist. Trollope was an admirable portrait-painter. Thackeray was a clairvoyant. Or, to put it differently, Dickens depicted his fellow-men as they are not: Trollope presents them as they appear to the world; Thackeray reads them through and through. ...

In this triumvirate – Dickens, Trollope, Thackeray – I would assign a very prominent place to the author of *Framley Parsonage*. He was himself a typical Englishman, bluff, hearty, straightforward; passionately fond of field sports, yet at the same time a thorough man of business and a thorough Londoner. He was intimately conversant with the life and haunts of the upper and upper-middle classes; and he had a very considerable knowledge of parliamentary life, and of parliamentary men. Also he made an exhaustive and affectionate study of the British parson; and the British parson, till Anthony Trollope took him in hand, was an unexplored field of research, notwithstanding that Parson Adams and Doctor Primrose are dear to us. Now, the British parson plays a very important part in English national life, especially in country parishes and provincial towns, and until the publication of *Barchester Towers*, he had been treated by our novelists as a mere lay figure. But in Anthony Trollope's hands he became one of the most lifelike characters in fiction. The meek domestic chaplain, the starving curate, the hunting rector, the courtly archdeacon, the henpecked bishop, and a hundred others throng 'thick and fast' upon our memory. It is a portrait-gallery in which no one canvas is exaggerated, and in which caricature has no place. And herein lies the secret of Trollope's strength. He never exaggerates. He has humour; but he never allows it to run away with him. He has pathos; but it is a manly pathos, reserved and self-contained, with no snivelling in it, and no display of white pocket-handkerchief. There is no more tragic figure in fiction than the Reverend Mr Crawley, nor any more tragic situation than that in which he is placed by the disappearance of the twenty-pound-note.[1] Yet with how few touches and in what sober tints it is painted! As with his tragedy, so it is with his pathos. It is as the pathos of life itself. ...

I do not know what Thackeray's method of work was; but of one thing I am certain – and that is, that his characters were to him absolutely real, that he believed in them, suffered with them, rejoiced with them, as though they were creatures of flesh and blood. His own heart beats under the lines, as he traces them with his hand. That is why they are so real to us; for no story-teller can possibly make his readers believe in characters which he does not believe in himself.

And this, I take it, is the inmost secret of the art of the novelist, sincerity. It is of no use to 'make believe' as the children say. It is of no use to dress up a company of puppets, and put fine speeches in their mouths, and pull the wires this way, and that way. It is of no use to describe scenery which you have never seen; or people living in a class of life to which you have no access; or emotions which you have never felt. Such work rings hollow; and although it may amuse for an hour, there is nothing satisfying in it, and nothing enduring.

I am ashamed to refer to myself in this connection; but when it comes to a question of work, of the story-teller's craft, and of the tools to be used in it, one can but fall back upon personal experience. I have repeatedly been asked how I set to work to write a novel, and the only answer I can give, in all seriousness, is that I lay in a stock of paper, a box of quill nibs and a big stone bottle of the best and blackest ink. 'But how do you invent the plot?' asks my questioner. It seems to me that I do not invent the plot. The plot comes of itself. It flashes upon me suddenly, unexpectedly, when I am walking, perhaps, or in some way actively employed. Sometimes it but half reveals itself. That is to say, it lacks some essential motive. In this case, it is useless to puzzle over it. I let it alone and, by and by, in the course of a few hours, or a few days, the solution flashes upon me in the same unexpected way. Unconscious cerebration may have been going on, but it was absolutely unconscious. And so with the characters. They present themselves just as real personages might walk into my library, and introduce themselves and their business. It seems to me that I look at them face to face, just as I should look at living visitors. I do not 'invent' their features, or their moral qualifications, or even their actions. I am conscious of no mental deliberation about what they shall do or say. They do absolutely as they please. They say what comes into *their* heads, not what comes into mine! To me, they seem as living men and women, having passions, prejudices, emotions and wills of their own.

'Why *did* you let Crosbie jilt Lily Dale?', I asked Anthony Trollope one day.[2]

'Why did I "let" him?', he repeated. 'How could I help it? He *would* do it, confound him!'

This was not said in jest. It was earnest. I know exactly what Trollope meant. Given the creation – if you care to give it so fine a name – given the creation of a certain character, all the actions of that character are as necessarily governed by the laws of his being as if he were a living and breathing entity.

(2)   [Mrs Oliphant reviews the *Autobiography* with characteristic appreciation of his regularity and industry, but she does not deny him title to genius.] There has been in England for many years no name that has been better known than that of Anthony Trollope. Out of the way, and almost closed to all outside intercourse must that house have been into which something from his hand did not tell among the pleasures and expectations of life, or furnish some material for talk and the drawing forth of individual opinion. The creations of his fancy have been to many of us like friends familiarly known. We have discussed the actions and the motives of those airy nothings to whom he gave not only local habitation and a name, but many of the experiences and difficulties of existence, with a warmth and partisanship which ought to be ridiculous from a common-sense point of view, but is not ridiculous at all, considering that half the persons we meet in life are less real and less interesting than these beings of the imagination. In this way the novelist becomes the acquaintance of all the world. We are thankful for his company not only when all is well with us, but when we are sick or sorry, and shut out less familiar friends. This is true even of the poorer professors of the art, but how much more of him in whose works there was always a true reflex of the actual existence in which he took a manful share – not that of a scholar in his study, but of a living and energetic member of the society he described. Mr Trollope was no specialist, to use a word which has not much acceptance with the English mind, yet in literature has always given its professors a decided advantage. He was not a philosopher like George Eliot, nor a humorist like Thackeray. His mind did not concentrate upon any individual view of existence, nor was there that relation between the different parts of his work which some great novelists have aimed at. We might almost say that his selection of subjects was accidental and that he took whatever came uppermost with a general sense of capacity to deal with what he took up, rather than a particular impulse within to search into the depths of human motive, or to discover its endless discrepancies and shortcomings. He was a story-teller rather than an analyst or moralist, although no man ever took more pains to show the way in which the mind justified to itself a certain course of action. Wherever he held his

lantern there came into light within its circle a little world, a microcosm, with everything going on in little which goes on at large in the universe. Spots that had been dim before thus came into sight, all throbbing with life and motion. When he did concentrate the light the illumination was worth almost as much as the best, and Barchester comes in many points little short of the streets and booths of Vanity Fair. But though he did not always do this, he was always capable at a moment's notice of clearing a little plot around him from out the undiscovered, and showing us groups as animated, as restless in their busy preoccupations, loving and hating and pursuing their personal objects with all the ease and unconsciousness of real life.

It would be vain to calculate what Mr Trollope might have done had he been shut up, by nature and circumstances, within one circle, and left us only the half-dozen stories which embody the History of Barset, with the more careful elaboration which leisure and concentration would have given. Our own opinion is that every artist finds the natural conditions of his working, and that in doing what he has to do according to his natural lights he is doing the best which can be got from him. But it is hopeless to expect from the reader either the same attention or the same faith for twenty or thirty literary productions which he gives to four or five. The instinct of nature is against the prolific worker. In this way a short life, a limited period of activity, are much the best for art; and a long period of labour, occupied by an active mind and fertile faculties, tell against, and not for, the writer. It is a sort of foregone conclusion that the man who does little is likely to do that little better than the man who does much.[3] Mr Trollope has suffered from this natural and by no means unjustified prejudice. He has been discussed since his death with a certain condescension and careless praise, as if the industry and regularity which were so conspicuous in him, and which are so meritorious in a moral point of view, were his chief qualities. But those individual characteristics have in reality no more to do with the grounds upon which a true estimate of Mr Trollope's genius is to be formed, than would have been the case had he been idle and irregular instead, turning day into night, and producing nothing except under the pressure of the printer's devil at the door. We have all heard of such in the history of literature, and curiously enough the public mind is more disposed to judge them favourably than it is to acknowledge the claims of those who pursue the literary profession with the same devotion and steadiness which is necessary in every other. We do not know how to account for the caprice of the ordinary standard on this point. In every other craft, however it may be dependent upon the higher gifts, the close and constant labour of the workman is put to the credit of his work. Not even the painter, the nearest parallel we can think of, is expected to wait for special inspiration or damned with faint praise as 'industrious' and 'meritorious', because he works a certain number of hours a day. But up to the present moment this is still the familiar thing to say of Mr Trollope. It might have been said of Scott, who, indeed, has gone through many phases of critical disapproval on the same ground – and in such company our story-teller need have little objection to go down to the judgement of posterity. ... Mr Trollope is perhaps unrivalled for this general landscape, the level of real life, in which no one towers disproportionately above his neighbours. We do not seek special scenes, or the development of special characters, when we return to the histories of the warden, the dean, or the doctor, but pursue our way well pleased about the Barchester streets, glad to meet a familiar face round every corner; or set out into the country to visit Archdeacon Grantly at his Rectory, or poor Mr Crawley in his poor parsonage with an untiring interest in everything, and pleasant recognition of all we meet. It is altogether different from the interest, either tragic or comic, which makes us see one figure everywhere, and passes with a little impatience through the less important surroundings to get to the central interest. In Mr Trollope's books the interest is diffused throughout all, it quickens here and slackens there with a genuine and natural fluctuation; nobody will fail specially to remark Mr Harding's delicate old figure in the road, the delightful, energetic bustle of the Archdeacon, or that less excellent, because more conventional, but most popular of all, Mrs Proudie, at the palace; but even their eminence does not make us at all indifferent to all the other innumerable human folk who inhabit the little episcopal town, and the fresh-breathing country with its muddy lanes and long distances. Even Thackeray, with his finer and more powerful touch, has not done just the same for the history of the age; for all his dealings are with Society, the modes of which are more artificial and its laws more continuous.. Old Lady Kew is so real that we know the very sound of her voice, and regard her with a mixture of affection and abhorrence, which is more genuine than our sentiments towards many of our most familiar friends, but there is not very much distinction between that wonderful old figure, and the old Baroness of the early Georgian age, whom we meet in *The Virginians*; the species continues for ever. And such is to a certain extent the case with all expositions of that fine mixture of the artificial and the savage, of hungry human self-interest and fictitious restraint, which is called Society. But Barchester is as entirely the England of our time as Bath in *Northanger Abbey* represents the England of Miss Austen's. The one picture is larger, not so delicate as the other, and they are as different in sentiment as in costume; but when the world is as far in advance of Trollope, as we are now of Miss Austen, it is scarcely possible to doubt that the little cathedral town, with its dignitaries, the country parsonages, the poor clergy, the little social circles all about, will form as important a contribution to the history of the time as there is to that of the beginning of the century: and it is difficult to say more for a novelist. ...

The readers of *Good Words* have had special links of connection with the friend whom we have all lost. Twenty years ago he began to contribute to these pages some of the short stories in which he was excellent. ... Since then many a page from his hand has entertained our readers, and the last of his published stories had just appeared in *Good Words* when his life, too, ended; not without warning, nor prematurely, yet at an age when he was still in full vigour, and might still have lived, and rode, and written, for many a day to come. It is curious to remember how recently he had played with the idea of an arbitrary conclusion to life at the age he just lived to reach, in the amusing and original chapter of imaginary history called *The Fixed Period*. It was probably because he felt how little occasion there was for dying, and how well adapted a man was to enjoy life at sixty-seven, that he put forth at that age the elaborate scheme of the colonial legislator for the honourable extinction of existence; but the coincidence is curious. The great novelist is dead, at peace and in honour with all men, leaving nothing behind him that is bitter or painful, but an honourable man, a reputation which there is every reason to believe will increase rather than diminish, and the example of a life full of useful exertion. He did much in his life to restore character and credit to the literary profession, while at the same time he was no mere writer, but a man thoroughly experimented in the world, and knowing the life which he illustrated. There is no

Westminster Abbey for the novelist, but its roll contains many a less notable name than that of Anthony Trollope, who has in his generation been as much the faithful servant of England as if he had fought half a hundred battles.

NOTES

1. 'Taking it as a whole, I regard this as the best novel I have written', said Trollope of *The Last Chronicle of Barset* (1867); he also considered the Revd Josiah Crawley one of his best creations along with the Pallisers (*Auto.*, xv and xx).

2. In *The Small House at Allington*, ch. xxx (1864).

3. No one knew better than Mrs Oliphant of the tension between the need to maintain factory-line production and time to pull back and lie fallow. She described her life as a servitude of incessant work and looked at times enviously on writers like George Eliot: 'Should I have done better if I had been kept, like her, in a mental greenhouse ...?' (*Autobiography and Letters*, ed. Mrs Harry Coghill (1974) p. 5).

An Editor's Discomfort

CUTHBERT BEDE

As was almost inevitable in his long career Trollope became an editor, and experienced what Thackeray had called the 'thorns in the cushion'. In the period of great magazine expansion during the 1860s James Virtue considered taking over the *Argosy* from Alexander Strahan or starting a new periodical, inviting Trollope to become editor: 'I am sure there is room for a good Magazine, under your management, it will be hard if we cannot hold our own against such as *Belgravia* [founded 1866] and *Temple Bar*.' Virtue calculated that a sale of 25,000 would enable the magazine to pay its way. Trollope says the circulation seldom rose above 10,000 (*Auto.*, xv; *Letters*, I, 357, 358). Trollope was to have £1000 p.a. and sole editorial responsibility. Names were canvassed over several months and included the 'Monthly Westminster', the 'Monthly Liberal' and 'Whitehall Magazine'; 'I think my own name "Trollope's Monthly" would be objectionable', wrote Trollope, adding rather tactlessly, 'because it means nothing when the connection between the magazine & the Editor has been dissolved' (*Letters*, I, 361). The name decided upon was *Saint Pauls, A Magazine*. Although 'He was a conscientious but not overbearing editor' (*Letters*, I, xviii), against stiff competition the magazine fought a steadily losing battle. Trollope's editorship lasted from Oct 1867 to July's issue 1870 and the magazine ceased publication in 1874. See John Sutherland, 'Trollope and St Paul's 1866–70', in *Anthony Trollope*, ed. Tony Bareham (1980) pp. 116–37; Patricia Srebrnik, 'Trollope, James Vitrue, and *St Paul's Magazine*', *Nineteenth Century Fiction*, xxxvii, 3 (Dec 1982) 443–63. From 'Some Recollections of Mr Anthony Trollope', *Graphic*, xxvi (23 Dec 1882) 707. Edward Bradley (1827–89), vicar of Stretton, Rutland, lecturer and purveyor of light literature under the pen name 'Cuthbert Bede'; his best-known books were novels of university life, *The Adventures of Mr Verdant Green An Oxford Freshman* (1853) and its two sequels, *The Further Adventures of Mr Verdant Green* (1854) and *Mr Verdant Green Married and Done For* (1857).

I never knew a more industrious literary man, or one of greater method, than the late Mr Anthony Trollope. He sat down to his novel-writing as a man of business would sit down to his desk and ledgers; and he told me that he always made a point of resolutely determining to cover so many sheets of foolscap within a given time; and that he had so trained himself to his task, that he could accomplish it within the prescribed limits. He told me that he never wrote at night, but always in the morning, rising early for the purpose, and having performed the best portion of his daily task by breakfast-time. He could then, with a clear conscience, take his pleasure at hunting or other recreations.

I met him at a country house, where he had come on a visit, bringing his hunters with him; and being then on his way to Casewick, to stay with his cousin Sir John Trollope, who, soon after, was created the first Lord Kesteven.[1] When I left the house after dinner it was nearly eleven o'clock, and Mr Trollope was then playing whist. After that there was smoking, and it was the small hours when he got to bed. I had promised to rejoin them at breakfast at half-past nine; and I found Mr Trollope already downstairs and busied with that morning's postal delivery. He was in hunting costume, and I complimented him on his freshness and industry, after his late hours of the preceding night, when he cheerily replied that he had never felt better in his life, and that he had got up at five o'clock. 'Since then,' he said, 'I have earned twenty pounds by my pen; besides writing several needful letters.' He had many other letters to attend to, which had just come by post, in addition to a bundle of proofs for the next number of the *St Paul's Magazine*, of which he was the first editor. One of the proofs was an article on the Irish Church,[2] and Mr Trollope wished to curtail its dimensions considerably, in which difficult and delicate work he begged for my assistance, which, of course was granted;

and, while I was engrossed with the Irish Church, he looked over other proofs and wrote several letters. I was much struck with the rapidity he showed in getting through this business, and also in keeping up a running conversation with those present, at the same time that he was reading proofs and writing letters. Then, after a hearty breakfast – which he had well earned – he rode off to the meet, and was out hunting for the whole day. But at night, I met him at dinner at another country house, some miles distant; and he was as fresh as ever, full of conversation, and an admirable guest. Then came whist, and the drive back to his friend's house, and more late hours; to be followed by the early rising and patient toil and methodical work.

I have heard it said of him, that he was 'good for sixteen hours' in a day; and, no doubt, he was, and could stick to work with the greatest pertinacity; but, on the various occasions on which I had the pleasure to meet him, the greater portion of the day was given to recreation – in the pursuit of which, however, he gathered materials for his writings, and his desk work appeared to be pretty well over by ten o'clock in the morning. He told me that it was in those first hours after a night's rest – or, what I called, 'only a few hours sleep' – that his brain most readily answered the demand that he placed upon it. I reminded him of Sir Walter Scott's plan of letting his projected work 'simmer' in his mind, while he was getting up and dressing; but Mr Trollope told me that he rarely troubled to do this, until he had actually sat down, pen in hand, and paper before him, when he could at once resume his task, or novel, at the point where he had left on the previous morning; and that so surely would his pen traverse the paper, that by breakfast-time so many thousands of words that he had 'told himself' (his favourite expression) would cover the white sheets, would all be written, and in such a way that they would need little or no correction.[3]

One evening I met him at a large dinner-party especially given in his honour by the great man in that part of country.[4] More than twenty sat down to dinner, and I found myself side by side with Mr Trollope, without a lady to separate us. Perhaps the lady who sat by him on the other side was thinking of his gifted mother, and her wonderful industry in novel writing, for she said, 'Do you believe, Mr Trollope, in inherited genius?' Before turning to answer her question, he whispered to me, 'I believe much more in cobbler's wax.' On another occasion also I heard him speak of what I may call his cobbler's wax theory, and what he meant by that expression is very clearly conveyed in what he has written concerning Thackeray. Speaking of that great writer's desire in 1848 to obtain the post of Assistant Secretary at the General Post Office, and how utterly unfitted he would have been for the office, especially if he had sought to add to it his literary duties, Mr Trollope – evidently speaking from his own personal experience – says: 'He might have done so could he have risen at five, and have sat at his private desk for three hours before he began his official routine at the public one. A capability for grinding, and aptitude for continuous task work, a disposition to sit in one's chair as though fixed to it *by cobbler's wax*, will enable a man in the prime of life to go through the tedium of a second day's work every day; but of all men Thackeray was the last to bear the wearisome perseverance of such a life' [*Thackeray*, p. 36]. In that sentence Mr Trollope has faithfully painted his own portrait as a literary worker.[5]

Though that work was very varied – novels, short tales, essays, travels, biography, classics, or what not – he seemed to be thoroughly happy in it, so long at it was of his own choosing, and was original. But the editorial harness-work of the *St Paul's Magazine* did not seem at all to his mind, and he spoke to me of the many ways in which he was bothered and harassed by it. He was so thoroughly kindly and genial that it was heartbreaking work to him to return a manuscript to its author, especially when the writer was of the fairer sex, with the stereotyped 'declined with thanks'. Of some of his editorial troubles, worries and experiences he has left a record in some short stories called 'An Editor's Tales', published in *St Paul's Magazine*.[6] He ceased to be an editor in 1870, with the fifth volume, though he contributed to its pages till it was withdrawn from publication. He was talking to me one day on this subject, and showing me some manuscripts which, for various reasons, were unsuitable for his magazine, when he said to me, 'I suppose that you have not much difficulty in getting your articles accepted, and do not know what it is to have them rejected?' I replied, 'Indeed I do! Very often my manuscripts come back to me, like chickens to roost. But my plan is to send them on by the same post to some other editor; then, if he returns them, to send them to Editor no. 3, and so on, and I usually find that my manuscripts obtain admittance somewhere, and are duly printed and paid for. What may suit one editor may not suit another, or

1. The General Post Office, St Martin's le Grand, 1850

2. (*top*) Frances Trollope, portrait by Auguste Hervieu, *ca*. 1832; (*bottom*) Kate Field,
crayon portrait by Vanderweyde, 1878

3. Thomas Adolphus Trollope and Anthony Trollope

4. Trollope in later years

5. Rose Trollope

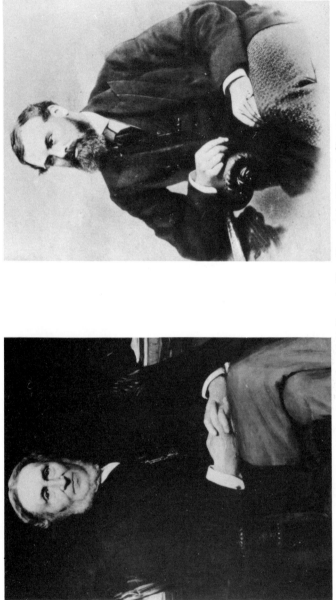

6. Two of Trollope's publishers: (*left*) Alexander Macmillan and (*right*) Frederic Chapman

7. Caricature portrait of Trollope by 'Sem'

8. Trollope's first biographer, T. H. S. Escott

may not suit him at that time. The rejection of a manuscript does not necessarily imply that it is not worth printing.' Said Mr Trollope, with much feeling, 'I do hope these manuscripts that I am returning will get printed and paid for – somewhere. I know what it is to feel that sickening at heart when the manuscript on which you have bestowed so much pains and thought is returned to you as unsuitable.'

I expressed my surprise at hearing him say so. He was then at the height of his fame; and I should have fancied that he would have been about the last man to have known what it was to have his magazine articles 'declined with thanks'. For, although he began young as a writer, he had not only his own talent, but the great *prestige* of his mother to secure for his papers a favourable reception. But he assured me that in the early years of his literary career he too frequently knew what it was to have his manuscripts rejected by editors and his theatrical pieces by managers – in fact, he never scored a single success with the stage.[7] He said that he had also known what it was to have his articles accepted, and then, for some reason, not to be paid for; and he told me that his first year's hard work at authorship only brought him in twelve pounds, and his second year twenty pounds. In fact, it was not until he was forty years of age that his pluck and perseverance met with their due reward, and his talent was conspicuously revealed to the world in his novel *The Warden*. This was published in 1855; and from that day Mr Anthony Trollope was a man of mark, and his first success was rapidly followed by that long and brilliant series of stories of modern life which made him one of the most popular novelists of the day. That he was one of the most industrious and methodical it is the purport of these few recollections to show. He was 'a glutton for work', and appeared thoroughly to enjoy it. He also enjoyed a joke. I had purchased (in Birmingham) an excellent photographic portrait of him, which the shopkeeper had accidentally labelled Mr M. F. Tupper'; and, when I showed it to him, Mr Trollope laughed heartily at being exhibited in the window as the author of *Proverbial Philosophy*.[8]

NOTES

1. Probably in Jan 1868. Trollope left London on Monday, 6 Jan for a hunting trip; he was at Stilton, Huntingdonshire on the 12th, and by the 17th at Casewick. Sir John Trollope was created Baron Kesteven in Apr 1868.

2. The article on the Irish Church appeared in *St Paul's Magazine*: John Herbert Stack, 'The Irish Church', I (Feb 1868) 564–7.

3. Misunderstandings arose after Trollope's death because he debunked waiting for inspiration and appeared to suggest he merely had to sit down at his desk and press a button. Bede puts the right interpretation on it: he had Zola's ability to drop the pen in mid-sentence and pick up where he had left off. Of course, as he says many times, he spent long hours thinking about character and event: the work the writer carries with him everywhere 'in all his walks abroad, in all his movements through the world, in all his intercourse with his fellow-creatures' (*Auto.*, x, xii).

4. Perhaps Charles Buxton (1823–71), MP for East Surrey (1865–71), liberal politician. Trollope corresponded with him while at Casewick (*Letters*, I, 413, 415) and consulted him over his decision to stand for Parliament, speaking of him as 'a man whom I greatly loved' (*Auto.*, xvi). According to Escott, the Buxtons and their friends brought him into the Essex hunting fraternity. See p. 116 below.

5. See *Auto.*, vii. Trollope's favourite metaphor for his writing practice together with his shoemaking analogy first recorded in a letter to Mrs Catherine Gould, 13 Apr 1860: 'My belief of book writing is much the same as my belief as to shoemaking. The man who will work the hardest at it, and will work with the most honest purpose, will work the best' (*Letters*, I, 100).

6. Published in book form 1870.

7. 'Theatrical Pieces' suggests more than one play. Trollope's early dramatic effort was a comedy in five acts, *The Noble Jilt* (1850), sent to Frances Trollope's friend, George Bartley, and promptly returned labelled 'Failure preordained' (*Commentary*, p. 142). For Bartley's opinion see *Letters*, I, 26–27; also Trollope's comment, I, 445–6. Sadleir produced an edition in 1923. But Escott also speaks of 'one or two unacted plays' in Trollope's early years (*Time* (1 Aug 1879) 629). His other foray into drama was *Did He Steal It?*, a play from *The Last Chronicle* (1869).

8. Martin Farquhar Tupper (1810–89), called to the Bar, 1835, but never practised law; his collection of maxims *Proverbial Philosophy* (1834–42) proved extremely popular and prompted other miscellanies.

No Keener Sportsman

VARIOUS

'Nothing has ever been allowed to stand in the way of hunting, – neither the writing of books, nor the work of the Post Office, nor other pleasures' (*Auto.*, iv). With the possible exception of G. Whyte-Melville few have described the sport with more realism. Trollope confesses he dragged it into many novels; 'I have always felt myself deprived of a legitimate joy when the nature of the tale has not allowed me a hunting chapter' (*Auto.*, iv). Not surprisingly, anecdotes abound of Trollope on horseback, booted and spurred even on his Post Office rounds, and later riding to hounds. He began hunting in Ireland, and after moving to Waltham joined the Essex Hunt, from which source most of the following memoirs are drawn, although he also hunted with the Pytchley and Fitzwilliam Hunts. He wrote about it and argued about it: eight hunting essays were published in the *Pall Mall Gazette* (Feb to Mar 1865) and thereafter appeared in book form as *Hunting Sketches* (1865), and he was involved in controversy with the historian E. A. Freeman. His letters abound with references to meetings, train timetables, stopovers, getting his horses down, lending togs to guests and 'supplying sherry and sandwiches and small-talk' (*Letters*, i, 463). 'Ploughing about thro the mud & rain' (*Letters*, i, 142) remained his sublime recreation. 'The cause of my delight in the amusement,' he wrote, 'I have never been able to analyse to my own satisfaction. ... I ride still after the same fashion, with a boy's energy, determined to get ahead if it may possibly be done, hating the roads, despising young men who ride with them, and with a feeling that life cannot, with all her riches, have given me anything better than when I have gone through a long run to the finish, keeping a place, not of glory, but of credit, among my juniors' (*Auto.*, ix). Having to give up the sport was great pain, but in Apr 1876 the decision had to be taken (*Auto.*, xix). (1) from Richard Francis Ball and Tresham Gilbey, *The Essex Foxhounds* (1896) pp. 159–65; (2) from *Milestones* by the Marquis of Huntly, Charles Gordon (1926) pp. 270–1; (3) from Sir George Leveson Gower, *Years of Content 1858–1886* (1940) p. 70. Leveson Gower (1858–1951), son of Edward Frederick Leveson Gower (1819–1907), brother of Lord Granville, and author of *Bygone Years* (1905); (4) from Mrs M. Evangeline Bradhurst, 'Anthony Trollope, the Hunting Man', *Essex Review*, 38 (1928) 186–7; (5) from Escott, *Anthony Trollope*, pp. 168–71. The striking element of this account is the acknowledgement of despondency in the comment attributed to Millais.

(1) Though he had keenly enjoyed hunting in Ireland, when he first came to Waltham Cross he had almost made up his mind that his hunting was over. As, however, the money came in, he very quickly fell back into his old habits, and found his house near enough to the Roothing country for hunting purposes, though his average distance to the Essex meets was twenty miles. ...

Trollope was perfectly fearless; but his defective sight led him often to choose some good man to show him the way. He was indifferent either to jumping on anyone, or being jumped upon. When he and his son Harry were out, it was good betting which would first blunder on the top of the other.[1]

A mishap to Trollope one day, when the hounds ran sharp across the Dagnam brook, is thus described by the novelist's intimate friend Colonel Howard:[2] 'You could not get at the brook to fly it; but I thought I saw my way to get into the brook through a little coppice. I jumped into the coppice safely; but they had been making a drain just inside the hedge, and Trollope's horse put his feet into it, pitched Trollope over his head, and he lay on his back with his head over close to the horse's front feet. In his first plunge to get out he got half-way over Trollope, and we had great difficulty in preventing him doing serious damage; however, I got off with a nasty cut on the forehead. We took him up to Mr John Sands, at the Priory. Mr Sands, who had only recently come there, was but little known; but his kindness on this occasion was an introduction, and he soon became one of us.'...

[Trollope had at last to give up hunting.] He adhered to his decision, and never again spoke willingly on hunting matters –having resolved to give up his favourite amusement, and that, so far as he was concerned, there should be an end of it. But the recollections of the sport remained to the last. He had in his possession the brush of a fox which had afforded a capital run one frosty afternoon from Lubberhedges. The first three up at the death were Trollope, John Ridley and James Stallibrass. When near his end, Trollope sent for Stallibrass, and gave him the brush, saying, 'When you are going to die, pass it on to Ridley.' This was done, and the brush is now in Mr Ridley's possession.

(2)   Anthony Trollope was a cadet of the Casewick family,[3] settled hard by Uffington, my mother's birthplace, and she knew him well. He stayed with her at Orton every winter, and brought his hunters with him. He was rather unkempt and untidy, with a big beard and beetling eyebrows. Of medium height and thick set, he cut a comical figure when arrayed in a somewhat soiled pink coat, cord breeches, and shiny mahogany top-boots, for the hunting-field; but he was an enthusiastic follower of the chase, and never went home before the hounds had given up for the day. He was rough-mannered, but good-hearted and genuine. It seemed impossible to understand how an author with such love of an open-air life could turn out the number of books Trollope wrote, and I asked him how he managed to do it. He replied that he made a rule to write not less than a certain number of words (I think he said a thousand) every day.[4] I have seen him set to work with pen and ink directly he came in from a hard day's hunting, and he would not join in a rubber of whist (a game he was very fond of) until he had finished his daily allotted task. He

gave amusing descriptions of his early impecunious days as a clerk in the Post Office.

(3)   From Lowick[5] I hunted with the Woodland Pytchley and occasionally with the Fitzwilliam. Anthony Trollope, the novelist, used to spend four or five weeks every year at the Rectory to hunt, and we always went out and often came home together.[6] He brought down a string of seven hunters, which excited my envy. He was a big, bearded, red-faced, jovial man with a loud voice and hearty manner. He told me that, when as a young man he was employed in the Post Office, he once had to take the mails from Paris to London in the depth of winter. It was in the days when the diligence carried the mails and it stuck fast in a deep snow drift a few miles from Calais. There was nothing for it but to unharness the best of the horses and to make his way to Calais through the driving snow with the mail bags slung before and behind him. He was fearful of losing his way and of missing the boat, but caught it just in time.

(4)   It is as a hunting man that these memories treat with him. Anthony Trollope's letters to his Essex friends – a large number of which have not yet been published – some of them to my aunt I am here printing – show what a good man across country he was, in spite of being sadly hampered by his imperfect sight.

It is doubtful if he could ever have enjoyed the spectacle of hunting hounds for more than a field away; nevertheless, he rode straight, and good cattle carried him well. There is a story of him when out with the East Essex Hounds; at the meet he asked an old friend if he were 'riding up' that day. On his explaining that he was not, owing to only having his second-best hunter, and that it had already gone through a half day's work that week, he advised Trollope to follow a much beloved member of the Hunt – a welter weight – who was always 'a good 'un to follow and a bad 'un to beat'. Trollope took the hint. At the end of the day his unwilling pilot complained bitterly to those around him: 'What an awful day I have had; that old Trollope rode on my horse's tail the whole time; if he had pecked in the least he'd have been on top of me. I had to go like winking.'

So, in spite of his short sight, hardly bettered by the huge spectacles he always wore, he got to hounds gallantly.

His well-known hunters, 'Banker' and 'Buff', one a dark chestnut, the other a blue roan, were more like coach horses than anything else, but his huge squat bulk required weight carriers, and they were safe conveyances and clever fencers over the trappy Essex ditches.

Trollope hunted chiefly with the Essex Hounds, his house at Waltham Cross being handy for the meets, and many a happy day he had in the Rodings. ...

On a hunting morning Trollope used to be in the best of spirits, and as he dressed it was his habit to wander into the rooms of his men friends while getting ready, chatting and laughing, for, he declared, it was such waste of boon companionship not to make the most of every minute available.

It was a great amusement to those in the house to listen to him when wandering back to his room; he talked to his garments, his poor sight making it hard for him to lay his hands on the various parts of his hunting kit, such as, 'Oh, Mrs Sock, where have you got to? Not under there? No. Perhaps the chest of drawers. Why, I do declare, there you are hiding near the curtain. I've got you, ha! ha! ha! Now, Mr Top Boot, where is your twin? Can't go hunting alone, you know. A fine thing to run away on a hunting morning.' Then snatches of song in a guttural voice, always horribly out of tune – 'A-hunting we will go, ho! ho!' with a delighted bellow on the final 'ho!' Then down to breakfast, where the children of the house were wildly impatient to be on their ponies, who were being walked round and round the stable yard with horse cloths thrown over their loins, their hoofs shining from grease, ready for the fray – and their young riders inclined to scamp their foods, being reminded 'no-one-can't-go-hunting who don't eat a good break-fast'.

(5)   At Waltham House, where his Post Office duties had made it convenient to settle, he was within practicable distance of several different meets. At Harlow, some ten miles from Waltham, were the kennels of the Essex pack, and with these he soon became a familiar figure. His earliest hunting friend, Charles Buxton, between 1865 and 1871 Member for East Surrey, on Trollope's re-establishment in the home counties, was himself still a keen rider to hounds; Buxton's friendship and introduction proved of special service to Trollope in connection with his favourite pastime. During Trollope's experience of the Essex

country, the district opened to him by his friends of the Buxton family was that known as the Roothings, chiefly hunted by the staghounds, but occasionally also the scene of a fox hunt. Famous for its stiff riding, it abounded in formidable fences and in deep ditches. In the sixties Trollope was a very heavy weight, and therefore frequently in difficulties; of these he made light, pulling himself together with surprising speed after a series of spills, and seldom failing to hold a good place at the end of a run. Of his fellow-Nimrods in the East Anglian region, there are still left Sir Evelyn Wood and Mr E. N. Buxton, from personal experience to testify to the undaunted alacrity with which, after having been lost to view in the field, Trollope scaled the sides of a Roothing dyke, reappeared in the saddle, and pushed on with unabated vigour.

In addition to his weight, fatal, of course, to anything like equestrian elegance, Trollope had to contend against a defect of vision which no artificial relief entirely obviated. Hence some of the difficulties that used to beset him with the Essex pack and with H. Petre's staghounds. His popularity in the field generally brought him timely relief in answer to his call for help. Such proved the case when, on one occasion, he had been making up lost ground after a fall in the middle of a ploughed field. The fellow-sportsman who then answered to his cry was no less a person than the present Field-Marshal Sir Evelyn Wood.[7] 'For heaven's sake,' exclaimed Trollope, 'be careful; I am afraid to move lest I should trample on my spectacles which have just fallen off my nose.' Quick as thought, the future Field-Marshal alighted from his horse, and retrieved the glasses. Having fitted them to his nose, Trollope rejoined the hunt with as much serene sturdiness as if the little contretemps had never occurred. Trollope's sporting performances in the eastern home counties had also a social side he found highly useful for the purposes of his novels.[8] Many of the sportsmen lived at London or elsewhere, renting at local inns a certain amount of stabling for their horses, together with suites of rooms for themselves during the season. They thus formed a club whose members, as often as convenient, dined together, and of which Trollope soon became free. It was a pleasant, cheery life that exactly suited the eminently clubbable Trollope. Glimpses of it are given in those passages of *Phineas Finn* describing the performances of that novel's hero on Lord Chiltern's Bone-breaker.

As Trollope wrote, so did he ride, confident that the animal he

bestrode, equally the novelist's Pegasus as his Irish mare, would
in each case carry him successfully from point to point. Whether
with the pen or on horseback, he took his own line. Neither checks
nor even falls prevented his finishing at the spot and the hour he
had from the first fixed. As much as he could desire of the sport he
loved, in a good country, and with social accessories just suited to
him; a constitution, naturally of iron, as yet practically untouched
by years, and revealing no unsound spot; a sense of official
importance gratified by the authority delegated to him from St
Martin's le Grand; the inheritance at the London club he most
frequented, the Garrick, of something like Thackeray's own
position; ascendancy firmly established and wide popularity
permanently won in the calling of novelist; freedom from all
present anxiety as to his circumstances, and every year bringing a
solid addition to his funded savings – all this surely formed a
combination, such as might have made him who commanded it
the happiest, as he was certainly the most fortunate, of men. And
yet Trollope's life was chronically saddened by recurrent moods
of indefinable dejection and gloom. A sardonic melancholy he had
himself imputed to Thackeray. In his own case the sardonic
element was wanting, but the melancholy was habitually there,
darkening his outlook alike upon the present and the future. 'It is,
I suppose,' he said, addressing the friend to whom, more than to
any other, he unbosomed himself, Sir J. E. Millais, 'some
weakness of temperament that makes me, without intelligible
cause, such a pessimist at heart.'

These seizures of despondency generally overtook him as he
was riding home from a day with the hounds. They began with the
reflection that he rode heavier in each successive season, and that
in the course of nature the hunting, repeatedly prolonged beyond
what he had fixed as its term, would have to be given up.[9] The
vague presentiment of impending calamity, as he himself put it,
came, no doubt, from nothing more than an increasingly practical
discovery of the Horatian truth: '*Singula de nobis anni praedantur
euntes*' [Our years keep taking toll as they roll on]. Against the
depressing influences thus engendered, Trollope lacked the natural
resources of his two most famous contemporaries. Thackeray, if
he had not always at his command spirits as high as Dickens, by
an effort of purely intellectual strength could generally secure the
enjoyment of life against the intrusion of unwelcome fancies and
gloomy thoughts. Anthony Trollope was without Dickens's

perennially boyish zest of existence or Thackeray's stubborn opposition to the first approach of the 'blue devils'. His manner, habitually abrupt and sometimes imperious, concealed an almost feminine sensibility to the opinions of others, a self-consciousness altogether abnormal in a seasoned and practical man of the world, as well as a strong love of approbation, whether from a stranger or friend. The inevitable disappointment of these instincts and desires at once pained and ruffled him beyond his power to conceal, and so produced what his physician and friend, Sir Richard Quain, once happily called 'Trollope's genial air of grievance against the world in general, and those who personally valued him in particular'.[10]

NOTES

1. Trollope himself confessed: 'My eyes are so constituted that I can never see the nature of a fence. I either follow someone, or ride at it with the full conviction that I may be going into a horse-pond or a gravel-pit' (*Auto.*, ix). John Tenniel, the artist and illustrator of *Alice in Wonderland*, took jumps, said John Leech, that he would not attempt, and Trollope was reckless enough to ride at a gate while it was being opened (F. Anstey, *A Long Retrospect* (1936) p. 267).

2. Samuel Lloyd Howard (1827–1901), JP and Deputy Lieutenant for Essex County. This may be the incident Trollope refers to as happening on 16 Jan 1875: 'I got into a muddy ditch, & my horse had to blunder over me, through the mud. He trod 3 times on my head. When I saw the iron of his foot coming down on my head, I heard a man on the bank say – "He's dead." I am strapped up with plasters as to my forehead, but otherwise quite uninjured. You may imagine that in the scrimmage I had a queer moment' (*Letters*, II, 644).

3. Sir John Trollope (1800–74), later Baron Kesteven (1868), MP for Lincoln, a descendant of Thomas Middleton Trollope, brother of Trollope's grandfather. Casewick, near Stamford, Lincolnshire, was Sir John Trollope's country home.

4. Considerably more. 'It had at this time become my custom, and it still is my custom, though of late I have become a little lenient to myself, to write with my watch before me, and to require from myself 250 words every quarter of an hour' (*Auto.*, xv). Allowing for a period spent in reading over the previous day's work and getting steam up this meant an average of about 2000 words.

5. Trollope used to stay with the Revd W. Lucas Collins, Rector of Lowick. George Leveson Gower had been sent to Lowick as Collins' pupil after Eton in 1874. He went to Oxford in 1876.

6. Bradford Booth records meeting Leveson Gower who called Trollope 'very human – a dear fellow' and explained that, although they would become separated during a hunt, he often manoeuvred to be at the novelist's side on the trot back (*Trollopian*, II (1947–8) 117).

7. Field-Marshal Sir Henry Evelyn Wood (1838–1919) pursued a distinguished military career, serving in the Crimean War in which he was severely wounded; awarded the VC in 1859 for service in India; served as Quartermaster-

General to the Forces, 1893–7, Adjutant-General, 1897–1901. He wrote many books on military affairs such as *The Crimea in 1854 and 94* (1895) and *British Battles on Land and Sea* (1914–15).

8. Besides the hunting in *Phineas Finn*, Escott mentions there are equestrian scenes in at least 14 other novels. Some of the best are in *The Kellys and the O'Kellys* (1848, chs xxi–xxii); *Orley Farm* (1862, chs xxviii–xxix); *The American Senator* (1877, chs ix–xi, xxii–xxiii); *Is He Popenjoy?* (1878, chs vii–viii); and *The Duke's Children* (1880, chs lxii–lxiii).

9. He disposed of his horses in Mar 1878. 'Alas, alas,' he wrote on 6 Mar to William Blackwood (John Blackwood's brother) 'my hunting is over. I have given away my breeches, boots – and horses' (*Letters*, II, 759). However, in old age he still rode sedately in London as the memory of Muriel Trollope records. See pp. 242–3 below.

10. Sir Richard Quain (1816–98), physician extraordinary to Queen Victoria, 1890, created baronet in 1891, editor of the *Dictionary of Medicine*, 1882, staunch clubbable type on terms with leading literary and political figures.

A Man One Would Hardly Choose to Confide In

J. HAIN FRISWELL AND OTHERS

A man of such decided opinions and frankness offended some and made lasting enemies – Yates for one, already noted – but the surprising thing is the relatively small number who recorded unfavourable verdicts. The sampling below is of such outbursts of irritation, usually from brief experiences of Trollope's bluster or, in the case of Charles Reade, the consequences of a misunderstanding largely his own fault. (1) from J. Hain Friswell, *Modern Men of Letters Honestly Criticised* (1870) pp. 135–44. Friswell (1825–78), prolific contributor to *Chambers's Journal*, *Saturday Review* and other journals; author of popular guides like *Familiar Words: A Collection of Quotations* and *The Gentle Life* (1864) which ran to 20 editions. His 'honesty' in the collection from which this view is taken produced a writ for defamation from G.A. Sala which cost the publishers £500. Friswell was sufficiently well known to find a page in the *DNB*, xx, 277–8 by G. C. Boase; (2) from Malcolm Elwin, *Charles Reade: A Biography* (1931) pp. 237–40. It is hardly surprising that Trollope and the contumacious Charles Reade, fellow Garrick Club member, should cross swords, but they did so in odd circumstances. While Trollope was in Australia, Reade off his own bat adapted *Ralph the Heir* (1871) and presented it to John Hollingshead, the theatre manager, as *Shilly-Shally*, a three-act comedy. The play duly went on at the Gaiety Theatre on 1 Apr 1872 where it played for a month. Garrick members noted that henceforth Trollope and Reade, although at the same whist table, never spoke to each other and addressed necessary bids through a third party. They were eventually reconciled; (3) from Marcus Stone, 'Boz Club Papers' (1906) p. 24, in Philip Collins, *Dickens: Interviews and Recollections* (1981) p. 188. Marcus Stone (1840–1921), the artist, illustrator of *Our Mutual Friend* (1865). Partiality for Dickens may have influenced his judgement here. At any rate the opinion is scarcely just: Trollope may have given latitude to his illustrators but he scrutinised the results closely and did not hesitate to state his views. He objected strongly to Hablôt Browne ('Phiz') illustrating *The Claverings* (1867) and gave detailed instructions for the drawings in *The Last Chronicle* (1867). See *Commentary*, pp. 264–7, and N. John Hall, *Trollope and his Illustrators* (1980).

(1)   Yet we all like Trollope much. He writes 'as a gentleman for gentlemen', as the phrase of the day has it, as if Homer, the led-blind man as they called the nameless one, wrote only for one class. But in this picked aged, you see, we label our works of genius. Every vapid shilling's worth *testibus Tyburnia* or *The Best Society* – you could not go farther from good literature, nor fare worse on the whole – describes itself as a 'first-class' magazine. That is why such are purchased only by third-class passengers, and those flunkeys and housemaids who shoulder us poor Bohemians in the second-class. Every paper is a first-class organ, and essentially in this meaning Mr Anthony Trollope is a first-class novelist, and yet he is very clever, and has had an effect on this age. 'Sir,' says a character in Jerrold's *Housekeeper*, 'I am a student of human nature.' 'Yes,' retorts his interlocutor, 'you study human nature as a housebreaker does a house, *to take advantage of its weakest parts.*'[1] Trollope has done this with our parsons. Of him we may say that he 'To parsons gave up what was meant for mankind.' For from the Bishop and his wife in *Barchester Towers* to that good old fellow, the Revd Mr Crawley, who puts the noble ballad of Lord Bateman into Greek verse, preserving the measure and the rhyme, Trollope is never tired of introducing us inside the clerical waistcoat. Do we think anything better of the parsons? We know parsons well, and, upon the whole – though we find them men like ourselves, sometimes not too elevated, not too self-sacrificial, not too noble – we can only think that the clerics drawn by Trollope are a disgrace, and almost a libel. We do not say that they are not true. They are photographically true, but they are never so from the highest and noblest sight-point. Van Dyke, whose portraits are true to nature, and Lawrence, in a lower way, never painted anything but a gentleman or a lady. So some few of our photographers elevate their photographic sitters.

They take them at their best. They look clever, well, at ease, capable. Other artists stand on a lower ground, and give us those sombre, hard-featured, commonplace English men and women who make our photographic albums a horror, and the portraits of our actresses in the shop windows a sin and a disgrace. Mr Trollope hath dealt somewhat after this fashion with our clergy. He has not done any better with our dukes and men in office; he has not flattered our pretty commonplace English girls, and as for our equally commonplace young Englishmen, let Johnny Eames bear witness that he pictured them as very ordinary Philistines and fools. And yet we all read him, and like him. What is the power he has over us? Simply there is but one answer. It is art – it may be commonplace art, but it is art. Mr Trollope is a literary workman of a sort; but a true workman.

His outward appearance symbolises, or rather pictures, his inner. When you look at his face, you exclaim, with Addison's Cato, 'Plato, thou reasonest well.'[2] For, as that great one said, the soul chooses a fit house wherein to dwell, you must own that the soul of Trollope has fitted itself with a proper and suggestive tabernacle. His portrait is gaunt, grim, partly grey and looks taller than he is; his eyes are noticeable, dark and brilliant; two strong lines down each side of his mouth, lost in a tufted American-like beard, give him a look of greater ill-nature than he possesses. He is unquestionably a gentleman, but of the middle-class look, by no means of *haut école*. He gives one an idea – that is, if one knows life and town pretty well – that he has seen hard service in the drudgery of some government office; he has a cut-and-dried official look, and seems capable of scolding and otherwise irritating his juniors. He looks his age – about fifty-five – and is a man one would hardly choose to confide in. A Winchester, and afterwards a Harrow boy, he gave little promise of inheriting any of the brilliant caustic genius of his mother, whose most truthful pictures of the United States made the Americans hate her; while her immortal figure of the widow Barnaby caused her sex never to forgive her.

His inherited genius is of a different kind, less incisive, much less vulgar, as people have it, but, as we think, far inferior. The sons of great ones generally show this. There are living men of letters who inherit the *nomen et preterea nihil* else of the father, and who yet pick up a decent living on their intangible estate. Neither Anthony, nor his brother Thomas Adolphus, who is five years his senior, owe anything to their mother's style or manner. Both are educated gentlemen, who have been too much and too well taught to be copyists. They both write well; in his way the historian T. A. Trollope perhaps the better of the two, but we repeat there is not even a *soupçon* of the old flavour of Mrs Fanny Trollope.

(2)   On 1 April 1872, John Hollingshead produced at the Gaiety Theatre a three-act comedy called *Shilly-Shally*, based by Reade upon a recent novel by Anthony Trollope, *Ralph the Heir*. Trollope, in his autobiography, himself admits that it was one of the worst novels he ever wrote and in its vulgar sentimentality there was nothing of the sensational or melodramatic such as usually attracted Reade. However, he had a low opinion of Trollope as a writer; in reply to a suggestion by James T. Fields that he should read Trollope's *North America* on its publication in 1862, he promised to do so 'since you tell me it is endurable. I had no intention of reading it otherwise, or anything else the man writes. He is mediocrity incarnate.' In spite of Hollingshead's assurance that 'he offered it to me, and I gladly accepted it', it seems likely that the manager proposed that Reade should adapt Trollope's novel.[3]...

Trollope was in Australia; he had sailed in May of the previous year, before the serial run of *Ralph the Heir* was completed. Reade, however, wrote informing him of his adaptation and its approaching production, but before there was time to receive a reply – here is another item of circumstantial evidence that the adaptation was commissioned by the management – Hollingshead decided to hasten the presentation. Trollope's indignation was comprehensible but nevertheless exaggerated. Under the existing copyright laws, he had no legal grounds for objection and might have considered himself lucky to have been victimised by a writer of Reade's reputation instead of an obscure pirate of the Barnett and Johnstone stamp. Unfortunately Trollope was as choleric in his different way as Reade, and adopted an attitude of outraged astonishment that a writer so pugnacious about the rights of authors could have perpetrated such a piracy. Without private acknowledgement of Reade's letter, Trollope wrote to the Press, disclaiming any share in the adaptation and denying that he had been approached in the matter.[4] As the defendant of a case in which the evidence has never been thoroughly sifted, Reade has been generally considered guilty of conduct indelicate, inconsiderate and inconsistent with his avowed principles, but it appears that, if Trollope had written courteously for Reade's explanation instead of rushing precipitately into print, the trouble might have been kept private and free from animosity. In fairness to Reade, his reply to Trollope, which was never resurrected in *Readiana* or any posthumous account of the affair, should be carefully considered.

[Trollope wrote courteously but firmly against Reade's action; letters were published in the *Pall Mall Gazette* (16 July 1872) p. 5, and the *Daily Telegraph* (6 Aug 1872) p. 3. Reade duly replied the same day.]

To the Editor of the *Daily Telegraph*
    Sir,
        Permit me a short reply to Mr Trollope's letter, dated 'Melbourne, 1 June'. When I wrote him that private letter, the spirit of which, by selection and suppression, he has misrepresented, *Shilly-Shally* was to be produced in October next, and meantime any objection of Mr Trollope's to father his own lines in the theatre would have been law to me. But the theatre demanded the play unexpectedly for a short run in April, and here I was in a difficulty.
        Obliged to decide one way or other, I did as I would be done by. It has been the custom of playwrights to take the novelist's invention and use it on the stage, and rob the novelist of all the dramatic credit and money due to him. But this practice has often been publicly denounced, and I must venture to think that the opposite of a double wrong must be right. So I took advice, and decided to give Mr Trollope half the receipts of *Shilly-Shally*, and, by the same rule, half the credit.
        Mr Trollope decomposes my theory, and objects to his name being connected with the play, though two-thirds of the lines are from his pen.
        I submit; and henceforth his only connection shall be with the receipts.
        But five years hence, when *Shilly-Shally* still keeps the boards, and most of its contemporaries, especially the most belauded, have gone to the dogs, I hope Mr Trollope and his friends will review my judgement with more respect, and my conduct with

more kindliness and candour, than they have done up to this date.[5]

> I am Sir,
>   Your obedient Servant,
>   CHARLES READE

To Reade, Trollope's anger appeared unfair and unreasonable, and injustice always irritated him. Hostility was met with hostility, for several years the two novelists, both close on sixty years of age, maintaining an absurd state of passive offence. Coleman relates that they carried the quarrel to the most farcical extremes, even playing whist together at the Garrick Club without speaking.[6] Eventually they sank their differences and resumed an amiable acquaintance which, though never developing into friendship, had endured for many years; but Trollope wrote his autobiography while the quarrel was still raging and his ungenerous notice of Reade reflected the rancorous feelings of the moment.

(3)   ... I found a very great and marked difference with other authors I had to deal with in those early days. I remember a notable instance with Anthony Trollope. I once had to illustrate a book of his which was already completed in manuscript, but the parsimony of a publisher only permitted me to have two numbers in print when beginning my illustrations.[7] In those two numbers I found two young ladies whom I had to draw, two of the principal characters in the book, of whose appearance there was not the least description. I applied to Anthony Trollope and said, 'Is Julia dark and Clara fair? How am I to distinguish one from the other?', and he replied, 'I do not know; do what you like.' Having been left to my own devices, I made Julia dark and Clara fair, but afterwards in the book I found there were certain references to Clara's dark hair. It was evident to me that these people were in no way alive to Trollope, whilst in the case of Dickens his people were always living people.

NOTES

1. Douglas Jerrold, *The Housekeeper* (1833).

2. The well-known quotation from v, i.

3. Hollingshead maintained that Reade had told him 'he had asked and obtained' Trollope's permission to present the play, and that 'he absolved me from all blame in the matter' (*My Lifetime* (1895) ii, 48). What Reade did, in fact, was to write to Trollope on 7 Mar 1872 to *tell* him, not ask him, about the play: 'I would not have taken this liberty without consulting you if you had been accessible.' Reade offered a prompt copy 'since you ought to make a good deal of money by it if produced in Australia under your own eye!' (*Letters*, ii, 558–9).

4. By the time Reade's letter arrived the play was under way. Not long after his letter to Trollope he advised Henry Merivale that the actors were engaged. They included John L. Toole, the comedian, whose performance as 'the tailor, Neefit...literally brought down the house and made the audience rock with delight' (Hollingshead, *Gaiety Chronicles* (1898) p. 211).

5. Reade ran into further problems. When the *Morning Advertiser* called *Shilly-Shally* indecent he sued and won £200 (G. S. Layard, *Life, Letters and Diaries of Shirley Brooks of 'Punch'* (1907) p. 534). For more details of the affair see John Hollingshead, *Gaiety Chronicles*, pp. 211–15; Bradford Booth 'Trollope, Reade and *Shilly-Shally*', *Trollopian*, i (Mar 1947) 46–7. Reade was involved in a similar dispute in 1877 over adapting Frances Hodgson Burnett's *That Lass o' Lowrie's* which he called *Joan*.

6. See John Coleman, *Charles Reade As I Knew Him* (1903) pp. 325–6.

7. *He Knew He Was Right* (1869).

He is a Perfect Cordial to Me

DICKENS, COLLINS, CARLYLE AND LEVER

(1) from *The Letters of Charles Dickens*, ed Mamie Dickens and Georgina Hogarth (1893) pp. 685–6; *WIR*, ii, 128–9; MS Free Library of Philadelphia, cited *Letters*, i, 423. Relations with Dickens were friendly but never close. Although in the course of affairs they often met, their literary circles were not the same and the prolongation of the 'Garrick Club Affair' in which Yates was embroiled kept them in separate grooves. They seldom corresponded except on business, but Dickens wrote warmly about the memorial fund to Robert Bell's widow: 'I knew she could have no stauncher or truer friend' (*Letters*, i, 379; *WIR*, ii, 128–9). The only tart word is reported by Yates, an unreliable witness where Trollope is concerned, suggesting that when Forster said of Yates's first novel it was as good as one of Trollope's, Dickens replied 'That is not very high praise' and sat down to his lunch (Yates, *Recollections*, ii, 161); (2) from R. P. Ashley, *Wilkie Collins* (1952) pp. 105–6. Wilkie Collins (1824–89), celebrated author of *The Moonstone* (1868) and other novels; (3) from *Thomas Carlyle: Letters to His Wife*, ed. Trudy Bliss (1953) p. 381; *WIR*, ii, 305. Trollope and Carlyle were not in sympathy. In

1851 Trollope wrote to his mother of *Latter Day Pamphlets* as a grain of sense smothered in a sack of trash (*Letters*, I, 29), and as early as *The Warden* (1855) he lamely parodied him as Dr Pessimist Anticant. When Trollope reviewed Ruskin's *Sesame and Lilies* in *Fortnightly Review*, I (15 July 1865) 633–5, Carlyle exploded privately; (4) from *Charles Lever: His Life in His Letters*, ed. E. Downey (1906) I, 226–32. Charles Lever (1806–72), expatriate Irish author of *Charles O'Malley* (1841) and other popular military and fashionable novels; consul at Trieste, 1867–72, wearing a general air of grievance at his lack of recognition. Trollope came to know him at Sir William Gregory's Irish estate, and spoke of him as 'my dear old friend' (*Auto.*, xiii). Certainly the few extant letters show cordiality, and Trollope wrote appreciatively of him to W. J. Fitzpatrick. See *The Life of Charles Lever* (1879) II, 269–70. Visiting his mother in Florence in 1857 Trollope renewed the friendship and, according to E. S. Pigott, 'helped Lever towards keeping Florence society in good spirits' (Lionel Stevenson, *Dr Quicksilver: The Life of Charles Lever* (New York, 1969, repr. of 1939 edn) p. 235).

(1) [To James T. Fields, aboard the *Russia*, bound for Liverpool, 26 Apr 1868.] You will see Anthony Trollope, I daresay. What was my amazement to see him with these eyes come aboard in the mail tender just before we started! He had come out in the *Scotia* just in time to dash off again in said tender to shake hands with me, knowing me to be abroad here. It was most heartily done. He is on a special mission of convention with the United States Post Office.[1]

[To Thomas Adolphus Trollope, (?) Sep 1868.] Anthony's ambition [in becoming a candidate for Beverley] is inscrutable to me. Still, it is the ambition of many men; and the honester the man who entertains it, the better for the rest of us, I suppose.

[To Thomas Adolphus Trollope, 6 May 1869.] I saw your brother Anthony at the Athenaeum not long ago, who was in the act of reading a letter from you. He is a perfect cordial to me, whenever and wherever I see him, as the heartiest and best of fellows.

(2) [Wilkie Collins to William Winter shortly after Trollope's death.] His immeasurable energies had a bewildering effect on my invalid constitution. To me, he was an incarnate gale of wind. He blew off my hat; he turned my umbrella inside out. Joking apart, as good and staunch a friend as ever lived – and, to my mind, a great loss to novel-readers.[2] Call his standards as a workman what you will, he was always equal to it. Never in any

marked degree either above or below his own level. In that respect alone, a remarkable writer, surely? If he had lived five years longer, he would have written fifteen more thoroughly readable works of fiction. A loss – a serious loss – I say again.

(3) [Carlyle to his wife, 27 July 1865.] Ruskin's *Sesame and Lilies* must be a pretty little thing. Trollope, in reviewing it with considerable insolence, stupidity and vulgarity, produces little specimens far beyond any Trollope sphere of speculation. A distylish little pug, that Trollope; irredeemably imbedded in commonplace, and grown fat upon it, and prosperous to an unwholesome degree. Don't *you* return his love; nasty gritty creature, with no eye for 'the Beautiful the', etc., – and awfully 'interesting to himself' he be. Adieu, Dearest; write to me; – sleep oh sleep!...

[Trollope had very much wished to meet Carlyle. G.H. Lewes brought this about on 4 July 1861, and afterwards wrote to Thomas Adolphus:] Yesterday Anthony dined with us, and as he had never seen Carlyle he was glad to go down with us to tea at Chelsea. Carlyle had read and *agreed* with the West Indian book, and the two got on very well together; both Carlyle and Mrs Carlyle liking Anthony, and I suppose it was reciprocal, though I did not see him afterwards to hear what he thought. He had to run away to catch his train.

(4) [Charles Lever to John Blackwood, Trieste, 3 Sep 1868.] ... I don't think Trollope *pleasant*, though he has a certain hard common-sense about him and coarse shrewdness that prevents him being dull or tiresome. His books are not of a high order, but still I am always surprised that he could write them. He is a good fellow, I believe, *au fond*, and has few jealousies and no rancours; and for a writer, is not that saying much?

[To John Blackwood, Trieste, 17 Oct 1868.] Of course I only spoke of O'Dowding Trollope in jest.[3] I never had the slightest idea of attacking a friend, and a good fellow to boot. I thought, and shall think it great presumption for him to stand in any rivalry with Lord Stanley, who, though immensely over-rated, is still far and away above we poor devils in action, though we can caper and kick like the devil.[4]

[To John Blackwood, Trieste, 19 Oct 1868.] I am so glad to get your long and pleasant letter that I return your fire at once. First of all for explanations. I never seriously thought of O'Dowding Trollope – he is far too good a fellow; and, besides, he is one of us – I mean scripturally, for in politics he is a vile unbeliever.[5]

NOTES

1. Dickens was returning from his triumphant reading tour of the United States when Trollope arrived at New York on 22 Apr 1868. One would like to record Trollope's comments on Dickens as being similarly magnanimous, but they usually have a tinge of asperity. Of this occasion he wrote to A. H. Layard smugly: 'I go to America to make a postal convention, not to make money by reading. I fear I shall bring back a very small bag' (*Letters*, I, 423).

2. One letter survives from June 1873 in which Collins thanks Trollope for inviting him round to meet Kate Field: 'Yes I have heard of the American lady – she is adored by everybody, and I am all ready to follow the general example' (*Letters*, II, 589). See Trollope's comment on Collins's fiction in *Auto.*, xiii.

3. Lever's O'Dowd sketches appeared in *Blackwood's Magazine* in 42 instalments (Sep 1866 to Mar 1872).

4. Lord Stanley of Alderley (Edward John Stanley, 1802–69) was Postmaster-General from 1860 to 1866.

5. Lever was a staunch Tory.

Oh, For Some More Brave Trollope

EDWARD FITZGERALD

From *The Letters of Edward Fitzgerald*, ed A. M. and A. B. Terhune (Princeton, NJ, 1980) II, 354, 565; III, 51, 403, 427, 458, 473; IV, 8, 10, 133, 144, 149, 182–3, 188, 229, 236, 276, 284, 314–15, 491, 503. Edward Fitzgerald (1809–83), poet, best known for his translation of *The Rubáiyát of Omar Khayyám* (1859), lifelong friend of Thackeray and such an admirer of Trollope's novels that he had them read aloud as they appeared. Trollope consulted him about materials for his book on Thackeray. It proved a difficult task: not long before he died Thackeray had said to his daughter Anne Isabella ('Annie'), later Lady Ritchie, 'When I drop let there be nothing written of me' (*Letters of Edward Fitzgerald*, IV, 491), so material was hard to come by. 'There is absolutely nothing to say – except washed out criticism', wrote Trollope (James Pope Hennessy, *Anthony Trollope* (1971) p. 196). Trollope's book got him into trouble with Annie. This pained

him, as did a harsh review in the *Pall Mall Gazette* (18 Oct 1879), taking up
Trollope's remark that the author had left a 'comfortable income' and naming
the sum as £30,000. See *Letters*, II, 812n. The rift with Annie was mended in 1882:
'I am very glad' wrote Trollope to Rose 'because my memory of her father was
wounded by the feeling of a quarrel' (*Letters*, II, 947). Annie's journal records
Trollope standing by the fireplace 'very big and kind ... I said I'm so sorry I
quarrelled with you. He said so am I my dear. I never saw dear Mr Trollope
again' (Winifred Gerin, *Anne Thackeray Ritchie: A Biography* (1981) p. 193; cited
Letters, II, 947).

[Fitzgerald to Stephen Spring Rice, 2 Mar 1860.] I am now
awaiting another Box from Mudie: when some Novels of
Trollope's will, I hope come. Have you ever read them? I was
afraid my Power of Novel reading was gone: but living here all
alone I am glad to go into Society so easily as one does in a good
Novel. Trollope's are very good, I think: not perfect, but better
than a narrower Compass of Perfection like Miss Austen's. ...

[To John Allen, 1 Nov 1868.] Now this precious Letter can't go
tonight for want of Envelope; and in half an hour two Merchants
are coming to eat Oysters and drink Burton ale. I would rather be
alone, and smoke my one pipe in peace over one of Trollope's
delightful Novels, *Can You Forgive Her?*. ...

[To Mowbray Donne, 16 Oct 1867.] I fancied I could always
read A. Trollope: but his last Barset [*The Last Chronicle*] has made
me skip here and there. The Account of old Harding with his
Violoncello in Volume II is – better than Sterne – in as much as it
is more unaffected and true. ...

[To W. F. Pollock, Mar 1873.][1] I am hoping for Forster's second
volume of Dickens in Mudie's forthcoming box. Meanwhile, my
Boy (whom I momently expect) reads me Trollope's *He Knew He
Was Right*, the opening of which I think very fine: but which seems
to be trailing off into 'longueur' as I fancy Trollope is apt to do.
But he 'has a world of his own', as Tennyson said of Crabbe. ...

[To W. F. Pollock, June 1873.] This is Sunday Night: 10 p.m. And
what is the Evening Service which I have been listening to? *The
Eustace Diamonds* [1873] – which interests me almost as much as
Tichborne.[2] I really give the best proof I can of the Interest I take
in Trollope's Novels, by constantly breaking out into Argument

with the Reader (who never replies) about what is said and done by the People in the several Novels I say 'No – no! She must have known she was lying!' 'He couldn't have been such a Fool! etc.' ...

[To W. F. Pollock, 30 Nov 1873.] I set my Reader last night on beginning *The Mill on the Floss* I couldn't take to it more than to others I have tried by the Greatest Novelist of the Day: but I will go on a little further. Oh for some more brave Trollope; who I am sure conceals a much profounder observation than those Dreadful *Denners* of Romance under his lightsome and sketchy touch – as Gainsborough compared to Denner. ...[3]

[To Anne Thackeray, Jan 1874.] I believe *you* can't read Sir Walter: I think that must be wrong; and I sincerely think I must be wrong in being utterly unable to relish G. Eliot. Now Trollope I can read forever – though I generally forget what I read: but I do think he is much profounder in Character than that dreadful Evans, only he goes along so easily that People think him shallow. I only wish he would write as long as Tichborne ought to last. ...

[To Anna Biddell, 10 Feb 1877.] I tried Miss Broughton's novels – one of them – *Nancy* [1873] – very clever – very vulgar –and already forgotten. Then I got one of Trollope's, *Phineas Redux* [1874], and have been glad to be back with him – a clever, and right-hearted, Man of the World. It is a Political Novel: much better than Disraeli's, I think: whose writings are to me what his Politics are – showy and shallow. ...

[To W. B. Donne, 14 Feb 1877.] And I have been reading Trollope's *Phineas Redux* here; infinitely better than Dizzy in the record of London Society, Clubs, Political Parties, etc., never a caricature as Dizzy is. ... [He writes in similar vein to Mrs Elizabeth Cowell, mid-Feb 1877.]

[To W. B. Donne, June 1878.] Trollope's *Popenjoy* [1878] I see in *All [The] Year Round*; the weekly critics speak coldly of it; I wish it, or its like, would continue as long as I live. ...

[To W. A. Wright, 5 Sep 1878.] – have just finished the only dull Novel I have read of Trollope's, *The Prime Minister* [1876]. ...

[To Frederick Tennyson, 22 Sep 1878.][4] I can't get on with any but Trollope's [novels], which I wish would continue my Life long. ...

[Several letters concern Trollope's request for information for his book on Thackeray; to Frederick Tennyson, 25 Feb 1879.] Trollope (Anthony) wrote to me for particulars of Thackeray between 1830 and 1840, being engaged to make a sort of Biography of WMT for Macmillan. I could tell him very little, having burned nearly all the Letters that he (WMT) wrote me during that time; and you may know that 'tis not easy to remember when called upon so to do. I am glad Trollope has the job if to be done at all: he is a Gentleman as well as an Author – was a loyal friend of Thackeray's, and so, I hope, will take him out of any Cockney Worshipper's hands. ... [He writes in similar terms to W. F. Pollock, 16 Mar 1879.]

[To W. F. Pollock, 25 June 1879.] Here is my Great Work: two Copies, of which please to give one to your Neighbour, Mr Trollope. I suppose he has scarce time, if inclination, to look into it; but I told him I would send him a Copy by way of acknowledgement of his Thackeray: on the understanding that neither of us was to say a word about either Book.[5]

[To R. M. Milnes, 16 July 1879.] Mr Trollope seems to me to have made but an insufficient Account of WMT, though all in gentlemanly good Taste, which one must be thankful for. ...

[To Frederick Tennyson, 20 Nov 1879.] Then we have a new Novel of Trollope's, *The Duke's Children* [1880] – always delightful to me – in *All The Year Round*, and it is comical to hear my little man reading about Dukes of Omnium, Major Tifto, etc. ...

[To Fanny Kemble, 8 Jan 1880.] At night comes my quaint little Reader with *Chambers' Journal* and *All The Year Round* – the latter with one of Trollope's Stories – always delightful to me, and (I am told) very superficial indeed, as compared to George Eliot, whom I cannot relish at all. ...

[To W. A. Wright, 20 Apr 1880.] Here is a good example of literary manufacture, I think. In Trollope's good Serial in *All The*

Year Round (The Duke's Children) a Lady Mabel talks of an American 'Miss Boncassen' of whom she is jealous, as 'A Convict's Daughter'.[6] Mr B., being a very enlightened American, expected to be chosen President. I knew, of course, that such a phrase was only pitched out in a fit of jealous spleen; still, it was once, as I remember, spoken as serious truth by many English some fifty years ago: and I wrote to Trollope that I wished he would in his three Volumes cancel, or alter, a phrase that could only rouse up disagreeable recollections. I know no more of him than from corresponding with him about Thackeray last year. I am sure he is quite sincere in saying he forgets all the details of his Book, though he remembers the upshot: which I am sorry he has told me beforehand. The weekly reading of his Novel is one of the pleasures I count on here. ...

[To W. F. Pollock, 1 Mar 1882 in answer to questions about Thackeray.] I can only revert to what I first promised: that I will answer as well as I can any questions put to me; or look over, and annotate any proof sent to me, as I did in Mr Trollope's case. MS I have not eyes for. ... Mr Trollope (unto whom I wish you would make my respects) wrote his Book under Annie's eyes (who misinformed him in many ways), and, as your Walter is a Gentleman as well as Mr T., I will do all for him I did for the other; and positively I can do no more. ...[7] [He writes in similar terms to Anne Thackeray Ritchie, 17 May 1882.]

NOTES

1. Sir William Frederick Pollock (see pp. 90–1 above).
2. The Tichborne case, involving Arthur Orton, son of a Wapping butcher, who appeared in Wagga Wagga, New South Wales, in 1865 to claim the baronetcy and estates in Hertfordshire of Roger Charles Tichborne lost at sea. Orton was found guilty of perjury and sentenced to 14 years' penal servitude.
3. Balthazar Denner (1685–1747), German artist, regarded by Fitzgerald as painstaking but uninspired.
4. Frederick Tennyson (1807–1908), the poet's elder brother, contributed to *Poems by Two Brothers* (1827), and also published *Days and Hours* (1854) and *The Isles of Greece* (1890).
5. Fitzgerald's book was *Readings in Crabbe* (privately printed, 1879).
6. Lady Mabel Grex: 'Of course I intended to accept him – but I didn't. Then comes this convict's grand-daughter' (ch. liv).

7. Walter Herries Pollock was considering a piece on Thackeray for *Scribner's Magazine*. Fitzgerald wrote to Anne Thackeray on 17 May 1882 that he had heard nothing further about the project (*Letters of Edward Fitzgerald*, IV, 503).

One of the Heartiest, Most Genuine, Moral and Generous Men We Know

ELIZABETH AND ROBERT BROWNING, GEORGE ELIOT AND GEORGE HENRY LEWES

The Brownings got to know Trollope through his mother and brother in Florence and were soon acquainted with his books. Reading *The Three Clerks* Elizabeth shed tears over the third volume and reported that Robert, 'who can seldom get a novel to hold him, has been held by all three, and by this the strongest' (*WIR*, II, 188). Trollope was welcomed into the Browning circle, which included Isa Blagden and W. S. Landor. He and Robert became warm friends, meeting frequently in club and at literary gatherings. William Allingham noted in his diary (26 May 1868) that Browning once offered Trollope the story that became *The Ring and the Book* to turn into a novel. They dined together at the Garrick two days before Trollope's stroke and Browning was among the mourners at the funeral. See *William Allingham: A Diary*, ed. H. Allingham and D. Radford (1907) p. 180; *Letters*, I, 115, 335–6. Trollope's closest literary friendship was with George Eliot. They sometimes exchanged notes about each other's work. Trollope found her work 'sometimes abstruse, sometimes almost dull, – but always like an egg, full of meat' (*Letters*, II, 627). On her part she claimed that but for Trollope she could hardly have pursued the extensive study for *Middlemarch* (*Commentary*, p. 367). Note the fine comment in her letter, 23 Oct 1863, printed below. At her death he wrote: 'I did love her very dearly. That I admired her was a matter of course' (*Letters*, II, 887). Of Lewes (1817–78) he wrote: 'There was never a man so pleasant as he with whom to sit and talk vague literary gossip over a cup of coffee and a cigar. That he was great philosopher, a great biographer, a great critic, there is no doubt' ('George H. Lewes', *Fortnightly Review*, n.s. 25 (1 Jan 1879) 15–24). The friendship, begun in Florence in May 1860, developed rapidly, and Lewes was touched when Trollope helped his son, Charles, enter the Post Office in Aug 1860. The boy, then nineteen, may well have reminded Trollope of his own difficult start in a career, especially when the job began to go wrong. 'Trollope, ever interested and ever kind investigated the matter and wrote Lewes a letter about the boy's failures' (May 1862). See Anna T. Kitchel, *George Lewes and George Eliot* (New York, 1933) p. 215. Through Trollope's persuasion Lewes became editor of the *Fortnightly Review* (May 1865), retiring the following year because of ill health.

From the many letters exchanged between the Leweses and Trollope a compilation has been made; sources and explanatory details are given in the text and notes. (1) from *Letters of Elizabeth Barrett Browning*, ed. Kenyon, ii, 391; (2) from *Letters of the Brownings to George Barrett*, ed. Paul Landis (1958) pp. 244, 247–8; (3) from *The George Eliot Letters*, 9 vols, ed. G. S. Haight (New Haven, Conn., 1954–78) iii, 326, 360, 362, 426, 470; iv, 8–9; viii, 302; iv, 59, 110, 170, 392, 394; v, 132; ix, 15; v, 351; vi, 20.

(1)   [Elizabeth Browning to Isa Blagden, Rome, 3 May 1860.][1] At last we see your advertisement. *Viva Agnes Tremorne* [her first novel, published 1861].[2] We find it in *Orley Farm*. How admirably this last opens! We are both delighted with it. What a pity it is that so powerful and idiomatic a writer should be so incorrect grammatically and scholastically speaking! Robert insists on my putting down such phrases as these: 'The Cleeve was distant from Orley two miles, though it *could not be driven* under five.' '*One rises up the hill.*' 'As good as *him.*' 'Possessing more *acquirements* than he would have *learned* at Harrow.' *Learning acquirements*! Yes, they are faults, and should be put away by a first-rate writer like Anthony Trollope. It's always worthwhile to be correct. But do understand through the pedantry of these remarks that we are full of admiration for the book. The movement is so excellent and straightforward – walking like a man, and 'rising up-hill', and not going round and round, as Thackeray has taken to do lately. He's clever always, but he goes round and round till I'm dizzy, for one, and don't know where I am. I think somebody has tied him up to a post, leaving a tether.

(2)   [Elizabeth Browning to George Barrett, Florence, 12 Oct 1860.] I have not been out since we arrived here – Yesterday we had a visit from Anthony Trollope, the clever novelist, who is at Florence visiting his brother. I like both brothers – The novelist is surpassingly clever as a writer – don't you think? And he has a very kind feeling for me, I understand from those who bear witness.

[Elizabeth Browning to George Barrett, Florence, 1 Nov 1860.] – I agree with you in adhering to Anthony Trollope – & indeed Robert & I both consider him first-rate as a novelist – *Framley Parsonage* is perfect it seems to me – The writer is just now in Florence & came to see us yesterday for the second time – I like both brothers very much. Anthony has an extraordinary beard to be grown in England, but is very English in spite of it, & simple, naif, direct, frank – everything one likes in a man – Anti-Napoleonist of course, & ignorant of political facts more than of course, & notwithstanding that, caring for *me* – which is strange, I admit –

(3)   [GHL Journal, 23 July 1860.] Among the two or three people I spoke to about [Charles] was Anthony Trollope and of him I only asked information, yet he most kindly interested himself and wrote to the Duke of Argyll for a nomination to compete for a vacancy in the Post Office.[3]

[GE Journal, 28 Nov 1860.] Last Tuesday, the 20th, we had a pleasant evening. Anthony Trollope dined with us, and made us like him very much by his straightforward, wholesome *Wesen*. Afterwards Mr Helps[4] came in, and the talk was extremely agreeable. He told me the Queen had been speaking to him in great admiration of my books, especially *The Mill on the Floss*.

[GE to François D'Albert-Durade, 6 Dec 1860.] Mr Lewes begs me to thank you for your kind attention to his request about the schools. Mr Trollope is a friend of course who has exerted himself so obligingly on behalf of our son Charles, that we should be glad to be able to procure him any useful information.

[GHL Journal, 15 Apr 1861.] Went down to Waltham to dine and sleep at Trollope's. He has a charming house and grounds, and I like him very much, so wholesome and straightforward a man. Mrs Trollope did not make any decided impression on me, one way or the other.

[GE to François D'Albert-Durade, 15 June 1861.] We seem destined to give you fruitless trouble about schools. Mr Trollope, since we wrote to you on his behalf, has changed his mind, having been dissuaded by the present tutor of his boys at Winchester from sending them abroad until they are much more matured.[5]

[GHL to Mr and Mrs Thomas Adolphus Trollope, 9 Dec 1861.] Of course you hear from Anthony. Is he prosperous and enjoying his trip? The book will have an enormous sale just now; but I fancy he will find more animosity and less friendliness than he expected, to judge from the state of exasperation against the Britisher which seems to be general.[6]

[GE to Sara Sophia Hennell, 14 Jan 1862.] I have read most of the numbers of *Orley Farm* and admire it very much, with the exception of such parts as I have read about Moulder and Co., which by the way I saw in glancing at a late *Spectator*, the sapient critic there selects for peculiar commendation. There is no mistake an author can make but there will be some newspaper critic to pronounce it his finest effort. Anthony Trollope is admirable in the presentation of even, average life and character, and he is so thoroughly wholesome-minded that one delights in seeing his books lie about to be read.

[GHL to Thomas Adolphus Trollope, 2 June 1862.] I have finished one volume of Anthony's *America*, and am immensely pleased with it – so much so that I hope to do something towards counteracting the nasty notice in the *Saturday*.[7]

[GE to François D'Albert-Durade, 23 Sep 1862.] *The Small House at Allington* is by our excellent friend Mr Anthony Trollope – one of the heartiest, most genuine, moral and generous men we know.

[GE to Charles Bray, 16 Apr 1862. She comments on Thomas Adolphus Trollope's letter to the *Athenaeum* (4 Apr 1863) about D. D. Home, the spiritualist.] His brother Anthony Trollope, on the other hand, is a Church of England man, clinging to whatever is, *on the whole*, and without fine distinctions, honest, lovely and of good report. I mention these points, although you may know them, lest, not knowing them, you should fall into some confusion of personalities and opinions.

[GE to Anthony Trollope, 23 Oct 1863.] Rachel [*Rachel Ray*] has a formidable rival in *The Small House*, which seems to me peculiarly felicitous in its conception, and good for all souls to read. But I am much struck in *Rachel* with the skill with which you have organised thoroughly natural everyday incidents into a strictly related, well-proportioned whole, natty and complete as a nut on its stem. Such construction is among those subtleties of art which can hardly be appreciated except by those who have striven after the same result with conscious failure. Rachel herself is a sweet maidenly figure, and her poor mother's spiritual confusions are excellently observed.

But there is something else I care yet more about, which has impressed me very happily in all those writings of yours that I know – it is that people are breathing good bracing air in reading them – it is that they (the books) are filled with belief in goodness without the slightest tinge of maudlin. They are like pleasant public gardens, where people go for amusement and, whether they think of it or not, get health as well.

[GE to Charles Bray, 15 Dec 1864.] I have seen people much changed by the Banting system.[8] Mr A. Trollope is thinner by means of it, and is otherwise the better for the self-denial.

[GE to John Blackwood, 18 Oct 1867.] I suppose you have seen in the papers that our friend Mr Trollope has resigned his place in the Post Office.[9] I cannot help being rather sorry, though one is in danger of being rash in such judgements. But it seems to me a thing greatly to be dreaded for a man that he should be in any way led to excessive writing.

[John Blackwood to GE, 7 Nov 1867.] I agree with you in thinking that Trollope giving up his official situation is a doubtful step, but I hope he has a good retiring allowance.

[GE to Sara Sophia Hennell, 2 Jan 1871.] I have not read *Sir Harry Hotspur*, but as to your general question I reply that there certainly are some women who love in that way, but 'Their sex as well as I, may chide them for it.'[10] Men are very fond of glorying that sort of dog-like attachment.

[GHL to Robert Lytton, 6 May 1871.] We have had Tour-guéneff here lately and seen much of him. He was an old fellow student of mine in Berlin in 1838 and we had not met since! He's a superb creature and a real genius. ... One of your appreciators and real well-wishers, Lady Castletown, pointed out to me what a group of genius and of what variety of genius there was standing in a small circle on that occasion – Tourguéneff, Viardot, Browning, Trollope, Burne-Jones and Polly.[11]

[Joseph Munt Langford to John Blackwood, 24 Dec 1872.][12] You will be surprised to hear that Harry Trollope has gone on a visit to Australia. In writing to Trollope perhaps you will be kind enough not to allude to this unless you hear it from someone else. Trollope will most likely and would unquestionably if you were with him tell you all about it but as he told me that besides myself he should talk about it only with Charles Taylor and O'Neil I do not feel at liberty to enter into the matter. It will be attributed no doubt to a business quarrel but the cause is one which has troubled our sex from the earliest periods and the young man has shown himself amenable to reason and obedient to parental authority.[13] Trollope has behaved with his usual promptness. It must trouble him though and he is involved in a quarrel with Charles Reade about dramatising *Ralph the Heir* – that is C. R. quarrels but Trollope will not. I am sorry for I have always stood up for Reade but in this case he was wrong from the beginning and has at last written a very bad letter headed 'Mr Trollope', getting himself more into the mud at every step he has taken.

[John Blackwood to GE, 18 Feb 1874.] Mrs Trollope came down from London last night to pay us a short visit. She is looking well and gave a very amusing account of her experiences of American and Australian travelling. Anthony seems to be flourishing and hunting. What an indefatigable fellow he is.

NOTES

1. Isabella (Isa) Blagden (1817?–73), one of the Anglo-Florentine circle who charmed Trollope and persuaded him to introduce her work to George Smith. Trollope wrote to Smith about her first book in Nov 1860: 'I do not suppose you will make a fortune by it; – nor, I suppose, will she' (*Letters*, i, 125). When her second novel appeared Rose Trollope wrote to Kate Field: 'I hope it will have more common-sense than the former one – it can't well have less' (from MSS in Boston Public Library, cited *Dearest Isa; Robert Browning's Letters to Isabella Blagden*, ed. Edward C. McAleer (Austin, Tex., 1951) xxix.

2. Isa was somewhat of a trial to her friends. While in Florence G. H. Lewes noted in his journal for 27 May 1860: 'Mrs Trollope [Tom's wife, Theodosia] called bringing with her an awful visitor, a Miss Blagden, who beset Polly' (*GE Letters*, iii, 471n). They liked her better on further acquaintance. By Aug 1863 Trollope was distinctly tetchy, writing to Kate Field: 'You will not be glad to hear me declare that your dear friend (and my dear friend also) Miss Blagden is a plague' (*Commentary*, p. 226).

3. Charles Lee Lewes (1842–91), Lewes's eldest son. For Trollope's interest in his Post Office career, see *Letters*, i, 109, 112, 117–18.

4. Sir Arthur Helps (1813–75), historian, novelist, playwright and essayist; Clerk of the Privy Council from 1860 until his death; prepared the Queen's *Leaves from the Journal of Our Life in the Highlands*, 1868; awarded Order of the Bath, 1871, Knight Commander, 1872; best known for pious discourses, *Friends in Council* (four series 1847–59) and *Realmah* (1868).

5. In the event, both sons attended Bradfield College, near Reading, from 1860; Henry left in 1863, Frederick in 1865 (*Letters*, 1, 136n).

6. Trollope was gathering material for *North America*; feeling against the British stemmed from the removal of Mason and Slidell from the British vessel *Trent*, 8 Nov 1861 (*Auto.*, ix).

7. *Saturday Review*, XIII (31 May 1862) 625–6 described *North America* 'as thin-spun, tedious, mooning a journal of travel as has been offered to the public for a long time'. Lewes responded with a sharp attack on the ethics of the *Review* and a long and not uncritical comment on Trollope's book (*Cornhill*, VI (July 1862) 105–7; *GE Letters*, VIII, 302n).

8. Trollope had gone on a diet. William Banting (1797–1878) popularised a protein diet in *A Letter on Corpulence, Addressed to the Public* (1863).

9. Trollope resigned with effect from 31 Oct 1867.

10. *Sir Harry Hotspur of Humblethwaite* (1870). A quotation from *A Midsummer Night's Dream*, III, ii. 218.

11. Ivan Sergeyevich Turgenev (1818–83), eminent Russian novelist. His letters to GE were signed 'J. S. Tourguéneff'.

12. Joseph Munt Langford (1809–84) was in charge of the London operation of *Blackwood's*. He was a fellow member of the Garrick Club.

13. GHL noted in his diary 1 Jan 1873: 'Trollope came to lunch. Told me of his trouble with Harry wanting to marry a woman of the town' (*GE Letters*, V, 357). Harry's scrape was quickly hushed up.

His Manners Were Rough and, So to Speak, Tumultuous

JAMES PAYN AND OTHERS

The constant theme of memoirs, by now apparent, is that although at first the lion roared disconcertingly, given time it would roll over with its paws in the air. Parallels were not infrequently drawn between Trollope and the animal kingdom. Sala speaks of the 'ursine envelope', Locker-Lampson has him 'hirsute and taurine of aspect', Kent mentions the 'leonine face', Sichel makes him 'growl'; yet always the accompanying comment asserts his fundamental good nature. (1) from James Payn *Some Literary Recollections* (1884) pp. 167–8, 173; James Payn (1830–99), energetic journalist, popular author of *Lost Sir Massing-berd* (1864) and many other romances, one of the Dickens circle, editor of *Cornhill*

Magazine, 1882–96, reader for George Smith, 1874–94. See R. C. Terry, *Victorian Popular Fiction 1860–80* (1983) pp. 133–66; (2) from W. P. Frith, *My Autobiography and Reminiscences* (1887) I, 496. William Powell Frith (1819–1909), the artist known for narrative paintings such as *Derby Day* (1858) and *The Railway Station* (1862). His canvas *The Private View of the Royal Academy* (1881) included Trollope and Oscar Wilde as literary contrasts; (3) from Walter Sichel, *The Sands of Time* (1923) p. 217. Walter Sichel (1885–1933), author of studies on Bolingbroke, Disraeli, Sheridan and Sterne; (4) from F. Locker-Lampson, *My Confidences* (1896) pp. 331–3, 336–7. Frederick Locker (1821–95) later Locker-Lampson, writer of *vers de societé*, his best-known work *London Lyrics* (1857); (5) from Julian Hawthorne, *Confessions and Criticisms* (Boston, Mass., 1887) pp. 140–3. Julian Hawthorne (1846–1934), writer of sensation novels, a biography of his father, *Nathaniel Hawthorne and His Wife* (1885). His *Memoirs* were edited by his wife in 1938.

(1)   Trollope was the least literary man of letters I ever met; indeed, had I not known him for the large-hearted and natural man he was, I should have suspected him of some affectation in this respect. Though he certainly took pleasure in writing novels, I doubt whether he took any in reading them; and from his conversation, quite as much as from his own remarks on the subject in his autobiography, I should judge he had not read a dozen, even of Dickens's, in his life.[1] His manners were rough and, so to speak, tumultuous, but he had a tender heart and a strong sense of duty. He has done his literary reputation as much harm by the revelation of his method of work as by his material views of its result. He took almost a savage pleasure in demolishing the theory of 'inspiration', which has caused the world to deny his 'genius'; but although he was the last, and a long way the last, of the great triumvirate of modern novelists (for Bulwer is not to be named in the same breath, and George Eliot stands *per se*), he hangs 'on the line' with them.[2]

[As editor of *Chambers's Journal* and later of *Cornhill*, Payn described himself as at the mercy of flat-earthers and loonies of all kinds. 'Until a man becomes an editor,' he said, 'he can never plumb the depths of literary human nature.' Trollope's *An Editor's Tales* (1870) were, Payn declared, as convincing a proof of his genius as anything he wrote.] I once expressed this opinion to Trollope, who assented to my view of the matter, but added, with a grim smile, that he doubted whether anybody had ever read the book except myself, by which of course he meant to imply that it had had a very small circulation as compared with that of his novels.[3]

(2)   [Frith and Trollope became good friends in the seventies. In May 1874 Frith joined with Millais and Tom Taylor in helping Trollope raise funds for the widow of Shirley Brooks.] I must confess that my theory of men and their resemblance to their works must fall to the ground in Trollope's case, for it would be impossible to imagine anything less like his novels than the author of them. The books, full of gentleness, grace and refinement; the writer of them, bluff, loud, stormy and contentious; neither a brilliant talker nor a good speaker; but a kinder-hearted man and a truer friend never lived.[4]

(3)   I was brought into some contact with four more literary celebrities, the first about this time, the others later. They are Anthony Trollope, Miss Braddon, Rhoda Broughton and Marie Corelli. Trollope I met at the house of a sporting relative, who was a friend of his. He struck me as outwardly a curmudgeon, inwardly the soul of good-fellowship. Tall, bearded, growling and spectacled, he was a tough customer for any stripling. I had cut myself shaving, and he took care to tell me so at the outset. But his bluntness was the superficial bluntness of my own razor, and when he found that I was an Harrovian he thawed and told me much of his schooldays both at Winchester and on the Hill. His talented mother maintained them all, much as was the case with Mrs Oliphant, whose son I knew at Balliol. Of Harrow he was not particularly fond, as there he had been bullied, and his last term had coincided with the appearance of the bailiffs on the lawn of Julians Hill.

(4)   Anthony Trollope, like his ancestor of old, was combative, and he was boisterous, but good-naturedly so. He was abrupt in manners and speech; he was ebullient, and therefore he sometimes offended people. I suppose he was a wilful man, and we know that such men are always in the right; but he was a good fellow.

Some of Trollope's acquaintance used to wonder how so commonplace a person could have written such excellent novels; but I maintain that so honourable and interesting a man could not be commonplace.

Hirsute and taurine of aspect, he would glare at you from behind fierce spectacles. His ordinary tones had the penetrative capacity of two people quarrelling, and his voice would ring through and through you, and shake the windows in their frames, while all the time he was most amiably disposed towards you under his waistcoat. To me his *viso sciolto* and bluff geniality were very attractive, and so were his gusty denunciations, but most attractive of all was his unselfish nature. Literary men might make him their exemplar, as I make him my theme; for he may quite well have been the most generous man of letters, of mark, since Walter Scott.

I used to encounter Trollope at the Cosmopolitan, at the Athenaeum and at the meetings of the Royal Literary Fund (where he was amusingly combative).[5] I have dined with him, and he has dined with me. I hope we had a mutual regard. He gave me the bulky manuscript of his *Small House at Allington* which I much value. Bound in dark morocco it has the aspect of our Family Bible.[6]

Trollope had a furious hatred of shams and toadyism, and he sometimes recognised and resented these weaknesses where they would hardly have been detected by an ordinary observer. He could not be said to be quarrelsome, but he was crotchety. It would have been as well if sometimes he had borne in mind Talleyrand's advice, *Surtout point de zele*.

... Not the worst part of a distinguished man's reputation is the esteem in which he is held by his friends, and in this Trollope was rich. He indulged in no professional jealousies; indeed he had none to indulge in. He only had much nobility of nature; he worked hard for well-nigh seventy years, and when the end was near he awaited it with becoming fortitude and resignation, and so gave up his honest ghost, which, as Montaigne says, proved what is at the bottom of the vessel. I think Trollope must have been able to sing his *Nunc dimittis* without much faltering.

(5)   During the winter of 1879, when I was in London, it was my fortune to attend a social meeting of literary men at the rooms of a certain eminent publisher.[7] The rooms were full of tobacco-smoke and talk, amid which were discernible, on all sides, the figures and faces of men more or less renowned in the world of books. Most noticeable among these personages was a broad-shouldered, sturdy man, of middle height, with a ruddy countenance and snow-white tempestuous beard and hair. He wore large, gold-rimmed spectacles, but his eyes were black and brilliant, and looked at his interlocutor with a certain genial fury of inspection.[8]

He seemed to be in a state of some excitement; he spoke volubly and almost boisterously, and his voice was full-toned and powerful, though pleasant to the ear. He turned himself, as he spoke, with a burly briskness, from one side to another, addressing himself first to this auditor and then to that, his words bursting forth from beneath his white moustache with such an impetus of hearty breath that it seemed as if all opposing arguments must be blown quite away. Meanwhile he flourished in the air an ebony walking-stick, with much vigour of gesticulation, and narrowly missing, as it appeared, the pates of his listeners. He was clad in evening dress, though the rest of the company was, for the most part, in mufti; and he was an exceedingly fine-looking old gentleman. At the first glance, you would have taken him to be some civilised and modernised Squire Western, nourished with beef and ale, and roughly hewn out of the most robust and least refined variety of human clay. Looking at him more narrowly, however, you would have reconsidered this judgement. Though his general contour and aspect were massive and sturdy, the lines of his features were delicately cut; his complexion was remarkably pure and fine, and his face was susceptible of very subtle and sensitive changes of expression. Here was a man of abundant physical strength and vigour, no doubt, but carrying within him a nature more than commonly alert and impressible. His organisation, though thoroughly healthy, was both complex and high-wrought; his character was simple and straightforward to a fault, but he was abnormally conscientious, and keenly alive to others' opinion concerning him. It might be thought that he was overburdened with self-esteem, and unduly opinionated; but, in fact, he was but over-anxious to secure the good-will and agreement of all with whom he came in contact. There was some peculiarity in him – some element or bias in his composition that made him different from other men; but, on the other hand, there was an ardent solicitude to annul or reconcile this difference, and to prove himself to be, in fact, of absolutely the same cut and quality as all the rest of the world. Hence he was in a demonstrative, expository, or argumentative mood; he could not sit quiet in the face of a divergence between himself and his associates; he was incorrigibly strenuous to obliterate or harmonise the irreconcilable points between him and others; and since these points remained irreconcilable, he remained in a constant state of storm and stress on the subject.

It was impossible to help liking such a man at first sight; and I believe that no man in London society was more generally liked than Anthony Trollope. There was something pathetic in his attitude as above indicated; and a fresh and boyish quality always invested him. His artlessness was boyish, and so were his acuteness and his transparent but somewhat belated good sense. He was one of those rare persons who not only have no reserves, but who can afford to dispense with them. After he had shown you all he had in him, you would have seen nothing that was not gentlemanly, honest and clean. He was a quick-tempered man, and the ardour and hurry of his temperament made him seem more so than he really was; but he was never more angry than he was forgiving and generous. He was hurt by little things, and little things pleased him; he was suspicious and perverse, but in a manner that rather endeared him to you than otherwise. Altogether, to a casual acquaintance, who knew nothing of his personal history, he was something of a paradox – an entertaining contradiction.

NOTES

1. Payn is mistaken. Trollope read prodigiously, kept a commonplace book of his reading, embarked on a literary history, constantly added to his library and fussed over it when he moved house. See *Letters*, II, 1022–32. He also kept abreast of recent fiction.

2. Payn, also supremely professional, thoroughly approved of Trollope's business-like approach and prided himself on his negotiations for overseas publication. See *Some Literary Recollections*, pp. 165–6.

3. Ibid., pp. 155, 173.

4. Both were on the same platform at a prize-giving at Spitalfields School of Art, 28 Nov 1876. Frith recalled 'Trollope made a good speech, and I made a bad one' (*My Autobiography*, III, 387).

5. Witness his attempted resignation (*Letters*, II, 816–18). However, he gave sterling service to the Royal Literary Fund, serving on its committee, helping vigorously to promote its charitable causes, organising dinners and speaking. See R. H. Super 'Trollope at the Royal Literary Fund', *Nineteenth-Century Fiction*, XXXVII, 3 (Dec 1982) 316–28.

6. Trollope presented the manuscript in Mar 1882 not long before he died.

7. Probably Chapman & Hall who published four of Trollope's novels that year.

8. Although witnesses vary as to the colour of Trollope's eyes all agree on his piercing glance.

He Glowed, A Conversational Stove

JULIAN HAWTHORNE AND OTHERS

It was not unjustly said of Trollope that he made a better host than guest. In his home surroundings at Waltham or Montagu Square he was less likely to hog the conversation and play the expected role of lumbering lion. It is a feature not uncommon in the lives of celebrities. In consequence hosts who suffered his party manners or those who, as discomfited diners faced him across the table, occasionally left pithy notes of the evening. Ill-natured he never was, but intemperate and even vulgar he certainly sometimes sounded. On one occasion an eye-witness noted the novelist in the grounds at Panshanger with shirtsleeves rolled, prepared for fisticuffs with a hapless tradesman. Indoors he might well give an impression of being ready at any moment to break out, waving an ebony cane, as one excerpt recalls, shouting down an opponent in conversation, and perhaps causing the ladies to steal away to the drawing-room with their cambric handkerchiefs to their brows. (1) from Julian Hawthorne, *Shapes That Pass: Memories of Old Days* (1928) pp. 134–5, 226–7; (2) from W. G. Elliot, *In My Anecdotage* (1925) pp. 94–5. William Gerald Elliot (1858–1930), noted actor who began his career at the Haymarket in 1882; (3) *The Amberley Papers: The Letters and Diaries of Lord and Lady Amberley*, ed. B. and P. Russell (1937) ii, 27. John Russell, Viscount Amberley (1842–1876), son of Lord John Russell. 'Kate', Lady Amberley (1842–74), a political hostess following the path of her mother, Lady Stanley, widow of the second Lord Stanley of Alderley, Postmaster-General, 1860–6; (4) from T. H. S. Escott, *Anthony Trollope*, pp. 151–3.

(1)   The London season was coming on. It began, for me, with a dinner at Eustacia's.[1] That was the name by which she desired her particular friends to call her. She was of northern England or Scottish blood, I believe, and of patrician lineage, but poor in purse. She made up for that in the brilliance of her person and spirit, which soon got her the wealth which such gifts and social station demanded. That is, she married a rich manufacturer with an income, large for those times, of sixty thousand pounds. When I first met her – at a dinner at Smalley's[2] – she conveyed an expression of life, resource, and sparkle that seemed like beauty; she was vigorous in body, fresh-coloured, with brown hair and blue eyes, strong features, a ready smile, and noticeable teeth; the

drawback was that the pink gums from which the teeth came were uncovered, when she smiled, by her short upper lip. Otherwise she might have stood as model for the Venus of Milo: there was a pagan vitality in her; and the Venus may have had gums like Eustacia's, for aught we know. She had a way, in conversation, of holding up her folded fan under her chin, with a coquettish suggestion. She was dressed and jewelled exceedingly, and her shoulders and bosom must have been beautiful, for she showed them with pagan frankness. I took her to be thirty at most; but Smalley afterwards told me sardonically that she was many times a mother and once already a grandmother, and could not have been less than fifty. One hears such things about an attractive woman, and ignores them. At the round table besides were old Lord Houghton (Monckton Milnes); Archibald Forbes, the great war correspondent; Anthony Trollope, in his successful, glowing, gusty, gesticulating old age, most likeable;[3]....

... Trollope, skilful, experienced and veracious to the verge of commonplace, had become popular ever since Thackeray had engaged him to write the first novel for the new *Cornhill Magazine* in 1860. He was homespun, but he wore well. He never took you underground, or to the mountain-tops, but cantered you along with the fox-hunt, or introduced you to an amiable clergy, and to ladies great and small, but always ladies; so that when you put down the book and went outdoors, you seemed to be still reading Trollope. His book of power was his *Autobiography*, perennially fascinating and touching. He was sincere and hearty, and after overcoming the inferiority complex of his youth, he was afraid of nobody except God and Mudie.

Nobody consciously patterned himself on Trollope; but in unguarded moments of composition you might find yourself goose-stepping him unawares. A hearty, wholesome, ruddy being he was personally, with a furious white beard and explosive speech, swinging his arms in impulsive gestures, and when, owing to occasional gout, he was carrying his ebony gold-headed cane, he would swish it about so that the bystander must beware: he glowed, a conversational stove. Coming to him from one of his books, he would surprise you. But his wife was his books, though not at all literary, and, in fact, declaring that she wished Anthony was not a writer.[4] 'He never leaves off,' she said complainingly, 'and he always has two packages of manuscript in his desk, besides the one he's working on, and the one that's being published.' But the good woman was always fashionably dressed, and money, unlike Dian's kiss, does not come unasked, unsought. But he and she were an affectionate couple; fox-hunting and matrimony cost him something, but he was faithful to both to the end.[5]

(2)   Mrs Lehmann was the daughter of Robert Chambers, the proprietor of *Chambers's Miscellany* in Edinburgh.[6] She had a host of delightful stories and was one of the best exponents of good Scottish humour I ever met. James Payn, the well-known novelist, was constantly at the Sunday dinner there, a fascinating man, and I shall never forget a dinner-party one night where the guests were Anthony Trollope, Pym, a witty solicitor – who saw all the fun in what is to follow – Sir John Millais, Sir Arthur Sullivan and Lord James of Hereford.[7] About four of us young 'uns were asked also to hear the clever sayings and wit that ought to have fallen from the mouths of the Great Ones, but unfortunately, as sometimes happens on these occasions when two or three such are gathered together, they were all rather shy of each other, and the dinner opened in perfect silence. At last, Sullivan made an effort, and began a discussion on the Law of Copyright, of which he evidently disapproved. Lord James looked at him fixedly, and then suddenly cut in: 'My dear Sullivan, you evidently haven't the faintest idea what you're talking about!' Silence. Then Millais, ostensibly to clear up the awkwardness, came in, and in loud tones narrated to the assemblage some slightly painful details of his household. Silence. To change the subject, a young man nervously remarked to Trollope, who had all the time been munching his dinner in silence: 'They tell me, Mr Trollope, that before sitting down to write one of your – may I say? – delightful novels, you always make a prefatory sketch!' 'Never did such a thing in my life sir, and never shall!' bawled the angry Anthony. Mrs Lehmann here deemed it wise to rise and retire to the drawing-room. It was a great evening!

(3)   Monday 8 April [1867]. We had a little dinner of Huxley, Anthony Trollope, Lady Russell, and Mr Knatchbull-Hugessen whom Amberley brought home fr. the H of C.[8] Dinner was very pleasant, Ly R. enjoyed it very much and was pleased to make acquaintance with Trollope and Huxley. A and I thought T's

voice too loud, he rather drowned Huxley's pleasant quiet voice which was certainly better worth hearing.[9]

(4) [Much is said of Trollope ranting and roaring in society. The value of this comment lies in sober assessment of Trollope in conversation compared with the table talk of other notables; Escott had several opportunities to observe across the decanter.] High genius always appreciates genius, whatever its personal setting. Dickens and Thackeray were, therefore, above the pettiness of belittling each other. Between Anthony Trollope, however, and Edmund Yates, with all their cleverness, there always existed a good deal of mutual depreciation and jealousy. Especially was this the case in and after 1868; for in that year F. I. Scudamore, who had been made a GPO Secretary over Trollope's head, took Yates for his assistant in arranging the transfer of the telegraphs from a private company to the State. Yates, therefore, thought he had as good a reason as Trollope for pride in his work as a Post Office servant; while, as for his social antecedents, if he had not been, like Trollope, at a public school, he had, before going to a German university, been in its best days under Dyne, at Highgate School. Neither man had many pretensions to real scholarship, but Yates had read and remembered the regulation Latin Classics well enough to quote them quite as aptly as Trollope. In facility and force of literary expression, he was at least Trollope's equal; in ready wit and resourcefulness he was his superior. But of the English life that Trollope depicted he knew nothing. The success of Thackeray and of Dickens he could understand and admire. Both of them describe different aspects, and hit off certain angles of personal character connected with that existence which Yates knew and had studied. But as for Trollope, with his parsons, sporting or priggish, his insipid young ladies and the green, callow boys upon whom experience was wasted, and opportunities thrown away – in a word, these washed-out imitations of Thackeray, as to Yates they seemed – it passed Yates's comprehension that the public should find any flavour to its taste in all this. It even stirred his indignation to hear of publishers paying such a writer prices approaching those commanded by the twin chiefs of his craft themselves.

It must be remembered, too, that Yates's notions of what constitutes conversational cleverness were largely those he had imbibed as a youth in the school of Albert Smith.[10] Hence the opinion recorded in his autobiography, that Trollope did not shine in society and had only humour of a very second-rate kind. Yates himself, like Dickens, talked well, and talked for effect. From both his parents he had inherited marked histrionic power, which showed itself in his performances as *raconteur*, in the inflections of his voice and the gesture of his hands. To Trollope such action and pose were altogether foreign. With real humour, indeed, he overflowed, as has already been shown from *The Macdermots* and *The Warden*, and as will be seen more fully later on, but, unlike Yates, he kept it for his books, and never wasted it on social effects. Moreover, Trollope had committed what Yates resented as an unpardonable sin by refusing to sit for his portrait in the 'Celebrities at Home' then appearing in the *World*. It should, however, be mentioned that, after this honour had been declined, Yates, in his magazine *Time*, published a highly eulogistic article about Trollope, whose proof, before it appeared, he sent Trollope, not only to read, but to revise and touch up as he pleased.[11] The Post Office, like other public departments, has had its literary ornaments, whose best traditions subsequently to the period now dealt with have been perpetuated by Mr Buxton Forman, in the domain of literary criticism, and by Mr A. B. Walkley, as an authority on the drama in all its developments. But, in the nineteenth century, Yates and Trollope ran each other a neck-and-neck race for priority as representatives of St Martin's le Grand in belles-lettres.

High animal spirits and irrepressible buoyancy entered largely into the Dickensian estimate of social wit and humour. Few, if any, of these qualities belonged to Trollope by nature, or had become his acquisition by habit. A writer who put so much felicity and fun into the lighter passages of his stories could not, indeed, but occasionally introduce happiness and pungency into his table talk. But, as Anthony Trollope himself remarked, 'the conversational credit of our family is maintained not by me but by my brother Tom'. Thomas Adolphus Trollope's academic training, natural subtlety, and turn for humorous paradox caused him, after a fashion always entertaining and often original, to play with the problems of metaphysics and theology, amid the applause of those Florentine circles where he was better known and appreciated than in any London drawing-rooms or clubs. His brother Anthony at his best brimmed over with shrewd common-sense. Occasionally, when asked a question, he put his answer in a memorable shape, but, apart from the distinction won by his pen, was welcomed in society not so much for a talker as for a listener.

NOTES

1. Probably in 1874.

2. George Washburn Smalley (1833–1916), an American journalist, chief of the *New York Tribune's* European staff, 1867–95, and influential literary ambassador between Britain and the United States. See next item.

3. Both longtime friends. Richard Monckton Milnes (1809–85), patron of many writers, editor of Keats, famed for his social gatherings, made Baron Houghton (July 1863), fellow member of the Cosmopolitan Club and, like Trollope, on the Treasurers' Committee of the Royal Literary Fund. See T. Wemyss Reid, *The Life, Letters and Friendships of Richard Monckton Milnes* (1890). Archibald Forbes (1838–1900), correspondent for the *Daily News*, author of *Memories and Studies of War and Peace* (1895).

4. Hawthorne alone among witnesses claims such a vital part for Rose in Trollope's life, but he is probably correct.

5. Augustus Hare notes in his journal, 17 May 1877, a party at Lord Houghton's attended by Princess Louise, sixth daughter of Queen Victoria. Among the guests Mrs Anthony Trollope struck him as 'a beautiful old lady with snow-white hair turned back' (*In My Solitary Life* (1953) p. 106).

6. Nina Chambers was married to Frederick Lehmann.

7. Horatio Noble Pym (d. 1896), bibliophile and raconteur, numbered Browning, Collins and James Payn among his friends. He wrote several books including *Memories of Old Friends* (1882) and *A Tour Round My Bookshelves* (1891). Sir Henry James, afterwards Lord James of Hereford (1828–1911), Attorney-General under Gladstone, 1873–4 and 1880–5. Arthur Seymour Sullivan (1842–1900), composer and collaborator with W. S. Gilbert. When Millais hosted an all-male party in May 1881, Sullivan won £6 from Trollope at cards (Arthur Jacobs, *Arthur Sullivan: A Victorian Musician* (1984) p. 157).

8. Edward Knatchbull-Hugessen (1829–93), Liberal MP for Sandwich, 1857; Lord of Treasury, 1859–60 and 1860–6; Under Secretary for Colonies, 1871–4; 1st Baron Brabourne, 1880. Lady (Frances Anna Maria) Russell (d. 1874). Thomas Henry Huxley (1825–95), eminent scientist and philosopher who published widely on natural history; best known for *Man's Place in Nature* (1863) and *Science and Morals* (1873); his *Collected Essays* appeared in 1894; President of the Royal Society, 1883–5.

9. The meeting actually took place on 9 Apr. It was just such occasions among intellectual luminaries like Huxley that brought out the truculent side of Trollope. See Barry A. Bartrum, 'A Victorian Political Hostess: The Engagement Book of Lady Stanley of Alderley', *Princeton University Library Chronicle*, xxxvi, 2 (Winter 1975) 133–46.

10. Albert Smith (1816–60), journalist and showman noted for his lecture 'The Ascent of Mont Blanc' (1851) and entertainment at the Egyptian Hall, Piccadilly (1852). Henry Vizetelly spoke of his 'noisy self-assertion and

boisterous behaviour' in company, *Glimpses Back Through Seventy Years: Autobiographical and Other Reminiscences* (1893) I, 319.

11. Trollope did not like society journalism. His long memory might also have been stirred. In Aug 1861 John Maxwell, the publisher, was keen to get Trollope as editor of *Temple Bar* and his representative tactlessly wrote offering 'the ostensible editorship' for three to five years at £1000 p.a. if he would supply a novel; all the real work would be done by the current sub-editor, Yates. Trollope wrathfully inscribed the letter 'Hands full. Would not undertake a mock Editorship' (Bodleian MS Don C10*; *Commentary*, p. 196; *Letters*, I, 157, 219). Escott refrains from mentioning that he wrote the article alluded to ('A Novelist of the Day', *Time*, 1 (Aug 1879) 626–32).

'You Are Not Man Enough To Eat Two Breakfasts?'

GEORGE SMALLEY

From George Smalley, 'English Men of Letters', *McClure's Magazine*, xx (Jan 1903) 298–9. George Washburn Smalley (1833–1916), well-known American journalist, chief of the *New York Tribune's* European staff, 1867–95, and something of a literary ambassador between the two countries; author of many books such as *Studies of Men* (1895), *London Letters and Some Others* (1896) and *Anglo-American Memories* (1911). Smalley helped negotiate publication of *Ayala's Angel* in the *Cincinnati Commercial*, Nov 1880–July 1881 (*Letters*, II, 896).

'A typical Englishman' Mr Anthony Trollope might be called. But there is no typical Englishman except on the stage, and then he is a caricature. There is not one type, there are many; and Trollope was a very good example of one of the best types. He had the bluffness which is supposed to be characteristic of the race; the hearty manner, the love of outdoor life; the loyalty and the red face which belong to the country squire. This man of letters seemed to have spent all his life in the country, growing turnips and preserving game. He had, in fact, spent part of it; but that part was in the hunting field, where he rode hard and straight, though never a very good horseman. He hunted three days a week during the season, going down by train from London and returning the same night. His books are full of his experiences in following the hounds, and there are no better hunting pictures. Whyte-Melville's are not better, though Whyte-Melville was a better man in the pigskin.[1]

But the Trollope whom American readers may be supposed to care for was not the Nimrod, not the Post Office inspector, but he who lived in Montagu Square and wrote the Barchester novels. At one time, and during many years, I saw much of him.[2] We lived in the same quarter of London. One morning, before I knew much about his habits, I went in to see him toward noon. He was at breakfast (a midday French breakfast), and asked me to join him. I said I had breakfasted much earlier. 'What,' he broke out; 'do you mean to say you are not man enough to eat two breakfasts?' His rule was to begin work at eight o'clock each morning, except Sundays and days when he hunted, and to work until eleven o'clock. Each morning, between these hours, he wrote eight hundred words; no more and no less.[3] He wrote almost a lady's hand – fine, rapid, firm, not always easy to read.

I have known four men who could compose in this way, as it were, to order, and who scoffed at the theory of waiting for inspiration. The four were Trollope, Sir Richard Burton, Browning and the American novelist Mr Marion Crawford. Each was master of himself at all moments, and could do his best at one time as well as another. Dickens was, perhaps, a fifth; he sat regularly at his desk from nine in the morning till one. If he found he could go on with the current novel, well and good; if not, he wrote letters or read, but for those four hours there he sat. They were all men of unusual physique, all used to the taking of much exercise, all with sound minds and sound bodies. Trollope used to write in his library, which filled a kind of extension to the Montagu Square house, halfway from the first to the second floor. It was more a workshop than a library, yet held a good many books, in open cases, which Trollope, with his niece's help, used to dust religiously twice a year.[4] London, with its fogs and soot-laden air, is not a place where valuable books can be exposed with impunity. He knew London inch by inch, and the counties in which the scenes of so many of his novels are laid, and for all social and personal traits had a microscopic eye. It is this power and habit of accurate observation which will immortalise his best novels – the Barchester series. They were for a time, after his death, little read: now they are read again with ever fresh pleasure.

NOTES

1. George Whyte-Melville (1821–78), doyen of hunting novelists, best known for *Digby Grand* (1832), *General Bounce* (1855) and *Kate Coventry: An Autobiography* (1856); published his *Riding Recollections* in 1878 which ran to several editions.

2. Trollope's first reference to Smalley is a dinner invitation in Feb 1877 (*Letters*, ii, 708). He had moved to Montagu Square in 1873.

3. Smalley underestimates the wordage, which was set at a page of some 250 words every quarter of an hour (*Auto.*, vii, xv) for about three hours, a regime slightly softened in later years.

4. Compare Escott's account of the library shelves full to overflowing ('The Works of Anthony Trollope', *Quarterly Review*, 210 (Jan 1909) 226).

At the Club

SIR WILLIAM HARDMAN, MARK TWAIN AND OTHERS

Stories cluster round Trollope as clubman. Not surprisingly, since he held memberships in the Garrick Athenaeum and Cosmopolitan, and had affiliations at one time or another with the Arts, Turf and Civil Service. Of his membership of the Garrick from 1861 he said 'The Garrick Club was the first assemblage of men at which I felt myself to be popular' (*Auto.*, ix). Elected to the Athenaeum in 1864, he was often found there in later years. When Thomas Wentworth Higginson, a Boston luminary, met Browning in 1878, 'It seemed wholly appropriate that he should turn aside presently to consult Anthony Trollope about some poor author for whom they held funds' (*Cheerful Yesterdays* (Boston, Mass., 1898) p. 287). See also Francis G. Waugh, *The Athenaeum Club and Its Associations* (1897) p. 44. Whist was a major pastime at both clubs, and Sir John Hare recalled, on his first introduction to the card-room of the Garrick, finding Trollope amongst its frequenters (T. E. Pemberton, *John Hare: A Biography* (1895) p. 163). See Trollope's essay 'Whist at Our Club', *Blackwood's Magazine*, cxxi (May 1877) 596–604. See also William Ballantine, *The Old World and the New* (1844) p. 208, for a reminiscence of cribbage with Trollope, Reade and the Marquis of Anglesea. The Cosmopolitan or 'Cos' met two evenings a week in a painter's studio off Berkeley Square. Its object, said J. L. Motley, 'seems to be to collect noted people and smoke very bad cigars' (*The Correspondence of John Lothrop Motley*, ed. George William Curtis (1899) i, 227). Sir Francis (Frank) Burnand described it as both 'a very exclusive literary, artistic and parliamentary club', and 'a superior sort of free-and-easy, where pipes could be smoked'. Here one night he met Trollope 'who, bearded and rough in manner, struck me as being a rough variation of the Tom Taylor type' (*Records and Reminiscences Personal and General* (1904) II, 242). Trollope recalled a mixed group there, among them several politicians, who 'used to whisper the secrets of Parliament with free tongues' (*Auto.*, ix). Sir Algernon West commented: 'Anthony Trollope's rather loud but genial laugh was constantly to be heard there' (*One City and Many Men* (1908) p. 169). One more club enticed him at the end of his life, the United Service Club, about which he said: 'I find all the old Generals very good fellows, and one of them yesterday called me Sir Anthony, which I thought very civil' (*Letters*, II, 920). Escott says Trollope also made one of the party at the Union Club (*Club Makers and Club Members* (1914) p. 177). (1) from *A Mid-Victorian Pepys: The Letters and Memoirs of Sir William Hardman*, ed. S. M. Ellis (1923) pp. 143–4. Hardman (1828–90), called to the Bar, 1852; served from 1865 until his death as Chairman of Surrey Quarter Sessions, for which he was knighted in 1885; also Recorder for Kingston from 1875; editor of the *Morning Post*, 1872–90; (2) from Bernard de Voto, *Mark Twain in Eruption* (New York, 1941) pp. 330–3; (3) from G. S. Layard, *A Great 'Punch' Editor: Being the Life, Letters and Diaries of Shirley Brooks* (1907) pp. 526, 545, 568. Charles William Shirley Brooks (1816–74) began his career as parliamentary reporter of the *Morning Chronicle*; his long association with *Punch* began in 1851; editor after Mark Lemon, 1870–4; (4) from Percy Fitzgerald, *The Garrick Club* (1904) pp. 78–9. Percy Hetherington Fitzgerald (1829–1925), journalist and biographer, friend of Dickens and minor novelist; founder of the Boz Club (1900); wrote widely on literary figures, Dickens, Forster, Boswell, Sterne and the Sheridans; among his books are *Recreations of a Literary Man* (1882) and *Memoirs of an Author* (1894).

(1)   Thursday, 12 June [1862]. Last night I dined at the Castle, Richmond, with the Alpine Club.[1] We found a jolly party round William Longman, the publisher, who is vice-president of the Club, Anthony Trollope sitting next to him. Longman is a glorious fellow, full of jokes and story, and beaming with good humour. Anthony Trollope is also a good fellow, modelled on Silenus, with a large black beard.[2] There was a call for Trollope, and Silenus made a funny speech, assuring the Club that he was most desirous of becoming a member, but the qualification was the difficulty, and both time and flesh were against him. He added that not very long since, in the city of Washington, a member of the US Government asked him if it were true that a club of Englishmen existed who held their meetings on the summits of the Alps. 'In my anxiety', he said, 'to support the credit of my country, I may have transgressed the strict limits of veracity, but I told him what he had heard was quite true. (*Great cheers.*)'[3]

I have been reading Anthony Trollope's new work on America – or North America, I should say.[4] It is amusing, but much too lengthy. He has manufactured two fat volumes of nearly 500 pages each out of a few months' tour. This will tell you at once how much he has said which had been better left unsaid. The women and children of the States seem to have impressed him very unfavourably. ...

The frightful infantine consumption of pickles seems to have produced a profound impression upon him. In fact, this stands out most prominently in my recollections of the two fat volumes, filled up by a background of gigantic hotels, towns with vast untenanted and tenanted blocks of buildings, West Fourteenth Avenue, and North Twenty-First Street, heaps of grain like coals in Lancashire, hot stoves, disagreeable be-crinolined women, hard-featured unpleasant men, railway cars without distinction of class, and a large amount of immature twaddle about the American Constitution and the War.

(2)   Sidney Lee's dinner was in a room which I was sure I had not seen for thirty-five years, yet I recognised it and could dreamily see about me the forms and faces of the small company of that long forgotten occasion.[5] Anthony Trollope was the host, and the dinner was in honour of Joaquin Miller, who was on the top wave of his English notoriety at that time.[6] There were three other guests: one is obliterated, but I remember two of them, Tom Hughes and Leveson-Gower.[7] No trace of that obliterated guest remains with me – I mean the *other* obliterated guest, for I was an obliterated guest also. I don't remember that anybody ever addressed a remark to either of us; no, that is a mistake – Tom Hughes addressed remarks to us occasionally; it was not in his nature to forget or neglect any stranger. Trollope was voluble and animated, and was but vaguely aware that any other person was present excepting him of the noble blood, Leveson-Gower. Trollope and Hughes addressed their talk almost together to Leveson-Gower, and there was a deferential something about it that almost made me feel that I was at a religious service; that Leveson-Gower was the acting deity, and that the illusion would be perfect if somebody would do a hymn or pass the contribution box. All this was most curious and unfamiliar and interesting. Joaquin Miller did his full share of the talking, but he was a discordant note, a disturber and degrader of the solemnities. He was affecting the picturesque and untamed costume of the wild sierras at the time, to the charmed astonishment of conventional London, and was helping out the effects with the breezy and

independent and aggressive manners of that faraway and romantic region. He and Trollope talked all the time and both at the same time, Trollope pouring forth a smooth and limpid and sparkling stream of faultless English, and Joaquin discharging into it his muddy and tumultuous mountain torrent, and – Well, there was never anything just like it except the Whirlpool Rapids under Niagara Falls.

It was long ago, long ago! and not even an echo of that turbulence was left in this room where it had once made so much noise and display. Trollope is dead; Hughes is dead; Leveson-Gower is dead; doubtless the obliterated guest is dead; Joaquin Miller is white-headed and mute and quiet in his dear mountains.

(3) [In a letter to Miss 'Torie' Matthews, 1st Sunday in 1873 (5 Jan).] Anthony Trollope was one of the guests last night. He roars more than ever since Australia. He was exceedingly jolly and Billy Russell was opposite to him, so they fired away good stories.[8] When they were at cards we heard Anthony's thunder, and then a wild Banshee cry from the Irishman, till we threatened them with the police. Then Anthony said we were conventional tyrants, and Russell said in a weeping voice that Ireland was accustomed to being trampled on.

[Diary, 4 Jan 1873.] Trollope most laudatory of me (to me privately) touching my verses and the like, and urgent that I should 'proclaim' myself much more. 'Tis not my way, but the advice was good.

[Diary, 3 May 1873.] Committee 'G.' (Garrick Club) We had some talk, in reference to certain blackballing, and most of us thought that we owed it to one another to give a hint when a blackball was deserved. Trollope thought not, and in strictness he is right, but we ought to be able to be confidential.

[Letter to Miss Matthews, 26 Oct 1873.] Trollope shouted after me at the G. yesterday to tell me that in the *Graphic*, the artist, not being able to draw horses, has introduced a picnic with champagne into the middle of a chapter about a fox chase!

(4) Anthony Trollope was somewhat recalled by the late Sir Walter Besant, of our day.[9] He had an outspoken manner, but

was good-natured and friendly, like many a novelist who has enjoyed extravagant success, and at one time there was no one so much read by 'polite society', for his lively sketches of social types, such as bishops, deans and fashionable ladies. He had to undergo the mortifying process of being gradually let down, and of falling into neglect. However, he had made hay, and saved it too, while the sun was shining, and no one had such profitable contracts with the United States and the Colonies. He was my sponsor at the Club, and took much trouble about me.[10] He was good enough to say that I was 'safe'. He had another 'candidate', and added, 'I wish I was half as secure about him.' Mr Garnett has described him very accurately, 'In form Trollope was burly, in manner boisterous. His vociferous roughness repelled many, but was the disguise of real tenderness of heart.'[11] He also speaks of his 'frank but aggressive cordiality'. This manner of his always struck me as being somewhat affected, assumed to hide either shyness or a certain feeling of not being at his ease.

In Ireland, as I know, he was always remembered with pleasure, principally for his sporting tastes. He would pick up some little animal for a song, one that was full of work, and generally contrived to have a day's hunting with this useful animal at very small cost. He was a great diner out, and agreeable talker. He loved the good things of life. He had a large head and forehead, with a large blond beard.[12] This, with his glittering spectacles, made him look like a professor or a benevolent doctor.

NOTES

1. The original Castle Inn at Richmond, rendezvous of a previous literary generation; Charles Lamb dined here in 1826 with Harrison Ainsworth.

2. Hardman, noted for his conviviality, was thought to resemble Henry VIII. Meredith, a close friend, portrayed him as Blackburn Tuckham in *Beauchamp's Career* (1876).

3. Festive gaiety prevailed at Alpine gatherings. Also in the early sixties Trollope hobnobbed with the arts community, as Sir William Richmond noted: 'In Jermyn Street, over a fruit shop, was a small suite of chambers, inhabited by Arthur Lewis, a man friendly to the Arts, a great lover of music, an admirable painter, a good whip, a brilliant huntsman, a captain in the Artists' Rifle Corps, and a most successful tradesman, whose weekly hospitality was proverbial. Part-singing was the great entertainment; those who took their share in it were called the Moray Minstrels. On the occasions when they met

celebrities jostled one another in friendly proximity. Leighton, Charles Keene, little Freddy Walker, Sandys, Holman Hunt, Millais, Anthony Trollope, Poole the fashionable tailor, together with a sprinkling of lords rather proud of being admitted into such intellectual society, made up a curiously democratic company' (A. M. W. Stirling, *The Richmond Papers* (1926) pp. 184–5).

4. *North America* (1862).

5. Mark Twain dates the meeting as 1 July 1872, but see Trollope's letter to Kate Field of 5 July 1873: 'Two of the wildest of your countrymen, Joachin Miller & Mark Twain, dine with me at my club next week. Pity you have not yet established the right of your sex or you could come and meet them, and be *as jolly as men*' (*Letters*, ii, 591).

6. Cincinnatus Hiner 'Joaquin' Miller (1839–1913), flamboyant poet known as 'the Oregon Byron', most famous for his *Songs of the Sierras* (1871). He recalled an outing with Trollope, Monckton Milnes (Lord Houghton) and other horsemen who always seemed to be having spills. 'But in all our hard riding I never had a scratch. One morning Trollope hinted that my immunity was due to my big Spanish saddle which I had brought from Mexico City. I threw my saddle on the grass and rode without so much as a blanket. And I rode neck to neck; and then left them all behind and nearly every one unhorsed' (*Joaquin Miller's Poems* (San Francisco, Cal., 1909–10) iv, 154).

7. The Hon. Edward Frederick Leveson-Gower. Twain's nose is twitching for English snobbery, but Trollope, of course, knew his guest well.

8. Sir William Howard ('Billy') Russell (1820–1907), *The Times* correspondent famous for his dispatches from the Crimea, 1854–5, from India, 1858, and the United States, 1861–2; knighted in 1895. He was noted for his good company; Thackeray observed that he would pay a guinea any day to have Russell dine at his Garrick table (*DNB Supp.*, iii, 242–3).

9. Sir Walter Besant (1836–1901) collaborated with James Rice in such successful novels as *Ready-Money Mortiboy* (1871); his best-known book was *All Sorts and Conditions of Men* (1882); he helped found the Society of Authors (1884).

10. Fitzgerald was elected on 1 Jan 1876. Trollope wrote to him on 23 Dec 1875: 'I shall be there & will do what little I can. I have another friend up on the same day. [W. P. Harding]. I do not fear much; – but there may always be accidents *against which the manly heart will be steeled*. In other words there may be a nasty man, against whom who can be provided?' (*Letters*, ii, 676).

11. *DNB*, lviii, 238–42. Richard Garnett (1835–1906). His patronising account is influenced by Trollope's self-disparagement in the *Autobiography*.

12. Most observers recall a dark beard streaked with grey; by the time he was forty-six, according to one witness, it was 'iron grey'.

Many-sided Geniality

W. LUCAS COLLINS

From W. L. Collins, 'The Autobiography of Anthony Trollope', *Blackwood's Magazine*, 134 (Nov 1883) pp. 557–96. Revd William Lucas Collins (1817–87), Rector of Lowick, Northamptonshire, 1873–87, the heart of hunting country, editor of Blackwood's *Ancient Classics for English Readers*. See *St Paul's Magazine*, 5 (Mar 1870) 664–8, for Trollope's review of the series. Trollope's contribution, *The Commentaries of Caesar* (1870), cemented their friendship. His sojourn under Collins's roof, quoted later in this recollection, produced *Dr Wortle's School* (1881) in which Lowick is 'Bowick' and the rectory a school. A portion of Trollope's correspondence indicates the warm regard they felt for each other. Collins is said to have observed on one occasion, 'Trollope, you are too good for this world' (*Commentary*, p. 357). A letter from Collins to John Blackwood on 31 May 1870 says: 'The Trollopes came on Thursday and left on Saturday. We like them very much, – him especially, he was so very pleasant to talk to, and at the same time so perfectly unassuming. What I like best in Mrs T is her honest and hearty appreciation of her husband' (MS National Library of Scotland, cited *Letters*, i, 496n). Once again here is proof that Trollope in company was not always tempestuous.

It is time to say something of his private life. His residence in Ireland had given him no opportunities of mixing in literary society; but in 1859 he was appointed to the charge of the Eastern District of England, and took a lease of a pretty old-fashioned brick house at Waltham Cross, which he afterwards bought and considerably improved. It was the same year in which he became connected with the *Cornhill Magazine*, and he found it very convenient for his frequent journeys to London. And now he began rapidly to make those literary and other friends who added so much to his keen enjoyment of life. A dinner at the publisher's was his first introduction to Thackeray, whom he regarded as the greatest novelist of the age.[1] Millais, G. H. Lewes, 'Jacob Omnium' ([Matthew] Higgins), Robert Bell, Fitzjames Stephen, Dallas, Sala, – for each and all of these he has a word of hearty appreciation. Of the late Sir Charles Taylor, the 'king of the Garrick Club' in his day, he speaks thus: 'A man rough of tongue, brusque in his manners, odious to those who dislike him, – he is the prince of friends, honest as the sun, and as open-hearted as charity itself.'[2] Had he any sort of consciousness how very nearly he was drawing a portrait of himself?

He was now in a position to satisfy that 'craving for love', which he almost apologises for as 'a weakness in his character'. It was a craving never gratified, as he pathetically complains, in the early years of his life. At the Garrick Club he at once became very popular. He was soon afterwards elected to the Athenaeum; and, when in town, generally made one at those midnight meetings at the Cosmopolitan, which no man more thoroughly enjoyed, and which were so enjoyable. At Waltham House, too, where he was very happy, though in different fashion from his London life, amongst his cows, and roses, and strawberries, he delighted to welcome at his quiet dinner-table some half-dozen of intimate friends. Those who were occasional guests there remember how, in the warm summer evening, the party would adjourn after dinner to the lawn, where wines and fruit were laid out under the fine old cedar tree and many a good story was told while the tobacco-smoke went curling up into the soft twilight.[3]

In 1861 he succeeded in getting from his official chief a nine-months' holiday, in order to pay a visit to America, for the avowed purpose of writing a book. It was during the Secession War, and his sympathies were strongly with the North; but the book when written, though fairly well received, was, as he here candidly admits, not a 'good book'. In truth, his vocation was to tell in admirable fashion a tale of modern English life; and whenever he was tempted by literary ambition to step off this familiar ground, he lost his secure foothold.

Six years afterwards he resigned his place in the Post Office, without waiting for a pension, to which a few more years' service would have entitled him. More than one motive seems to have led him to this determination. He found the double work becoming a burden to him; he had lately applied unsuccessfully for the vacant office of Under-Secretary, and he had undertaken a task which he very soon relinquished – the editorship of the new *St Paul's Magazine*.

Very early in the days of his clerkship, he had amused a cynical old uncle who once asked him what profession he would like best, by replying that he should like to be a member of Parliament. In his maturer mind he had always retained the idea that 'to sit in the

British Parliament should be the highest object of ambition to every educated Englishman'.[4] He had, he confesses, 'almost an insane desire to sit there'. Accordingly, he was hardly freed from official trammels when he began to look out for a seat. At first his name was suggested for one of the divisions of the county of Essex; but he withdrew at once, with the unselfish chivalry of his nature, in favour of a candidate who seemed to have higher claims. Finally, he stood for Beverley. He did not get in. How should he? No one was less calculated to win the 'most sweet voices' of borough electors. ...

In 1871 Mr and Mrs Trollope determined to pay a visit to their eldest (*sic*) son, who had settled on a sheep-farm in Australia.[5] As they meant to be absent not less than a year and a half, and as the connection with the Post Office – one of the motives for his residence in the eastern district – had now ceased, and he was preparing to give up hunting altogether, it was determined to sell the house at Waltham, and migrate to London. This wrench from many pleasant old associations was not effected without 'many tears'. When he returned to England, after visiting New Zealand and the Australian colonies (having, of course, written a book upon Australia, and a novel on board ship on his way home), he took up his residence for some years in Montagu Square, where he entered again with zest into London society, and amused many of his leisure hours in arranging and cataloguing with some care his not inconsiderable library of books, in which he took increasing delight. It might have been thought that the unhappy association of his school days would have left little taste for Greek or Latin literature; but it was not so. The study of Greek he never seriously resumed; but he read through, with an amount of industry really wonderful, when we remember how very limited were his leisure hours, almost the whole of the Latin authors. One result of this was his volunteering to take in hand *Caesar's Commentaries* for the series of *Ancient Classics for English Readers*, issued under the editorship of the Revd W. Lucas Collins – one of those chance literary acquaintanceships which ripened, as he says, into a warm friendship, though made late in life. A proof of the many-sided geniality of the man was that he had friends in all professions, and moving in various spheres of life: and few who were drawn into immediate contact with him failed to prize his affection. The little volume on 'Caesar' was a labour of love in a double sense: the MS was given as a birthday present to the late editor of this Magazine

– another of those many friends first made in the way of business, but who soon became personally endeared to him in a degree which was fully reciprocated. The corrected proof was accompanied by a brief note, from which we are allowed here to quote. 'I think the 1st of June is your birthday; at any rate, we will make it so for this year, and you will accept this as a little present.'[6] He was continually doing such kindly acts, often in a manner that had all the gentleness of a woman; and only those who knew him well were aware how much of this there was in his nature underlying a somewhat rough outside. One friend who, in temporary ill health, was thrown upon the doubtful cookery of London lodgings, well remembers how he would look in continually, on his way to his club, for a few minutes' pleasant chat, carrying in his hand a pheasant, or some such little delicacy as might tempt an invalid's appetite. But such instances of thoughtful kindness live in the memories of many, and this is not the place to dwell upon them. The same love of Latin literature which produced the *Caesar* led him to publish, in 1880, a *Life of Cicero*, for whom he had an enthusiastic admiration. The book is pleasantly written; but it must be again said that when he was tempted to desert fiction for history, he did not show himself at his best.

This autobiographical record was finished (we are told in the preface) in April 1876: but the list of his published works given by himself in the last chapter includes *John Caldigate*, published in 1879. The following year he gave up his London residence, and retired to a pretty house, built in somewhat rambling fashion by a French emigrant in 1760, just outside the village of Harting in Sussex. He no longer enjoyed his old robust health, and the demands of London society had become somewhat too severe for him. It had been his habit for many years to vary his London life by a few weeks' ramble in the Black Forest, or in Switzerland; but in the spring of 1881 he made a short tour in Italy with Mrs Trollope and some friends, paying a visit to his brother at Rome. Though at times his old buoyant spirits made a stout fight against bodily infirmity, he was then far from well, and knew and confessed it. He had also entered into business relations – not necessary here to particularise – which worried and disgusted him: for such matters he had, as he confesses, neither taste nor aptitude.[7] Indeed it was remarkable that one who knew the world so thoroughly – who could write such a book as *The Way We Live Now*, which he admits to be over-coloured, and which is to us the least agreeable of all his novels – should have been himself the most trustful and unsuspicious of men. The fact was this, – taking the world as a whole, he knew that meanness, and baseness, and greed of all kinds were rampant in it; but in the case of a private friend, – one might almost say in any individual case with which he had to deal, – he could not believe that the man would be guilty of such things. His loyalty to his friends was so perfect that it tended sometimes, in his energetic nature, to make him prejudiced and unjust. A slight of himself he could readily forgive; but a slight to a relative or near friend was in his eyes the unpardonable sin.

The next year he paid two visits to Ireland, and on his return from the first of these he seemed the better for the change. He always retained a strong interest in the country, and the news of the Phoenix Park massacre affected him very strongly. It had been his constant prayer that he might not survive his powers of work, without which, he says in the closing chapter – 'there can be no joy in this world'. And it was at this time that he conceived the idea embodied in that curious story *The Fixed Period*, which first saw light in the pages of 'Maga'.[8] The law of his imaginary republic of Britannula was to provide that 'men should arrange for their own departure, so as to fall into no senile weakness, no slippered selfishness, no ugly whinings of undefined want, before they shall go hence and be no more thought of'. In their sixty-seventh year they were to be 'deposited' in a kind of college, and after the interval of the twelvemonth be put to a painless death. When an intimate friend once ventured to refer to this Utopian euthanasia as a somewhat grim jest, he stopped suddenly in his walk and, grasping the speaker's arm in his energetic fashion, exclaimed: 'It's all true – I *mean* every word of it.' He was fond of quoting, in the way of preference of a speedy to a lingering death, Lady Macbeth's words –

> Stand not upon the order of your going,
> But go at once.

One of his shorter stories – *Dr Wortle's School* – was written in a country rectory-house, which had been lent him by a friend for three weeks of the summer holidays. He is understood to have expressed a wish, which his son has duly respected, that his correspondence should not be published. But a few characteristic

lines, written by him on this occasion, may be quoted without
violating the spirit of his injunction:

> That I, who have belittled so many clergymen, should ever
> come to live in a parsonage! There will be a heaping of hot coals!
> You may be sure that I will endeavour to behave myself
> accordingly, so that no scandal shall fall upon the parish. If the
> bishop should come that way, I will treat him as well as e'er a
> parson in the diocese. Shall I be required to preach, as
> belonging to the rectory? I shall be quite disposed to give
> everyone my blessing. ... Ought I to affect dark garments? Say
> the word, and I will supply myself with a high waistcoat. Will it
> be right to be quite genial with the curate, or ought I to
> patronise a little? If there be dissenters, shall I frown on them,
> or smile blandly? If a tithe pig be brought, shall I eat him? If
> they take to address me as 'the Rural Anthony', will it be all
> right?[9]

He loved his profession. 'There is perhaps no career in life', he
says, 'so charming as that of a man of letters.'

NOTES

1. See *Auto.*, xiii for accounts of Thackeray and Trollope.
2. These tributes are in the *Auto.*, viii.
3. Compare the memories of Waltham by Anne Thackeray and the Pollocks
(pp. 87–8, 90–1 above).
4. These comments and the whole sad story of his parliamentary bid may be
found in *Auto.*, xvi. Compare the comments in *Dr Thorne*: 'To be or not to be a
Member of the British Parliament is a question of very considerable moment in a
man's mind.' He briefly reviews the drawbacks before concluding 'the prize is
one very well worth the price paid for it' (ch. xvii). Likewise, before the portals of
the House of Commons, he confesses in *Can You Forgive Her?* 'It is the only gate
before which I have ever stood filled with envy, – sorrowing to think that my
steps might never pass under it. ... It is the highest and most legitimate pride of
an Englishman to have the letters MP written after his name' (ch. xlv).
5. Their younger son, Frederick James Anthony, who emigrated to Australia
in 1865 at the age of eighteen.
6. 'It is a dear little book to me', said Trollope (*Letters*, i, 517), which is why
one unkind comment so wounded him. See *Auto.*, xviii. Blackwood
replied: 'It affects me as a great personal compliment & mark of regard never to be
forgotten' (*Letters*, i, 517–18). Collins wrote to Blackwood in Apr 1870 that he
had written encouragingly to Trollope: 'I have pointed out, as modestly as I

knew how, some few points where I think he might improve it, but mere trifles' (*Letters*, I, 506).

7. A reference to his joining the Board of Chapman & Hall.

8. *Blackwood's*, Oct 1881 to Mar 1882.

9. His working diary for *Dr Wortle's School* shows 'Mr & Mrs Peacocke' 8 Apr to 29 Apr 1879 [Bodleian MS Don C 10]. The lines Collins quotes are in *Letters*, II, 822–3.

A Thorough Englishman

MABEL E. WOTTON AND VISCOUNT BRYCE

(1) from *Word Portraits of Famous Writers*, ed. Mabel E. Wotton (1887) pp. 313–16. This is an account drawing upon recollections by an unnamed friend in 1873. An acknowledgement to Henry Merivale Trollope, George Augustus Sala and Frederic Chapman favours authenticity. The detail about the silk handkerchief being gnawed is corroborated by another account (see p. 62 above), and others testified to the impression of height. Like most tributes this centres upon the novelist's representative Englishness; (2) from James Bryce, *Studies in Contemporary Biography* (1903) pp. 118–23, 124–7, 271. To the bluff, hearty, forthrightness that belonged to the English, Bryce adds the essential characterstic of common-sense down-to-earth ordinariness and makes a virtue out of it. Bryce, who knew the political arena well, makes the rather surprising observation that Trollope might have succeeded in Parliament. James Bryce (1838–1922), jurist, historian, politician, served as Chancellor of the Duchy of Lancaster, 1892, and President of the Board of Trade, 1894. Membership of the Alpine Club after 1879 certainly brought him into contact with those who knew Trollope. He wrote classic studies, *The American Commonwealth* (1888) and *Modern Democracy* (1921). See also his obituary notice on Trollope in the *Nation*, XXXVI, 914 (4 Jan 1883) 10.

(1)   [The recollection is dated 1873.] I remember a man hitting off a very good description of Trollope's manner, by remarking that 'he came in at the door like a frantic windmill'. The bell would peal, the knocker begin thundering, the door be burst open and the next minute the house be filled by the big resonant voice enquiring who was at home. I should say he had naturally a sweet voice, which through eagerness he had spoilt by holloing. He was a big man, and the most noticeable thing about his dress was a black handkerchief which he wore tied *twice* round his

neck. A trick of his was to put the end of a silk pocket-handkerchief in his mouth and to keep gnawing at it – often biting it into holes in the excess of his energy; and a favourite attitude was to stand with his thumbs tucked into the armholes of his waistcoat. He was a full-coloured man, and joking and playful when at his ease. Unless with his intimates he rarely laughed, but he had a funny way of putting things and was usually voted good company.

Trollope said his height was five feet ten, but most people would have thought him taller. He was a stout man, large of limb and always held himself upright without effort. His manner was bluff, hearty and genial, and he possessed to the full the great charm of giving his undivided attention to the matter in hand. He was always enthusiastic and energetic in whatever he did. He was of an eager disposition, and doing nothing was pain to him. In early manhood he became bald; in his latter life his full and bushy beard naturally grew to be grey. He had thick eyebrows, and his open nostrils gave a look of determination to his strong capable face. His eyes were greyish-blue, but he was rarely seen without spectacles, though of late years he used to take them off whenever he was reading. From a boy he had always been short-sighted.

Standing with his back to the fire, with his hands clasped behind him and his feet planted somewhat apart, the appearance of Anthony Trollope, as I recall him now, was that of a thorough Englishman in a thoroughly English attitude. He was then, perhaps, nearing sixty, and had far more the look of a country gentleman than a man of letters. Tall, broad-shouldered and dressed in a careless though not slovenly fashion, it seemed more fitting that he should break into a vivid description of the latest run with the hounds than launch into book-talk. Either subject, however, and for the matter of that I might add *any* subject, was attacked by him with equal energy. In writing of this man, this, indeed, is the chief impression I recall – his energy, his thoroughness. While he talked to me, I and my interests might have been the only things for which he cared; and any passing topic of conversation was, for the moment, the one and absorbing topic of the world. Being short-sighted, he had a habit of peering through his glasses which contracted his brows and gave him the apperance of a perpetual frown, and, indeed, his expression when in repose was decidedly severe. This, however, vanished when he spoke. He talked well, and had generally a great deal to say; but his talk was disjointed, and he but rarely laughed. In manner he was brusque, and one of his most striking peculiarities was his voice, which was of an extraordinarily large compass.

(2)   Personally, Anthony Trollope was a bluff, genial, hearty, vigorous man, typically English in his face, his ideas, his tastes. His large eyes, which looked larger behind his large spectacles, were full of good-humoured life and force; and though he was neither witty nor brilliant in conversation, he was what is called very good company, having travelled widely, known all sorts of people, and formed views, usually positive views, on all subjects of the day, views which he was prompt to declare and maintain. There was not much novelty in them – you were disappointed not to find so clever a writer more original – but they were worth listening to for their solid common sense, tending rather to commonplace sense, and you enjoyed the ardour with which he threw himself into a discussion. Though boisterous and insistent in his talk, he was free from assumption or conceit, and gave the impression of liking the world he lived in, and being satisfied with his own place in it. ...

[Bryce notes his regular work habits disciplined by Post Office routine.] He turned his Civil Service experiences to account in some of his stories, giving faithful and characteristic sketches, in *The Three Clerks* and *The Small House at Allington*, of different types of government officials, a class which is much more of a class in England than it is in America, though less of a class than it is in Germany or France. His favourite amusement was hunting, as readers of his novels know, and until his latest years he might have been seen, though a heavy weight, following the hounds in Essex once or twice a week. ...

Like most of his literary contemporaries he was a politician, and indeed a pretty keen one. He once contested in the Liberal interest – in those days literary men were mostly Liberals – the borough of Beverley in Yorkshire, a corrupt little place, where bribery proved too strong for him. It was thereafter disfranchised as a punishment for its misdeeds; and his costly experiences doubtless suggested the clever electioneering sketches in the story of *Ralph the Heir*. ... Trollope showed his continued interest in public affairs on the platform at the great meeting in St James's Hall in December 1876, which was the beginning of a vehement party struggle over the Eastern Question that only ended at the

General Election of 1880.[1] He was a direct and forcible speaker, who would have made his way had he entered Parliament. But as he had no practical experience of politics either in the House of Commons or as a working member of a party organisation in a city where contests are keen, the pictures of political life which are so frequent in his later tales have not much flavour in reality.

He was fond of travel, and between 1862 and 1880 visited the United States, the West Indies, Australia and New Zealand and South Africa, about all of which he wrote books which, if hardly of permanent value, were fresh, vigorous and eminently readable, conveying a definite and generally correct impression of the more obvious social and economic phenomena he found then existing. His account of the United States, for instance, is excellent, and did something to make the Americans forgive the asperity with which his mother had described her experiences there many years before. Trollope's travel sketches are as much superior in truthfulness to Froude's descriptions of the same regions as they are inferior in the allurements of style. ...

[A comment follows on fictional categories naming Trollope's as novels of manners.] But the conspicuous merit of Trollope's novels, in the eyes of his own countrymen, is their value as pictures of contemporary manners. Here he may claim to have been surpassed by no writer of his own generation. Dickens, with all his great and splendid gifts, did not describe the society he lived in. His personages were too unusual and peculiar to speak and act and think like the ordinary men and women of the nineteenth century; nor would a foreigner, however much he might enjoy the exuberant humour and dramatic power with which they are presented, learn from them much about the ways and habits of the average Englishman. ...

[Bryce goes on to praise Trollope for evoking ordinary life among the English upper middle class.] People have often compared the personal impressions which eminent writers make on those who talk to them with the impressions previously derived from their works. Thomas Carlyle and Robert Browning used to be taken as two instances representing opposite extremes. Carlyle always talked in character: had there been phonographs in his days, the phonographed 'record' might have been printed as part of one of his books. Browning, on the other hand, seemed unlike what his poems had made a reader expect: it was only after a long tête à tête with him that the poet whose mind had been learned through his works stood revealed. Trollope at first caused a similar though less marked surprise. This bluff burly man did not seem the kind of person who would trace with a delicate touch the sunlight sparkling on, or a gust of temper ruffling, the surface of a youthful soul in love. Upon further knowledge one perceived that the features of Trollope's talent, facile invention, quick observation and a strong common-sense view of things, with little originality or intensity, were really the dominant features of his character as expressed in talk. Still, though the man was more of a piece with his books than he had seemed, one could never quite recognise in him the delineator of Lily Dale. ...

NOTE

1. British foreign policy was greatly occupied with the Eastern Question from 1875 and throughout 1876 when popular uprisings in Bulgaria were put down by the Turks with ruthless severity. Lord Shaftesbury presided at a meeting in July 1876 condemning the 'Bulgarian Atrocities'. Other meetings followed, including this one at St James's Hall on 7 Dec 1876. Trollope's contribution went down well according to report: 'Mr Anthony Trollope spoke of the splendid chance we gave Turkey by the Crimean War, but England would not, he said, repeat the experiment. (*Cheers*) The Turk was incurable, because he did not see the difference between good and evil as we saw it; to him tyranny, cruelty and oppression were absolutely good. He was the worst citizen in the world, because arms were his glory, and he had no glory except in arms. He must be made to live in Europe under other laws, and to conform to other customs than his own (*Hear, hear*)' (*Pall Mall Gazette* (8 Dec 1876) 8).

Lampoon, Satire and Verse Tribute

HENRY O'NEIL AND OTHERS

A man's fame may often be measured by the parodies, jokes and cartoons published at his expense. Trollope was many times publicised in this way in the last decade or so of his life. The best known cartoon is by 'Spy' (Sir Leslie Ward) (see item 4 below). Other cartoons included Frederick Waddy's in *Once a Week*, IX (1 June 1872) 499; Trollope was cartooned astride a train engine rushing through Australia by the Melbourne *Punch* in Aug 1871, reproduced by C. P. Snow, *Trollope* (1975) p. 141. Another cartoon appeared in the *Observer* (S. Africa) 13 Sep 1877 as frontispiece to Trollope's *South Africa*, ed. J. H. Davidson (Cape Town, 1973). Trollope was the subject of Linley Sambourne's 'Punch's Fancy Portraits No. 17', *Punch* LXXX (5 Feb 1881). *Punch* also ran a parody, 'The Beadle or the Latest Chronicle of Small-Beerjester by Anthony Dollop' between 5 June and 16 Oct 1880. Swinburne, characteristically, produced for his circle his own obscene version of a Barsetshire tale (see *The Swinburne Letters*, ed. Cecil Lang (New Haven, Conn., 1959) II, 87, 108, 141). Trollope was also satirised by the Australian author Thomas Alexander Browne (1826–1915) who wrote under the pen-name 'Rolf Boldrewood'. In *The Miner's Right*, serialised in *Australian Town and Country Journal* (Jan–Dec 1880), a character called 'Anthony Towers' is feted at a déjeuner: 'the old Turk gratefully acknowledged it in his book on Australia by a faint allusion and a statement that the cookery was better than the speeches' (ch. xli). Browne, as Police Magistrate at Gulgong, New South Wales, had presided at a lunch in the novelist's honour in Oct 1871. The following selection includes a vigorous dialogue by Trollope's old friend Henry O'Neil; this and the initial two items are reproduced for the first time. (1) from Cecil Hay, *The Club and Dining Room* (1870) I, 236–7; (2) from Mowbray Morris, 'Anthony Trollope', *Graphic*, XXVI (30 Dec 1882) 719; (3) Henry O'Neil, *Satirical Dialogues* (1870). Henry Nelson O'Neil (1817–80), ARA, illustrator of Milton's poems; his 'Lectures on Painting' were delivered at the Royal Academy, 1866; author of *Modern Art in England and France* (1869). O'Neil painted the portrait of Trollope now in the Garrick Club smoking room. Trollope wrote O'Neil's obituary in *The Times* (15 Mar 1880) 6; (4) from Sir Leslie Ward, *Forty Years of 'Spy'* (1915) pp. 104–5. Leslie Ward (1851–1922), portrait painter and caricaturist for *Vanity Fair*, 1873–1909; (5) from 'Men of the Day No. LX Anthony Trollope', *Vanity Fair*, IX (5 Apr 1873) 111. The article is signed 'Jehu Junior', pseudonym for T. G. Bowles, proprietor and editor. See L. E. Naylor, *The Irrepressible Victorian: The Story of Thomas Gibson Bowles* (1965).

(1)   [The item is headed 'Literary Clubs – the Garrick'.] We turn away, and as we are leaving the apartment we suddenly confront Mr Grizzly, the novelist, who has just come in to order his dinner two hours hence – pleasantest of romance writers, and gruffest and roughest of conversationalists. Mr Grizzly, so far both as money and fame go, is eminently one of the most successful men of the day. His books bring in immense sums, and his productive powers are unprecedentedly great. If there is any author in town who has reason to speak well of his profession, it is assuredly Mr Grizzly. And yet if you lounge into the smoking room three or four hours hence, you will find him occupied in conversation with a select circle of listeners, strenuously and

almost malignantly decrying the novelist's 'trade' – that is the
word which Mr Grizzly uses.[1] Mr Grizzly maintains that
anybody can write a novel who chooses to try. He has a son he will
tell you, and he means to bring him up in his own calling. How
will he set about it? Well, he will call him into his study every
morning at 7.30 a.m., give him the rough sketch of a plot, pens,
paper and ink, and tell him that he is not to stir for breakfast till he
has completed so much manuscript to his, Mr Grizzly's,
satisfaction. It only remains to see whether the experiment is
successful. But Mr Grizzly is rather fond of talking in this manner,
simply with an eye to effect, and as his friends will tell you, it is
only now that he has become infected with the *cacoethes* of politics,
that he finds it convenient to decry literature.

(2)   He was not wont, as many others use,
        The noble life of Letters to abuse;
        Its darker ways and works he did not choose.[2]

        Nor his the idle tortures of unrest,
        Blind doubts and fears that haunt the unhealthy breast;
        Riddles that ne'er have been, nor shall be guessed.

        Not on such themes his fancy loved to brood;
        He looked on life, and saw that it was good
        Or bad, according to the gazer's mood. ...

        What though the man were rugged to the view
        And blunt of speech; no one who knew him knew
        A soul more gentle, generous, and true.

        The world can show us many an ampler page,
        Records of deeper grief and nobler rage,
        Of loftier thoughts from poet and from sage.

        But eyes now bright shall wax with searching blind,
        Ere they may hope another friend to find,
        In hand more steadfast, and in heart more kind.

(3)   [The satire has a dedication to Anthony Trollope. The first
dialogue is between an Author and a Painter, the second between
a Philosopher and a Man of the World, the third between a
Liberal and a Conservative. It is the first which gives a fair

impression of Trollope's views and manner. Topics range over
marriage and simple life, the merits of town and country life, and
painting versus literature. The Painter bemoaning single life is
offered a variety of alternatives; marry a widow or an old maid
with a fortune, each of which he rejects to the Author's irritation:]

> I know a thing more needful, and 'tis this –
> A willing heart; with that you're free to wed
> At any time of life, so you be led,
> In making choice, rather by common sense
> Than by those feelings which most influence
> The heart in its selection, when youth throws
> Over the future its 'couleur de rose'.

[Next they debate town and country, the Painter exclaiming
against 'stuccoed villas without end', the unhealthy atmosphere,
and the noise:]

> And when I call to mind the constant noise
> Of German bands and organs ...[3]

[When do you rise? asks the Painter. 'At five' the Author replies,
which is when the Painter goes to bed. I write after midnight, he
continues, the fittest time for contemplation, when do you?]

> At sunrise. Even were your judgment right,
> There's a long interval 'twixt day and night;
> Why not employ the evening, you old Turk,
> At what you're pleased to call your mental work?

[The Author lectures the Painter on the dangers of self-indulg-
ence; one must be dedicated and,]

> > looking neither to the left or right,
> March straightway to the goal.

[He presses the point about early rising:]

> If life be such a blessing, then to lie
> In bed till noon, however great the pleasure,
> Is not the way to profit by the treasure.
> I have no wish to prate about myself,
> But I have works enough, piled on the shelf,
> To last three years at least, and strive to keep
> Thus ever in advance. Were I to sleep
> Till ten, as you do, where should I be now?

[Late nights and laziness having been roundly condemned, the debate turns to the comparative merits of Art and Letters. The Painter is aggrieved that:]

> What takes a painter six months to express
> A bard performs in six days, more or less

[and speciously he argues that art has its loftier aims. Next he inveighs against critics as to which the Author responds:]

> What art without its drawbacks? I don't paint,
> But think you're scarcely just in your complaint.
> To spurn one's trade is only fit for fools, –
> Good workmen never quarrel with their tools.
> Think you my *métier* is without its evils?
> Have we not publishers, and printers' devils,
> Who, by the malice of a fiend possest,
> Won't leave their wretched slaves a moment's rest?
> As for your scorn of critics – How, my friend,
> To dwell on such things can you condescend?
> It ill becomes a painter or a poet,
> However fierce and just his wrath, to show it.
> When you have gained the public ear or eye,
> Such literary wasps you should defy,
> Nor let your peace be ruffled by their sting;
> For as to crushing them to death, the thing
> Is quite impossible, nor wisely meant.
> Critics, like wasps, were sent with good intent, –
> Aesthetic scavengers, 'tis theirs to sweep
> The road of Art, and clean its pathways keep.

Painter

> And yet, what's worthy I have oft seen made
> Food for their broom.

Author

> Good God! why that's their trade.
> Nor is their conduct, after all, amazing.
> Think you that they could live by simply praising
> What everybody hates? Without some bouncing,
> How 'mongst the minnows could they sport as Triton,
> Or hide their ignorance of what they write on?

I don't uphold their calling: spite of fudge
On Art – a painter is the fittest judge;
For if we follow what the critics say, –
Not one, but all, – we're sure to go astray.

Painter

I could forgive their speech, howe'er uncouth,
Would they but condescend to speak the truth;
Nor let their hate or friendship interfere
To make their judgments more or less severe

Author

If you dislike their insolence and freedom,
Surely there's no necessity to read 'em.

[The dialogue comes to an end with the Painter's last question; one can live in town, manage without a wife, forget the critics, but what about the need for money and yearning for fame? The Author first replies curtly, 'The remedy is labour', but then he elaborates with truly Trollopian commonsense:]

Time holds, o'er human fame, a sovereign sway;
Years pass, and where's the idol of today?
As for the present, earnest labour sure
Can yet an ample competence secure,
To serve all present and all future need;
Beyond that point, desire for wealth is greed –
A vice which never can be satisfied
Without some loss of self-respect and pride.

[The last exchange, a subject dear to Trollope's heart, concerns the avoidance of extremes:]

If fame thou dearly prizest,
A middle course, believe me, is the wisest.

Painter

You reason sweetly, let me shake your fist
And then you'll join me in a game of whist.

Author

I'm well content; but promise at eleven
You'll go to bed, and rise again at seven.

Painter
I'll promise nothing. Promises are risky
At all times. Waiter! Potass and Scotch Whiskey![4]

(4)   With Anthony Trollope I was more fortunate, for my kind friend, Mr James Virtue, the publisher, invited me to his charming house at Walton, where I was able to observe the novelist by making a close study of him from various points of view. We went a delightful walk together to St George's Hill, and while Trollope admired the scenery, I noted the beauties of Nature in another way, committed those mental observations to my mental notebook, and came home to what fun I could get out of them.

The famous novelist was not in the least conscious of my eagle eye, and imagining I should let him down gently, Mr Virtue did not warn him, luckily for me, for I had an excellent subject. When the caricature appeared, Trollope was furious, and naturally did not hesitate to give poor Virtue a 'blowing-up', whereupon I in turn received a stiff letter from Mr Virtue. It surprised me not a little, that he should take the matter so seriously; but for a time Mr Virtue was decidedly 'short' with me. Luckily, however, his displeasure only lasted a short period, for he was too genuinely amiable a man to let such a thing make a permanent difference to his ordinary behaviour.

I had portrayed Trollope's strange thumb, which he held erect whilst smoking, with his cigar between his first and second fingers, his pockets standing out on either side of his trousers, his coat buttoned once and then parting over a small but comfortable corporation.[5] The letterpress on this occasion I consider was far more severe than my caricature, for I had not praised the books with faint damns [what took place between Virtue and the novelist would have made an interesting 'Interview and Recollection', but there is no record of the encounter. Unflattering though the drawing may have been – in Pope Hennessy's words 'an affronted Santa Claus who has just lost his reindeer' (*Anthony Trollope*, p. 325) – Ward has some justification for pointing at the more mean-spirited commentary (see item 5). Business relations between Trollope and Virtue resumed after publication of the offensive cartoon, with Virtue printing *Lady Anna*, *South Africa* and *How the 'Mastiffs' Went to Iceland*. Trollope left a gracious tribute to Virtue's 'perpetual good humour' (*Auto.*, xv).]

(5)   [Text accompanying the 'Spy' cartoon:] A novelist who
would be generally read in this country and in these days should
write books with the ordinary young lady always in his mind,
books sufficiently faithful to the external aspects of English life to
interest those who see nothing but its external aspects, and yet
sufficiently removed from all the depths of humanity to conciliate
all respected parents. Mr Anthony Trollope has had by far the
greatest success in doing this. He is a student and delineator of
costume rather than of humanity. He does not, as George Eliot
does, pry into the great problems of life or attempt to show the
mournful irony of fate. He is not a deep thinker, but he is an acute
observer, and with the knack of divining what most impresses the
commonplace people who most delight in novels. He is a correct
painter of the small things of our small modern English life so far
as it presents itself to the eye – deeper than this he does not go –
and he is never guilty of a solecism in point of social forms. His
gentlemen and ladies are like gentlemen and ladies, and their
existence is the existence of people of decent manners. His
language is not strong or nervous, but it ripples smoothly along in
a well-bred monotone. For Anthony Trollope has lived a quiet
life, and writes like a quiet man. He is fifty-eight years of age, and
for the greater part of that time has occupied one of those snug
berths under government which are more favourable to good
digestion and a placid interest in the struggles mental, moral and
physical of unprovided-for men and women than calculated to
develop a great power of grasping the inner meaning of those
struggles. He began to write just as he was leaving his first youth
behind him; he has produced since a large number of novels of an
invariably unobjectionable and a variably interesting kind; and
he shows no sign of ceasing to produce them. He has visited
various foreign countries for official purposes; he is, if with an
undoubted consciousness of his own merits, good-natured and
genial as becomes a successful man; and he is very fond of
hunting. His manners are a little rough, as is his voice, but he is
nevertheless extremely popular among his personal friends, while
by his readers he is looked upon with the gratitude due to one who
has for so many years amused without ever shocking them.
Whether his reputation would not last longer if he had shocked
them occasionally is a question which the booksellers of future
generations will be able to answer.

NOTES

1. In rather more agreeable fashion Trollope portrays club types in 'Whist at Our Club', *Blackwood's*, 121 (May 1877) 597–604.

2. Another poetic effusion, 'To Anthony Trollope; on Re-reading his Barsetshire Novels', by Charles Graves, appeared in the *Literary Digest*, LI (14 Aug 1915) 310. It began:

> Good chronicler of Barset, weaver of genial yarns,
> Homely and unaffected as the verse of the Dorset Barnes,
> When the outlook is depressing, when journals bleat and scare,
> I turn to your kindly pages and find oblivion there.

3. A prophetic note. The noise of a German band playing under the window of his hotel room was said to have contributed to Trollope's fatal stroke.

4. High spirits were evidently apparent when O'Neil hosted a party in Mar 1877 at which Trollope and Sir Henry James had a furious debate: 'Trollope raging and roaring with immense vehemence against the system of cross examination as practised and James defending it with charming calmness and good-nature' (MS Nat. Libr. of Scotland, cited *Letters*, II, 950).

5. Trollope was a devoted smoker, as has been noted, and liked to share cigars among his friends. At times the price bothered him; in Dec 1872 he threatened to take up a pipe: 'If I can not smoke a small cigar under eight pence, I will not smoke them at all' (*Letters*, II, 573). He smoked about four cigars a day, later cut down to three. To A. Arthur Reade, seeking information for a book *Study and Stimulants* (1883), he wrote in Feb 1882: 'I have been a smoker nearly all my life. Five years ago I found it certainly was hurting me, causing my hand to shake, and producing somnolency. I gave it up for two years' (*Letters*, II, 946).

Australia and New Zealand

GORDON TROLLOPE AND OTHERS

Trollope visited Australia twice, from May 1871 to Dec 1872, and from Mar to Oct 1875. The first journey got off to a bad start with the ship delayed for 18 days. Once aboard Trollope had his writing desk set up, however, and in usual fashion began work on the current novel, *Lady Anna* (finished before the boat reached Melbourne, published 1874). While exploring he produced eleven letters for the *Daily Telegraph* (published Dec 1871 to Dec 1872) and the required travel book, *Australia and New Zealand* (1873). Wherever he went receptions were organised, and although regretting his winter hunting at home he was given some sport by his hosts in Melbourne. He looked up many old friends and made new ones, particularly the educator and author George William Rusden (1819–1903). He stayed with his sheep-farmer son, Fred, in Oct to Nov 1871 and again in June 1872. Some of the travelling, particularly in New Zealand, was difficult; once more Rose showed her mettle, for she accompanied him on several long journeys in all weathers. His second visit, without Rose, was for that reason less agreeable, but travelling via Ceylon he was guest of his old friend, Sir William Gregory, now the Governor. Again his writing desk was in demand, and he worked at *Is He Popenjoy?* (1878), finishing, true to form, as he landed in Melbourne. He contributed twenty letters to the *Liverpool Mercury*, and for good measure completed *The American Senator* (1877) on the way home. He was to create two novels out of his Australian experiences: *Harry Heathcote of Gangoil* (1874) and *John Caldigate* (1879). Publication of *Australia and New Zealand* (1873) caused widespread comment in Australia, notably in the *Melbourne Argus* of 21 June which rallied Trollope for his presumption but concluded: 'With all its faults of manner ... the work shows both acuteness of observation, industry in the collection, and method in the arrangement of facts'. See *Australia*, ed. P. D. Edwards and R. B. Joyce (Queensland, 1967) pp. 36–7; Marcie Muir, *Anthony Trollope in Australia* (Adelaide, 1949) pp. 82–92. (1) from Gordon Trollope, 'Trollope in Australia', *Sydney Bulletin* (2 Apr 1930). Gordon Clavering Trollope (1885–1958) was to inherit the Trollope baronetcy, which eventually passed to his elder son, Anthony Owen Clavering Trollope (b. 1917) and 16th baronet; (2) from Muir, *Anthony Trollope in Australia*, pp. 18, 27, 54–5, 64–6, 68–9, 96–7; (3) from *With Anthony Trollope in New Zealand*, ed. A. H. Reed (Dunedin, NZ, 1969) pp. 42–3, 45, 47, 99–101.

(1)   The prime object of his coming was to see his grazier son; but on his first visit he bore a commission from his publisher to write a book about the country.[1] His monumental *Australia and New Zealand* was the result, a book which has been much misquoted, chiefly by those who have never read it. He was paid £1300 for it, yet the publisher made handsome profits out of its success, and it is said to have put up the price of Australian securities in London at the time. It was not written, as often supposed, after a flying visit to the capitals; it was, as he himself tells in his *Autobiography*, 'the result of 15 months' unflagging labour'. He travelled extensively in Australia, making close and careful observation of our conditions, and he spent some considerable time with his son on Mortray station, out of Grenfell (NSW), and thereabout made much of his study of our bush life. The still extant stump of a tree in the garden of the homestead there is a memento of him. He used to sit under the tree's shade in the early mornings making his daily output of literary work before breakfast.

Curiously Trollope seems to have given offence to many Australians, though it is hard to account for the frequent misconception of his attitude towards us. He wrote the country up

far more than he wrote it down, and probably was more
enthusiastic over the natural beauties of the place than anyone
else has been, before or since. But generous as he was in his praise,
he was outspoken in his criticism, and people resented being taken
to task for their boastfulness, or 'blowing', as he called it.[2]
Jealousies were even stronger in those times than they are today,
and he managed to give offence to all sides by misguided
comparisons. His little wife, too, may have helped the misapprehension along. She hated the country, and said many unkind
things about it which probably have been heaped on to his
competent shoulders.[3] ...

[The writer disputes that Trollope said unkind things about the
country.] In any case the uncharitableness of the statement sorts
very ill with the kindliness of the man as we know him in his works
and as I have heard him described by his friends. He was a sincere
lover of beauty, his tastes running chiefly to colour and form. His
chief delight was character, particularly feminine character. His
novels teem with kindly and understanding sketches of his
women, and his book on Australia speaks warmly and appreciatively of the sex out here. His son married an Australian girl, and
Anthony showed her invariable respect and affection. He used to
love to sit and hear her sing, and there are still in existence some of
the lovely ballads of the day which he gave to her. He so much
regretted not having a daughter of his own that he went the length
of adopting a girl into his family. In all, it seems unthinkable that
he should have used such unkind words about women as he is
accused of having done. The story is grotesque.

Beyond this big book he did not introduce Australia much into
his work. *Harry Heathcote of Gangoil* is an exclusively Australian
story, but it is rather poor. The local part of *John Caldigate* is better.
One wonders what he intended with a fragment of a sketch–plot
which the present writer found in the cover pocket of a manifold
writer at Mortray, where Trollope left it behind him.

He left something more material than that there. He sank in the
station as much money as he received for the whole of the
Barchester series of novels.[4]

(2)   [From a report in the *Brisbane Courier*, 16 Sep 1871.] The
tour of that distinguished gentleman, Mr Anthony Trollope, is as
carefully watched and recorded by the Press as a royal progress.

The record would be incomplete without our little bit, which we shall supply because it happens to be good – and not because we are ambitious to be any man's 'Bozzy'. It is nearly a fortnight since Mr Trollope paid Gladstone a flying visit while en route to Rockhampton.[5] Mr Trollope visited that dreary and desolate region yclept the Valley, and actually sat on the Bench at the Court-house, while one Boney, an aborigine, was being tried by Mr Rich for being illegally on the premises of Mr Breslin. We are happy to record that the great author gave evidence of his sanity by retiring before the case was finished, being doubtless tired of it, though he was polite enough to excuse his departure on the ground that he did not want to be left behind by the steamer – another proof that he is anything but a maniac. On board the steamer, he sought a little relief under the poop awning from the heat of the sun, and the mental oppression induced by his visit to the Court-house and stroll through the Valley. Here he was pursued with Latin quotations by a high legal functionary whose intellectual front is always bared to distinguished visitors. He was next beset by a group of villagers, in whose presence the great author hung down his head and carefully poked the deck with his staff of British oak. He listened carefully while a gentleman descanted in unctuous and eloquent measures on the early history of Gladstone, the beauties of its harbour, the interest felt in it by its illustrious godfather. The lying tradition that he (Mr Gladstone) had given a cheque to the church here was paraded for the 999th time, when lo! – the eloquence of the smooth-tongued villager received a check. The great author quietly remarked that 'Mr Gladstone had also given a check to the Church at home.' The steamer's bell rang, and the villagers returned precipitately to the shore, while a stentorian voice admonished the steward to bring soda and brandy. ...

[In New South Wales he was greeted by the *Sydney Punch*, Oct 1871.] As noiselessly as the creatures of your own delightful fancy that have stolen into our hearts for years and made their home there, you have come amongst us, the brave master, the kindly magician, the eloquent teacher. The very city seems nobler when we think that you are walking its streets, and that its citizens may look upon one who has given so much happiness to millions.

[A hunting excursion was the occasion of ribald comment in the *Melbourne Weekly Times*, 1 June 1872.] There is one thing in connection with the hunt that affords me slight, though not malicious satisfaction. Mr A. Trollope was there, and Mr A. Trollope had an opportunity of testing a three-railer. Mr Trollope had, I am informed, been rather depreciatory in his remarks regarding Victorian hunting, and was especially anxious to lead the way *through a gap*. When last seen the distinguished novelist had acquired some experience of Australian soil which he is not likely to be very triumphantly descriptive over.[6] ...

[An incident in Tasmania not recorded by Trollope was cited by the *Cornwall Chronicle*, 12 Feb 1872.] His Excellency the Governor, accompanied by Mr Trollope[7] ... etc. ... paid a visit to Corra Linn on Friday, and had it not been for the prompt action of Mr Rankin, who was driving the carriage and pair, they were in danger of serious injury. In driving down to the bridge one of the horses, a young one, became restive and required a strong pull to hold him in. The reins, rounded ones, broke at a critical moment and the horses were pulled to the right to a low part of the road. Mr Rankin called out that the reins were broken and the Governor and the other gentleman leapt out simultaneously. His Excellency and the Master of Blantyre rushed to the horses' heads and secured them, then with the assistance of Mr Chichester and Mr Trollope, the wheels of the carriage were scotched by stones, the horses were taken out, and the reins underwent temporary repair. ...

[An account of Trollope at a reception in Perth, source unnamed.] Trollope was the guest of Mr E. Landor and of Mr Lochee, staying with Mr Landor to write with greater ease.[8] At Mr Lochee's house he was the guest at a special evening reception at which Miss Lochee made her debut.[9] To this formal party Anthony Trollope accompanied Mr E. Landor and his family. He insisted upon wearing ordinary day garb, with a blue shirt. He firmly refused to don the orthodox garb, and brushed aside abruptly all Mr Landor's suggestions that he should wear evening dress. The great author's entry caused as much sensation as if a political leader of extreme radical beliefs were to be officially invited to dine with the Governor-General today, and were to arrive in a red shirt and red tie, as embellishments to his morning coat. Indeed the red shirt would probably be forgotten by Mr Lochee's friends. At supper, sitting next to Miss Lochee,

Trollope, whose gestures were awkward, upset a cup of coffee over the young lady's new white silk grenadine frock.

(3) [Trollope's visit to Invercargill, New Zealand, was recalled by Miss Edith Hodgkinson, daughter of a well-known citizen.] I was twelve years old when Anthony Trollope visited Invercargill, and his charm had already won me, for at ten I had read *Framley Parsonage* and part of *The Small House at Allington* in the *Cornhill*.[10] ... He was the guest, if I mistake not, of the Revd Pybus Tanner, First Anglican minister of Invercargill, a man as saintly as Trollope's Mr Crawley, and I should say, far easier to live with.

A strange contrast – the clergyman, and the chronicler of clergymen – the one of barely medium height ... with aquiline nose and large, wistful eyes, more soul than body; and the stalwart man of letters, whose tread shook the church, as he marched down the aisle to take his seat near the pulpit. In Mr Allen's article Trollope disclaims being either an Antinous or a six-footer.[11] Well, if he was not actually six feet in height, he succeeded in looking much more. A burly, upstanding man with a massive head, made more leonine by the whiskers and beard of old Victorian days; these, with his hair greying, an English complexion as of one living much in the open, and kindly blue–grey eyes to match. Such was Anthony Trollope as I saw him those brief moments. And I can imagine his voice, hearty and genial, to match his aspect.

[Trollope's arrival at Lawrence was covered by the *Tuapeka Times* of 15 Aug 1872.] Mr Anthony Trollope, with Mrs Trollope, and Mr W. H. Pearson, arrived at Lawrence shortly after one o'clock p.m. on Monday last.[12] They had an exceedingly rough passage between Roxburgh and Tuapeka. Mr Pearson must have been able to furnish Mr Trollope with valuable information regarding the goldfields, as he has never before visited them. However, the fact that he has existed in that lively village of Invercargill without losing the possession of his faculties, renders him peculiarly fitted to pilot a stranger through any country under the sun. Mr Trollope, we believe, while in Lawrence visited the Athenaeum, and of course was highly gratified to learn that the inhabitants of this fair corner of the earth read sometimes.[13] ...

[The Trollopes travelled from Lawrence to Milton through a severe snowstorm. E. M. Lovell-Smith gave this version of the

journey.][14] Leaving Lawrence in the coach, the travellers arrived
at a cutting at Waitahuna to find the road blocked with snow.
Pulling up his team, Pope procured some shovels from Edie's farm
nearby and set to work to clear away the snow. Working away
with a will, Anthony Trollope remarked that he was 'more at ease
with a pen than a shovel'. After the snow had been cut to a depth
of a foot or so, the driver led a coachhorse back and forth over it
until it was trampled down enough to allow the coach to proceed.
Further along the road Pope found the snow to be so deep that it
would take a month to melt away, so he decided to take the coach
over the crest of the hill. Upon reaching the top, the horses were
taken out of the coach and placed in charge of the other male
passenger. Then Pope and Trollope proceeded to pull the coach
down-hill by hand; not that it needed much pulling, and guided it
safely to the bottom of the hill. Mrs. Trollope wore a crinoline,
and as she walked down the hillside, her petticoats underneath
became balled up with the soft snow. 'She was an enormous size,
and a wonderful sight to behold', remarked Pope in later years,
when referring to the novelist's trip with his wife.

[An interview reported in the *Wellington Independent*, 17 Sep 1872.]
Shall I try to describe him? He is tall, squarely built, slightly florid
faced, portly in figure, yet singularly light in his step, and with a
buoyancy and springiness reminding one of the free and elastic
gait of Bishop Selwyn. A bright hazel eye looks at his interlocuter
through spectacles, and a pleasant decided kind of voice is
suggestive of being that of a man who has seen for himself, taken in
all surrounding circumstances, weighed them, compared them,
and drawn his conclusions according to the evidence.
  It is surprising how in half-an-hour's conversation you can
discover how much he knows of the state of affairs. I mean social
affairs in New Zealand – those things that affect and more or less
completely guide and dominate the circumstances and condition
of people. He knows the pictures and interiors of middle-class life
here, and status and pay of people's servants, when they have any,
the price of labour, the condition of the working man, the cost of
living, the rate of rents, the general condition and well-being of the
mass of people as exhibited by what he has seen during his brief
but most observant journeyings. ... He and Mrs Trollope are
living at Government House, and I hear he proposes taking a long
ride through different parts of the country if the departure of the
San Francisco mail in October will permit him. Someone

acquainted with the country should be sent as a guide to take him to the Hot Springs, to Lake Taupo, Rotorua, &c.[15]

[During his second visit to Australia Trollope took part in launching the New Guinea Scientific Exhibition and celebrating the Queen's birthday at a military review in Sydney. His departure occasioned warm tribute during a picnic at Warragamba reported by the *Sydney Morning Herald*, 23 Aug 1875.] After the Queen had been toasted the Chief Justice proposed Trollope's health in the following words: 'Gentlemen, we are not, as you are aware, assembled in this beautiful place, in the midst of this inspiring scenery, for the idle purpose of airing our oratory, even if any of us were equal to an occasion such as this unquestionably is. But we are here for the purpose of doing honour to one who occupies a leading place among the most distinguished men of letters of the British Empire. Wherever, gentlemen, throughout the world, our great British tongue is spoken, there our guest, who has done us the honour to accept our hospitality today, is known, admired and loved as the most popular of modern English novelists. On his last visit to us he applied his great powers of observation to the condition and circumstances of these Australian colonies; and although he may have, in the estimation of some, drawn too flattering a picture of our qualities. ... and may have displeased others by his manly outspoken frankness, there can be but one opinion that he produced the very best book on Australia that has ever been published.' (*Loud cheers.*)

NOTES

1. Fred was allowed to go to Australia in 1865 when he was nearly 18, on condition he came back to England at 21 before deciding on permanent settlement there. Fred returned in 1868 and emigrated in the spring of 1869. He bought Mortray, a small sheep station near Grenfell, New South Wales. On 14 Dec 1871 he married Susannah Farrand, daughter of the police magistrate at Forbes. A rather sad letter from Trollope to Millais on his second visit in 1875 records: 'I write for four hours a day, then ride after sheep or chop wood or roam about in the endless forest up to my knees in mud. I eat a great deal of mutton, smoke a great deal of tobacco and drink a moderate amount of brandy and water. At night I read, and before work in the morning I play with my grandchildren, of whom I have two and a third coming. Fred, my son here, is always on horseback and seems to me to have more troubles on his back than any human being I ever came across. I shall be miserable when I leave him

because I do not know how I can look forward to seeing him again without again making this long journey. I do not dislike the journey, or the sea, or the hardship. But I was 60 the other day, and at that age a man has no right to look forward to making many more journeys round the world' (*Letters*, II, 659).

2. On this score his hosts were particularly sensitive. Trollope at any rate felt bound to return to the subject of 'blowing' on his second visit to Australia, pointing out that coals of fire had been heaped on his head in Victoria for daring to suggest to the colonists that they be aware of blowing their own trumpet (*The Tireless Traveller, Twenty Letters to the Liverpool Mercury by Anthony Trollope, 1875*, ed. Bradford Booth (California, 1941) p. 90).

3. At times the going was hard and the itinerary demanding. See *Australia*, ed. Edwards and Joyce, 'Appendix 1, Trollope's Itinerary', pp. 746–56. For Rose it must have been disappointing to have to miss her son's wedding ceremony for the sake of the itinerary.

4. Fred Trollope ran into financial difficulties with his ranching. A prolonged drought and an under-capitalised venture forced him to sell out in 1876 and thereafter he joined the Lands Department where he spent the rest of his working life. His story is traced in Edwards, *Anthony Trollope's Son in Australia*.

5. Of Gladstone, which some favoured as a capital of Queensland, Trollope waxed lyrical: 'From green glades within a quarter of a mile of the wharf one looks down upon a sea lake surrounded by wooded mountains, and feels all the pride of distant desolation and forest silence' (*ANZ*, I, 43–4).

6. This hardly measures up to Trollope's own exuberant account in *ANZ*, II, 291–96. The newspaper report, however, did have the grace to acknowledge 'This meeting will long be remembered for the great number of accidents that took place. All the best hunters in Victoria were out, and several horses, as clever as horses can be, came to grief' (*Australia*, p. 740n).

7. The Governor was Sir Charles Du Cane (1825–89), Tory MP for North Essex, Governor of Tasmania, 1869–74. An expedition to the Chudleigh caves is reported by the Hobart *Mercury*, 12 Feb; it was a rough journey of some sixteen miles described by Trollope (*Australia*, ch. xxxvi).

8. E. W. Landor, Police Magistrate at Perth, Western Australia; a distant cousin of Walter Savage Landor. After his stay Trollope sent Landor's wife an inscribed copy of *The Claverings*. This anecdote, notes Marcie Muir, may have been an embellishment of distant recollection (*Trollope in Australia*, pp. 68–9). Trollope does reflect, however, on being separated from his luggage in New Zealand. 'A hero, but nothing short of a hero, might perhaps sit down comfortably to dinner with the full-dressed aristocracy of a newly visited city in a blue shirt and an old greasy shooting-jacket' (*ANZ*, II, 327).

9. The party seems to have been got up with an eye to lionising Trollope himself by influential citizens. The Chief Justice of New South Wales, Sir James Martin (1820–86), was in the chair. Trollope had sent him a copy of his book on Australia. In his speech Trollope said of his book: 'It is not an accurate book, it is not an exhaustive book; but it is an honest book. It betrays no confidences, I am certain. It wounds no sensibilities; it contains nothing of which I feel ashamed, and I am sure it contains nothing which could give any human being pain' (Muir, *Trollope in Australia*, p. 98).

10. Trollope's visit to New Zealand resulted in a dramatic account of the journey from Invercargill to Wakatip and on to Queenstown and Dunedin in

dead of winter (*ANZ*, ii, xx). He knew they were asking for trouble, but was determined to see the scenery. 'I hate going back, and I made up my mind that if the mud and snow were no worse than British mud or British snow, we would make our way through' (*ANZ*, ii, xx, 325).

11. A reference to C. R. Allen 'A Word for Anthony Trollope', *Otago Daily Times* (23 Jan 1927) cited *With Anthony Trollope in New Zealand*, ed. Reed, p. 42.

12. *En route* to Dunedin the traveller put up at one corrugated-roofed inn and heard the host remark 'So this is Mr Anthony Trollope' to which the hostess assented. The man went on 'he must be a — fool to come travelling in this country in such weather as this' (*ANZ*, ii, 336). W. H. Pearson was Commissioner of Crown Lands.

13. At Lawrence, also known as Tuapeka, Trollope noted, as he had done elsewhere, well-used libraries: 'Carlyle, Macaulay and Dickens are certainly better known to small communities in New Zealand than they are to similar congregations of men and women at home' (*ANZ*, ii, 336–7).

14. E. M. Lovell-Smith, *Old Coaching Days* (Christchurch, NZ, 1931), cited Reed, *With Anthony Trollope*, p. 47. The coachman Tommy Pope was, Trollope said, 'as good a coachman as ever sat upon a box' (*ANZ*, ii, 337). Small wonder Rose Trollope remembered the journey with some disfavour.

15. Trollope did indeed visit hot springs at Rotorua and leaves the continent with a charming picture of himself bathing in the hot pool with three Maori damsels. 'Then I plunged into a cold river which runs into the lake a few yards from the hot spring, and then returned to the hot water amidst the renewed welcomings of the Maori damsels' (*ANZ*, ii, 476).

Cobbler's Wax on the Seat

FREDERIC HARRISON, JOHN MORLEY AND MRS HUMPHRY WARD

(1) from Frederic Harrison, *Studies in Early Victorian Literature* (1895) pp. 201–3, 220–3. Harrison (1831–1923), author and positivist; active in the Working Men's College with F. D. Maurice and Thomas Hughes; contributed widely to periodicals and wrote a life of Ruskin (1902), and studies of *Cromwell* (1888) and *Chatham* (1905). Although he knew Trollope well, his affinities with the more intellectual group round John Morley led him to be somewhat condescending. For all that, his memoir, first published in the *Fortnightly Review*, is affectionate and just; (2) from a review of the *Autobiography* in *Macmillan's Magazine*, xlix (Nov 1883) 53–6, by John Morley and Mrs Humphry Ward, both sympathetic but not really on Trollope's wavelength. Morley (1838–1923) succeeded G. H. Lewes in Jan 1867 as editor of the *Fortnightly Review* and held the post for 15 years; editor of *Pall Mall Gazette*, 1880–3; his considerable literary output included social and

political journalism, and books such as *The Life of Richard Cobden* (1881) and *The Life of Gladstone* (1903); raised to the peerage as Viscount Morley of Blackburn, 1908. Mary Augusta Ward (Mrs Humphry Ward) (1851–1920), journalist, playwright, novelist, contributed regularly to *Macmillan's*, *Quarterly Review* and others; acclaimed for her novel *Robert Elsmere* (1888).

(1)   I knew him well, knew his subjects, and his stage. I have seen him at work at the 'Megatherium Club', chatted with him at the 'Universe', dined with him at George Eliot's and even met him in the hunting-field.[1] I was familiar with the political personages and crises which he describes; and much of the local colouring in which his romances were framed was for years the local colouring that I daily saw around me. Most of the famous writers of whom I have been speaking in this series (with the exception of Charlotte Brontë) I have often seen and heard speak in public and private, but I cannot be said to have known them as friends. But Anthony Trollope I knew well. I knew the world in which he lived, I saw the scenes, the characters, the life he paints, day by day in the same clubs, in the same rooms, under the same conditions as he saw them. To reread some of his best stories, as I have just done, is to me like looking through a photographic album of my acquaintances, companions and familiar reminiscences of some thirty years ago. I can hear the loud voice, the honest laugh, see the keen eyes of our old friend as I turn to the admirable vignette portrait in his posthumous *Autobiography*, and I can almost hear him tell the anecdotes recounted in that pleasant book. ...

Does the present generation know that frank and amusing book –one of the most brisk and manly autobiographies in our language? Of course it is garrulous, egoistical, self-complacent in a way. When a famous writer, at the close of a long career of varied activity, takes up his pen to tell us how he has lived, and how his books were written, and what he has loved, seen, suffered and striven for – it is his business to be garrulous; we want him to talk about himself and to give us such peeps into his own heart and brain as he chooses to unlock. That is what an 'autobiography' means. And never did man do this in a more hearty, manly, good-tempered spirit, with more good sense, with more modest *bonhomie*, with a more genial egoism. He has been an enormous worker; he is proud of his industry. He has fought his way under cruel hardships to wealth and fame: and he is well satisfied with his success. He has had millions of readers; he has been well paid; he has had good friends; he has enjoyed life. He is happy in telling

us how he did it. He does not overrate himself. He believes some of
his work is good: at least it is honest, pure, sound work which has
pleased millions of readers. Much of his work he knows to be poor
stuff, and he says so at once. He makes no pretence to genius; he
does not claim to be a hero; he has no rare qualities – or none but
industry and courage – and he has met with no peculiar sufferings
and no cruel and undeserved rebuffs. He has his own ideas about
literary work – you may think them commonplace, mechanical,
mercenary ideas – but that is a true picture of Anthony Trollope; of
his strong, manly, pure mind, of his clear head, of his average moral
sense: a good fellow, a warm friend, a brave soul, a genial
companion.

With all his artless self-complacency in his own success, Trollope
took a very modest estimate of his own powers. I remember a
characteristic discussion about their modes of writing between
Trollope and George Eliot at a little dinner party in her house.
'Why!' said Anthony, 'I sit down every morning at 5.30 with my
watch on my desk, and for three hours I regularly produce 250
words every quarter of an hour.' George Eliot positively quivered
with horror at the thought – she who could write only when she felt
in the vein, who wrote, rewrote and destroyed her manuscript two
or three times, and as often as not sat at her table without writing at
all. 'There are days and days together', she groaned out, 'when I
cannot write a line.' 'Yes!' said Trollope, 'with imaginative work
like yours that is quite natural; but with my mechanical stuff it's a
sheer matter of industry. It's not the head that does it – it's the
cobbler's wax on the seat and the sticking to my chair!'[2] ...

The relations of London 'Society' to the parliamentary and
ministerial world as described in Trollope's later books are all
treated with entire mastery. It is this thorough knowledge of the
organism of English society which specially distinguishes Trollope. It is a quality in which Thackeray alone is his equal; and
Thackeray himself has drawn no complex social organism with
such consummate completeness as Trollope's Barchester Close. It
is, of course, purely English, locally true to England only. But it is,
as Nathaniel Hawthorne said, 'solid and substantial', 'as real as if it
were a great lump out of the earth', – 'just as English as a beefsteak'.

What makes all that so strange is this, that when he began to
write novels, Trollope had far less experience than have most
cultivated men of cathedral closes, rectories and county families.
He had never been to a college, and till past middle life he never had

access to the higher grades of English society. He never at any time, and certainly not when the Barchester cycle began, had any footing whatever in clerical circles, and but little intimate acquaintance with young ladies of birth and refinement in country homes.[3] He never was much thrown with the young bloods of the army, of the universities, or of Parliament. He rarely consorted with dukes or county magnates and he never lived in the centre of the political world. Yet this rough, self-taught busy Post Office Surveyor in Ireland, perpetually travelling about the country on the inspections of his duty, managed to see to the very marrow of the prelates of a cathedral, to the inner histories of the duke's castle and the squire's home, into the secret musing of the rector's daughter, and into the tangled web of Parliamentary intrigue. He did all this with a perfectly sure and subtle touch, which was often, it is true, somewhat tame, and is never perhaps of any great brilliance, but which was almost faultlessly true, never extravagant, never unreal. And, to add to the wonder, you might meet him for an hour; and, however much you might like his bluff, hearty, resonant personality, you would have said he was the last man to have any delicate sympathy with bishops, dukes, or young ladies.

His insight into Parliamentary life was surprisingly accurate and deep. He had not the genius of Disraeli, but his pictures are utterly free from caricature or distortion of any kind. In his photographic portraiture of the British Parliament he surpassed all his contemporaries; and in as much as such studies can only have a local and sectional interest, they have probably injured his popularity and his art. His conduct of legal intricacies and the ways of lawyers is singularly correct; and the long and elaborate trial scene in *Phineas Redux* is a masterpiece of natural and faithful descriptions of an Old Bailey criminal trial in which 'Society' happens to be involved. Yet of courts of law, as of bishop's palaces, rectory firesides, the lobbies of Parliament, and ducal 'house parties', Trollope could have known almost nothing except as an occasional and outside observer. The life of London clubs, the habits and personnel of a public office, the hunting-field, and the social hierarchy and ten commandments observed in a country town – these things Trollope knew to the minutest shade, and he has described them with wonderful truth and zest.

There was a truly pathetic drollery in his violent passion for certain enjoyments – hunting, whist and the smoking-room of his club. I cannot forget the comical rage which he felt at Professor

Freeman's attack on fox-hunting. I am not a sporting man myself;
and, though I may look on fox-hunting as one of the less deadly
sins involved in 'sport', I know nothing about it. But it chanced
that as a young man I had been charged with the duty of escorting
a certain young lady to a 'meet' of fox-hounds in Essex. A fox was
found; but what happened I hardly remember; save this, that in
the middle of a hot burst, I found myself alongside of Anthony
Trollope, who was shouting and roaring out 'What! – what are
you doing here?' And he was never tired of holding me up to the
scorn of the 'Universe' Club as a deserter from the principles of
Professor Freeman and John Morley. I had taken no part in the
controversy, but it gave him huge delight to have detected such
backsliding in one of the school he detested.[4] Like other sporting
men who imagine that their love of 'sport' is a love of nature, when
it is merely a pleasure in physical exercise, Trollope cared little for
the poetic aspect of nature. His books, like Thackeray's, hardly
contain a single fine picture of the country, of the sea, of
mountains, or of rivers. Compared with Fielding, Scott, Charlotte
Brontë, Dickens, George Eliot, he is a man blind to the loveliness
of nature. To him, as to other fox-hunters, the country was good or
bad as it promised or did not promise a good 'run'. Though
Trollope was a great traveller, he rarely uses his experiences in a
novel, whereas Scott, Thackeray, Dickens, Bulwer, George Eliot,
fill their pages with foreign adventures and scenes of travel.[5] His
hard riding as an overgrown heavyweight, his systematic whist
playing, his loud talk, his burly ubiquity and irrepressible energy
in everything – formed one of the marvels of the last generation.
And that such a colossus of blood and bone should spend his
mornings, before we were out of bed, in analysing the hypersensi-
tive conscience of an archdeacon, the secret confidences whispered between a prudent mamma and a lovelorn young lady, or
the subtle meanderings of Marie Goesler's heart – this was a real
psychologic problem.

(2)   Trollope's uprightness of nature comes out in another view,
much to be commended to men of letters. He tells the story of a
critic of the day who showed him the manuscript of a popular
novel, which the author of it had given in a handsome binding to
the critic as an acknowledgement of a laudatory review. It is no
secret now that Dickens was the author, *Our Mutual Friend* the
novel, and the critic a gentleman now dead, and mentioned

elsewhere in the book.[6] Trollope told the critic bluntly that the present should neither have been given nor taken. He was surely right, and his remarks on the general subject of journalistic criticism are extremely salutary. His own criticisms on some contemporary writers of fiction are shrewd and sound, so far as they go, – with a single exception. To Charles Reade he is ludicrously unjust.[7] Mr Reade has the gifts both of the artist and the story-teller; and when he chooses, he is the master of a singularly pure and correct style. Trollope himself was a good hand at drawing a woman, but Charles Reade, under many whimsicalities, has drawn women with a finer and subtler stroke than Trollope could ever reach, with all his brooding and his castle-building. To Mr Disraeli, too, Trollope is more unkind than he ought to be. Mr Gladstone is believed to hold as low an opinion of his rival's novels as Trollope does, but he hardly approaches the subject without bias. Disraeli's novels have no doubt 'that flavour of hair-oil, that flavour of false jewels, that remembrance of tailors', which so offends the honest Trollope. But the best of them have humour and wit, have touches of imagination and the picturesque, that have made so good a critic as Mr Leslie Stephen deplore the waste of such genius for literature on the idle and degraded pastime of being a Prime Minister.

In yet another sense besides those that have been already named Trollope always showed a sterling manliness. 'I do not think,' he says, 'that I ever toadied any one, or that I have acquired the character of a tuft-hunter. But here I do not scruple to say that I prefer the society of distinguished people, and that even the distinction of wealth confers many advantages.' Of course every man of sense would choose the society of the most distinguished people that he could find willing to consort with him on fair terms – distinction, it is understood, being truly and wisely interpreted. Trollope's notion of real distinction was no unworthy one. Mr Mill once expressed a desire to make his acquaintance, and it was arranged that Trollope should go down to dine at Blackheath on Sunday afternoon.[8] He came up from Essex for the express purpose, and said to a younger friend who was convoying him down, 'Stuart Mill is the only man in the whole world for the sake of seeing whom I would leave my own home on a Sunday.' The party was only a moderate success. The contrast was too violent between the modesty and courtesy of the host and the blustering fashions of Trollope. These came out the worse when they figured in the same room with the gentle precision of Mill and the pleasant gravity of Cairnes.[9] It was a relief to get the bull safely away from the china shop. Trollope did not recognise the delicacy of Truth, but handled her as freely and as boldly as a slave-dealer might handle a beautiful Circassian. He once had an interview with a writer whom he wished to make the editor of a Review. 'Now, do you,' he asked, glaring as if in fury through his spectacles, and roaring like a bull of Bashan, 'do you believe in the divinity of our blessed Lord and Saviour Jesus Christ?'[10] He had not a perfect sense of the shades and delicacies of things, nor had he exactly the spirit of urbanity. 'Peace', says Cowper of the Scholar –

> Peace to the memory of a man of worth,
> A man of letters and a man of manners too,
> Of manners sweet as virtue always wears.

We cannot say all this of Trollope, but of the three qualities he had at any rate two, and they were the two most important. He had worth and he had some care for letters. He was a staunch friend, and children delighted in him. Peace to his memory.

NOTES

1. The Universe was based on the Cosmopolitan Club. 'The name was supposed to be a joke, as it was limited to ninety-nine members. It was domiciled in one simple and somewhat mean apartment. ... Its attractions were not numerous, consisting chiefly of tobacco and tea' (*Phineas Redux*, ch. xxxiv).

2. This was a stock conversational gambit, never deployed to better effect than here. In a review of the *Autobiography* the moment is embellished with delightful detail: 'He expounded this theory of the seat of inspiration one afternoon in the drawing-room at North Bank to George Eliot and some others, with an inelegant vigour of gesture that sent a thrill of horror through the polite circle there assembled' (*Macmillan's*, XLIX (Nov 1883) 47–56). The cobbler image occurs in a letter to Mrs Catherine Gould, 13 Apr 1860, as quoted by James Russell in a letter of 20 Sep 1861; to G. W. Rusden, 8 June 1876. See *Letters*, I, 100; P. D. Edwards, *Notes and Queries*, n.s. 15 (Nov 1968) 419–20.

3. An overstatement. There were clerical associations on both parents' sides, and certainly the Harrow society Trollope was exposed to as a child was educated and professional.

4. See reminiscence by E. A. Freeman, pp. 220–7.

5. Scarcely tenable. Globetrotting gave Trollope raw material for much fiction, often directly incorporated in such novels as *The Bertrams* (1859), *The*

Claverings (1867), *Nina Balatka* (1867), *Linda Tressel* (1868), *Harry Heathcote of Gangoil* (1874), *John Caldigate* (1879), not to mention the short stories.

6. The critic was E. S. Dallas (1828–79), a Garrick friend of Trollope's, regular writer for *The Times* and editor of *Once a Week*. Dallas commissioned *The Vicar of Bullhampton* for his magazine and deferred publication in favour of a story of Victor Hugo's much to Trollope's indignation. The episode is told in *Commentary*, pp. 296–8.

7. As they stand, Trollope's comments among those on contemporary authors are not unduly harsh, although he does harp ironically on the theme of literary honesty (*Auto.*, xiii). Perhaps it was fortunate that a passage in which he makes no bones about Reade's role in the *Shilly-Shally* business had been suppressed.

8. Morley was a friend and supporter of John Stuart Mill (1806–73), distinguished philosopher and economist; founder of the Utilitarian Society, 1822–3, chief contributor to the *Westminster Review*; his best-known works included *On Liberty* (1859), *Representative Government* (1861), *Utilitarianism* (1863) and *The Subjection of Women* (1869).

9. John Eliot Cairnes (1823–75), Mill's close friend, Professor of Political Economy, University of London; author of *Political Essays* (1873) and *Some Leading Principles of Political Economy* (1874). Cecilia Meetkerke took exception to the crude presentation of Trollope in this part of the article.

10. Morley is recalling how he was interrogated by Trollope for the editorship of the *Fortnightly Reivew*. Morley held the post from 1867 to 1882.

Not One Scrap of Sentimentality About Him

WALTER HERRIES POLLOCK

From 'Anthony Trollope', *Harper's New Monthly Magazine*, LXVI (May 1883) 907–12. Walter Herries Pollock (1850–1926), son of Sir William Frederick Pollock, who was Queen's Remembrancer and Trollope's neighbour in Montagu Square. Miscellaneous writer and critic, Pollock was editor of the *Saturday Review*, 1883–94, and one of several young writers Trollope encouraged. When he married Emma Jane Pipon in 1876 Trollope sent a wedding present of books with a typically generous letter: 'When you bring your wife home I will come and inscribe your names. You will find that I have burdened you with a great many Elizabethan plays. When you have read them all and thoroughly digested them, so as to be able to answer satisfactorily all questions as to plot, language, character and customs, I will send you some more' (*Letters*, II, 677).

Mr Anthony Trollope's name was so essentially associated with the novel of modern life, dealing mainly with London or country-house life of people well up in the social scale, that hardly one of his many readers suspected him of suddenly turning his hand to semi-historical romance. Yet if they had remembered certain of *The Tales of All Countries*, they would have seen at once that if Mr Trollope had not as yet distinguished himself in the line of romantic fiction of the ordinary three-volume length, it was certainly not for want of a romantic vein in his composition.[1] Romance also of a kind, and very deep and true of its kind, may no doubt be found in his more familiar novels – in, for instance, the character and history of Mr Crawley in *The Last Chronicle of Barset* – but it is of a special kind; of the kind that a man of such invention and observation as Mr Trollope had could detect in the most everyday surroundings, and could bring out in what seemed the most everyday manner. I say 'seemed', because I think that the ease with which he wrote, the uniform swing or beat of style which he always adopted, were not unapt to prevent the art of his method and the genius which underlay that art from being perceived and appreciated. ...

The least boastful of men, he had not so much a pride as a conviction regarding his own method, and found it difficult to understand why any author did his actual writing with pain and labour. When publishers came to see him with a view to arrangements about a novel from his pen, he would open several drawers in his writing-desk, each containing a work written in the way above described, and offer them their choice. I remember his once going though the process of opening the drawers for my edification; but I also remember that when he was giving me some of the kind and wise counsel which was always at the disposal of his friends, whether of his own age or much younger than himself, one of the first things he asked with regard to a story which I was then wanting to write was whether I thought of it all day; whether when I walked the characters were always in my mind; whether my whole attention, when not given perforce to other things, was devoted to them and to what might possibly befall them. This he said, was the only way in which the people and events of a novel could be made to live, and in this way it was that every one of his own characters was so life-like.[2] It has been supposed and said, and I fancy the supposition and saying arose from the causes above referred to, that his range was, after all, narrow, and that his was a merely photographic art. There are, in the first place, photographs and photographs; in the second, a photographer, however full of artistic feeling he may be, does not need invention. That Trollope had invention, and much invention, anyone who reads his best-known books – to say nothing of *Nina* [*Balatka*, 1867] and *Linda* [*Tressel*, 1868] – with any care can very easily see for himself; but it may be well to state that some of the very studies which were especially described as 'photographs of life and society' were as much due to invention as any plausible representation of contemporary life and manners can be due to invention. This was largely the case with his studies of ecclesiastical and episcopal character, with which he was so closely and widely identified that on one occasion being thrown in company with a bishop to whom he was personally unknown, he introduced himself with, 'My lord, may I venture to claim your acquaintance? – I am Anthony Trollope.' The claim was at once and most genially admitted, and presently the bishop, looking downward said: 'I am the first bishop that ever came out in pantaloons. If you set down aught of me, set down that.' Another ecclesiastical anecdote of him is curious and characteristic. He was by no means given to talking of his own accord about his own works, past and present; indeed, I do not remember to have ever heard him do so except on this occasion, when he was writing *The Last Chronicle of Barset*, and he took an opportunity of observing that there was an end of Mrs Proudie.[3] ...

[There follows a similar account to that given on pp. 233–4 below.] Unluckily, it is hopeless to give any idea in writing of the manner in which all Trollope's stories, all his words of advice and encouragement, all his kindly greetings and casual talk, were uttered – the mixture of bluff geniality, of prompt decision, of slight and thoroughly superficial roughness. The very existence of the last-named quality was curiously in contrast not only with the great kindness and delicacy of feeling that was one of his most striking characteristics in private life, but also with the extraordinary insight and fineness with which he set forth girls' and women's characters in his novels. ...

Nobody could see anything of him without feeling that he was in the presence of an exceptionally high-minded as well as an

exceptionally gifted man, a man of strong feelings as of strong
sense, but a man who well knew how to keep his feelings in check,
and a man whose practice as well as his theory was Christian. He
told me once a story – and the story was pathetic enough as he told
it with all its details – of a certain work of his having been claimed
by someone else, and of the inevitable exposure which followed
the claim; and his own feeling was of pity for the claimant.[4] This,
told without the impression which his own manner of telling it
conveyed, seems a trifling thing by which to illustrate the noble
qualities of a man who was great in more than one sense; but the
absolute simplicity of it, the complete incapacity to imagine that
anyone telling such a story could tell it with any other feeling,
made an enduring impression on me; and it seemed to me strange
to reflect that had he for purposes of fiction had to describe a man
with a particle of meanness in him, telling such a story, he would
have brought out the meanness in the most easy and most lifelike
way. What he would have seized on with quick instinct as a
novelist was out of his ken as a man.

Something has been said as to the wide grasp of Mr Trollope's
powers and intellect, and this applied to what his mind took in as
well as to what it gave out. He was, in the truest sense of the word,
a well-read man, and he used always to read for a given time in the
early morning, before sitting down to his task of composition. His
judgement upon the works of the masters of fiction of a past time
was keen and close, if in some instances – as when, for instance, he
questioned the truth of the pathos in *The Bride of Lammermoor* – it
seemed unexpected. This particular instance was the more
surprising because, as may be guessed from many passages in his
novels, he was peculiarly sensible to the influence of pathos,
whether in fiction or on the stage. He had always had an idea of
writing a history of fiction – whether general or confined to
England had not been decided – and this, so far as fiction past was
concerned, would have been an admirable piece of work.[5] So far
as it dealt with fiction of his own time, it could not but have been
less satisfactory. The conviction as to his own method being the
right one, while it no doubt went for a good deal in the
completeness and ease of his work, also no doubt warped his
judgement of contemporary masters of the novelist's art. ...

This is not the time to attempt an analytical criticism of his
different kinds of work. What I wish I could do is to give anything
like an adequate idea of the man, and of the hold which he all

unconsciously acquired on the affections of all who were fortunate enough to be thrown in his way. To younger men his ways and manner had the special charm that, without for a moment losing dignity, he put them on an equality with himself. He happened to be older, and therefore more experienced, than they were – I do not think it ever occurred to him that he was more clever or more gifted – and whatever help might come to them from his greater experience was at their service as between comrade and comrade. It was impossible for the shyest young man to be with him without feeling at ease. Once a young writer who was admitted to his friendship went to him and said, 'A book of yours has been sent to me for review, and I don't think I ought to review it, but I have come to ask you.' He leaned back in his chair and looked hard through his spectacles, as was his wont, and said, 'No, my boy, I don't think you ought to review a book of mine, any more than I ought to review a book of yours', and then went on to deliver himself of sentiments regarding the business of reviewing generally, as to which it can only be wished that they were more generally shared and acted upon.

Besides the wisdom which one could always draw upon by paying him a visit in his study after his appointed hours of work, there was an atmosphere of cheerfulness, of good humour, of light-heartedness and of good feeling about him which could not but do one good. He loved fun; he loved laughing; he loved his kind. There was not one scrap of sentimentality about him, but there was plenty of sensibility, as well as sense. What his loss means to the reading world at large we all know. What it means to those who knew him well, who remember his kindness, his wisdom, his cheerfulness and the sense of good that was got from being in his company – what it means to those who mourn the loss of a friend as well as of a great novelist, cannot be estimated.

NOTES

1. A useful counterpoint to common views about his beefy realism; the romantic vein had, of course, been there from the beginning with *The Macdermots of Ballycloran* (1847), a tragic study of an impoverished Irish landowner.

2. 'So much of my inner life was passed in their [his characters'] company, that I was continually asking myself how this woman would act when this or that event had passed over her head, or how that man would carry himself

when his youth had become manhood, or his manhood declined to old age' (*Auto.*, xvii). See also his essay 'A Walk in a Wood', *Good Words*, xx (Aug 1879) 595–600.

3. This is a fuller version of the anecdote in the *Auto.*, xv. The *Autobiography* was published in Oct 1883, five months after this appreciation. Clearly it was a regular story in Trollope's repertoire. Augustus Hare recalled in his journal for 11 Jan 1881 how his friend, Mrs Duncan Stewart, amused a group with the tale of Mrs Proudie's death (*In My Solitary Life*, p. 166).

4. Perhaps the case of the young girl in the West Country who claimed to have written *Framley Parsonage* (1861); George Smith had the painful chore of telling the girl's father she had deceived him (Leonard Huxley, *The House of Smith, Elder* (1923), pp. 112–13).

5. See N. John Hall, 'An Unpublished Trollope Manuscript on a Proposed History of World Literature' (from the Trollope family papers in the University of Illinois Library), *Nineteenth-Century Fiction*, 29 (Sep 1974) 207–10. This was an even more ambitious project than the 'History of English Prose Fiction' referred to here, begun in 1866; see *Commentary*, Appendix iii, pp. 420–1.

He Was a Knowing Psychologist

HENRY JAMES

From *Partial Portraits* (1888) pp. 97–105. Henry James (1843–1916) reviewed Trollope's novel *The Belton Estate* (1865) harshly in the *Nation* (4 Jan 1866) 21–2, claiming that to get involved in one of his love stories was very like sinking into a gentle slumber. On the voyage aboard the *Bothnia* mentioned here he wrote to his family on 1 Nov 1875: 'We had also Anthony Trollope, who wrote novels in his state room all the morning (he does it literally every morning of his life, no matter where he may be) and played cards with Mrs Bronson all the evening. He has a gross and repulsive face and manner, but appears *bon enfant* when you talk with him. But he is the dullest Briton of them all.' Soon after another meeting James 'found him a very good, genial, ordinary fellow – much better than he seemed on the steamer when I crossed with him' (*Henry James Letters*, ed. Leon Edel (1974–5) i, 486; ii, 94, cited *Letters*, ii, 666). Clearly, as he knew the man and his work better, he came to appreciate both. The appreciation of the novelist after publication of the *Autobiography* remains a model of understanding, full of insights despite a number of nowadays untenable assertions about his photographic realism and lack of irony. A portion of the essay, first published as 'Anthony Trollope', *Century Magazine*, n.s. 4 (July 1883) 385–95, is reproduced here. Although from a Jamesian perspective Trollope violated certain canons of art ('he never took himself seriously', 'having as little form as possible', etc.), James praises his imagination and realism, and is not afraid of hailing his 'genius'. The article establishes Trollope's remarkable fidelity to real life without sensation or extravagance – by 'homely arts' – and draws on many of the novels. James has high praise for his characterisation, especially Harding, Grantly, Crawley and Louis Trevelyan, and of his drawing of the English girl James observes 'he took possession of her, and turned her inside out'. James concludes his article admirably by saying 'Trollope did not write for posterity; he wrote for the day, the moment; but these are just the writers whom posterity is apt to put into its pocket. ... Trollope will remain one of the most trustworthy, though not one of the most eloquent, of the writers who have helped the heart of man to know itself' (pp. 132–3).

When, a few months ago, Anthony Trollope laid down his pen for the last time, it was a sign of the complete extinction of that group of admirable writers who, in England, during the preceding half century, had done so much to elevate the art of the novelist. The author of *The Warden*, of *Barchester Towers*, of *Framley Parsonage*, does not, to our mind, stand on the very same level as Dickens, Thackeray and George Eliot; for his talent was of a quality less fine than theirs. But he belonged to the same family – he had as much to tell us about English life; he was strong, genial and abundant. He published too much; the writing of novels had ended by becoming, with him, a perceptibly mechanical process. Dickens was prolific, Thackeray produced with a freedom for which we are constantly grateful; but we feel that these writers had their periods of gestation. They took more time to look at their subject; relatively (for today there is not much leisure, at best, for those who undertake to entertain a hungry public), they were able to wait for inspiration. Trollope's fecundity was prodigious; there was no limit to the work he was ready to do. It is not unjust to say that he sacrificed quality to quantity. Abundance, certainly, is in itself a great merit; almost all the greatest writers have been abundant. But Trollope's fertility was gross, importunate; he himself contended, we believe, that he had given to the world a greater number of printed pages of fiction than any of his literary contemporaries. Not only did his novels follow each other without visible intermission, overlapping and treading on each other's heels, but most of these works are of extraordinary length. *Orley Farm*, *Can You Forgive Her?*, *He Knew He Was Right*, are exceedingly voluminous tales. *The Way We Live Now* is one of the longest of modern novels. Trollope produced, moreover, in the intervals of larger labour a great number of short stories, many of them charming, as well as various books of travel, and two or three biographies. He was the great *improvvisatore* of these latter years. Two distinguished story-tellers of the other sex – one in France and one in England – have shown an extraordinary facility of composition; but Trollope's pace was brisker even than that of the wonderful Madame Sand and the delightful Mrs Oliphant. He had taught himself to keep this pace, and had reduced his admirable faculty to a system. Every day of his life he wrote a certain number of pages of his current tale, a number sacramental and invariable, independent of mood and place. It was once the fortune of the author of these lines to cross the Atlantic in his company, and he has never forgotten the magnificent example of plain persistence that it was in the power of the eminent novelist to give on that occasion.[1] The season was unpropitious, the vessel overcrowded, the voyage detestable; but Trollope shut himself up in his cabin every morning for a purpose which, on the part of a distinguished writer who was also an invulnerable sailor, could only be communion with the muse. He drove his pen as steadily on the tumbling ocean as in Montagu Square; and as his voyages were many, it was his practice before sailing to come down to the ship and confer with the carpenter, who was instructed to rig up a rough writing-table in his small sea-chamber. Trollope has been accused of being deficient in imagination, but in the face of such a fact as that the charge will scarcely seem just. The power to shut one's eyes, one's ears (to say nothing of another sense), upon the scenery of a pitching Cunarder and open them upon the loves and sorrows of Lily Dale or the conjugal embarrassments of Lady Glencora Palliser, is certainly a faculty which could take to itself wings. The imagination that Trollope possessed he had at least thoroughly at his command. I speak of all this in order to explain (in part) why it was that, with his extraordinary gift, there was always in him a certain infusion of the common. He abused his gift, overworked it, rode his horse too hard. As an artist he never took himself seriously; many people will say this was why he was so delightful. The people who take themselves seriously are prigs and bores; and Trollope, with his perpetual 'story', which was the only thing he cared about, his strong good sense, hearty good nature, generous appreciation of life in all its varieties, responds in perfection to a certain English ideal. According to that ideal it is rather dangerous to be explicitly or consciously an artist – to have a system, a doctrine, a form. Trollope, from the first, went in, as they say, for having as little form as possible; it is probably safe to affirm that he had no 'views' whatever on the subject of novel-writing. His whole manner is that of a man who regards the practice as one of the more delicate industries, but has never troubled his head nor clogged his pen with theories about the nature of his business. Fortunately he was not obliged to do so, for he had an easy road to success;[2] and his honest, familiar, deliberate way of treating his readers as if he were one of them, and shared their indifference to a general view, their limitations of knowledge, their love of a comfortable ending, endeared him to many persons in England and America. It is in the name of some chosen form that, of late years, things have been made most disagreeable for the novel-reader, who has been treated by several votaries of the new experiments in fiction to unwonted and bewildering sensations. With Trollope we were always safe, there were sure to be no new experiments.

His great, his inestimable merit was a complete appreciation of the usual.[3] This gift is not rare in the annals of English fiction; it would naturally be found in a walk of literature in which the feminine mind has laboured so fruitfully. Women are delicate and patient observers; they hold their noses close, as it were, to the texture of life. They feel and perceive the real with a kind of personal tact, and their observations are recorded in a thousand delightful volumes. Trollope, therefore, with his eyes comfortably fixed on the familiar, the actual, was far from having invented a new category; his great distinction is that in resting there his vision took in so much of the field. And then he *felt* all daily and immediate things as well as saw them; felt them in a simple, direct, salubrious way, with their sadness, their gladness, their charm, their comicality, all their obvious and measurable meanings. He never wearied of the pre-established round of English customs – never needed a respite or a change – was content to go on indefinitely watching the life that surrounded him, and holding up his mirror to it. Into this mirror the public, at first especially, grew very fond of looking – for it saw itself reflected in all the most credible and supposable ways, with that curiosity that people feel to know how they look when they are represented, 'just as they are', by a painter who does not desire to put them into an attitude, to drape them for an effect, to arrange his light and his accessories. This exact and on the whole becoming image, projected upon a surface without a strong intrinsic tone, constitutes mainly the entertainment that Trollope offered his readers. The striking thing to the critic was that his robust and patient mind had no particular bias, his imagination no light of its own. He saw things neither pictorially and grotesquely like Dickens; nor with that combined disposition to satire and to literary form which gives such 'body', as they say of wine, to the manner of Thackeray; nor with anything of the philosophic, the transcendental cast – the desire to follow them to their remote relations – which we associate with the name of George Eliot. Trollope had his elements of fancy, of satire, of irony; but these qualities were not very highly developed, and he walked mainly by the light of his good sense, his clear, direct vision of the things that lay nearest, and his great natural kindness. There is something remarkably tender and friendly in his feeling about all human perplexities; he takes the good-natured, temperate, conciliatory view – the humorous view, perhaps, for the most part, yet without a touch of pessimistic prejudice. As he grew older, and had sometimes to go farther afield for his subjects, he acquired a savour of bitterness and reconciled himself sturdily to treating of the disagreeable. A more copious record of disagreeable matters could scarcely be imagined, for instance, than *The Way We Live Now*. But, in general, he has a wholesome mistrust of morbid analysis, an aversion to inflicting pain. He has an infinite love of detail, but his details are, for the most part, the innumerable items of the expected. When the French are disposed to pay a compliment to the English mind they are so good as to say that there is in it something remarkably *honnête*. If I might borrow this epithet without seeming to be patronising, I should apply it to the genius of Anthony Trollope. He represents in an eminent degree this natural decorum of the English spirit, and represents it all the better that there is not in him a grain of the mawkish or the prudish. He writes, he feels, he judges like a man, talking plainly and frankly about many things, and is by no means destitute of a certain saving grace of coarseness. But he has kept the purity of his imagination and held fast to old-fashioned reverences and preferences. He thinks it a sufficient objection to several topics to say simply that they are unclean. There was nothing in his theory of the story-teller's art that tended to convert the reader's or the writer's mind into a vessel for polluting things. He recognised the right of the vessel to protest, and would have regarded such a protest as conclusive. With a considerable turn for satire, though this perhaps is more evident in his early novels than in his later ones, he had as little as possible of the quality of irony. He never played with a subject, never juggled with the sympathies or the credulity of his reader, was never in the least paradoxical or mystifying. He sat down to his theme in a serious, business-like way, with his elbows on the table and his eyes occasionally wandering to the clock.

To touch successively upon these points is to attempt a portrait, which I shall perhaps not altogether have failed to produce. The source of his success in describing the life that lay nearest to him, and describing it without any of those artistic perversions that come, as we have said, from a powerful imagination, from a cynical humour or from a desire to look, as George Eliot expresses it, for the suppressed transitions that unite all contrasts, the essence of this love of reality was his extreme interest in character. This is the fine and admirable quality in Trollope, this is what will preserve his best works in spite of those flatnesses which keep him from standing on quite the same level as the masters. Indeed this quality is so much one of the finest (to my mind at least), that it makes me wonder the more that the writer who had it so abundantly and so naturally should not have just that distinction which Trollope lacks, and which we find in his three brilliant contemporaries. If he was in any degree a man of genius (and I hold that he was), it was in virtue of this happy, instinctive perception of human varieties. His knowledge of the stuff we are made of, his observation of the common behaviour of men and women, was not reasoned nor acquired, not even particularly studied. All human doings deeply interested him, human life, to his mind, was a perpetual story; but he never attempted to take the so-called scientific view, the view which has lately found ingenious advocates among the countrymen and successors of Balzac. He had no airs of being able to tell you *why* people in a given situation would conduct themselves in a particular way; it was enough for him that he felt their feelings and struck the right note, because he had, as it were, a good ear. If he was a knowing psychologist he was so by grace; he was just and true without apparatus and without effort. He must have had a great taste for the moral question; he evidently believed that this is the basis of the interest of fiction.

NOTES

1. Trollope was returning from his second trip to Australia. He sailed aboard the *Bothnia* out of New York on 20 Oct 1875, arriving at Liverpool on 30 Oct. Among the passengers was Katherine Colman DeKay Bronson (1834–1901), an American hostess and friend of Browning and other celebrities, who seems to have brought out Trollope's lumpish good humour. He wrote to her on his return to Montagu Square asking after several of his fellow passengers: 'What of half a score of other interesting young ladies who liked autographs from old men and more tender acknowledgements from those who were younger?' He also penned a roguish 'advertisement' for her amusement, calling for 'a delicate-chested clergyman of the Church of England, the state of whose health requires the Nile' (*Letters*, ii, 665–6). One is reminded of his high jinks on board the *Mastiffs* visiting Iceland.

2. In the light of his long apprenticeship and many early disappointments 'an easy road to success' is scarcely tenable.

3. James has toned down the phrase originally used in his *Century* article which read 'complete appreciation of reality'.

The Most Enthusiastic of Men

T. H. S. ESCOTT

From 'A Novelist of the Day', *Time*, i (Aug 1879) 626–32. From the time as a boy when he marvelled at the apparition who strode into his father's drawing-room at Budleigh Salterton (see p. 48 above), Escott was fascinated, and attached himself over the years until he constituted himself in some sort Trollope's unofficial biographer. Trollope saw and approved of what Escott had to say about him in *Time*: 'Many thanks for the excessive kindness of your remarks,' writes Trollope, 'Agree with you about myself of course I cannot! or if I did I should not dare to say so' (*Letters*, ii, 835–6). Here, as in his book *England: Its People, Polity, and Pursuits* (1879), Escott made the point that Trollope's novels were close replicas of the times: 'They give hundreds and thousands of men and women, of all ages and of all ranks, exactly what they want – light easy reading, that requires no special thought, that is at once a pure recreation, and that presents to them, as if reflected in a mirror, the society amidst which they live' (ii, 402; cited *Letters*, ii, 859). This was to remain the standard view until Sadleir and the Trollope revival. Graciously accepting a copy of the book, Trollope looked forward to Escott's 'coming time'. Two years later he joked about Escott's moving up the literary ladder when he was made (with Trollope's help) editor of

the *Fortnightly* (*Letters*, II, 979–80). What is important to note is that whatever he
privately thought of Escott's judgements, he was not disposed to dissent from,
correct, or disagree with, what was said; this, despite Escott's blunders and
creative recollection, makes him worth reading for Escott has the gist of the
matter: directness, frankness, spontaneity – these are qualities in Trollope which
made him a 'character', but at the same time a buried gentleness and
fundamental understanding (he who had struggled mightily and come through)
made him basically a man like in spirit to his own Harding; this is why, as his
granddaughter was told, to know him was to love him.

'The style is the man'; and there is a sense in which the remark has
more truth about it than may generally be suspected. There is no
need to dwell here on the deeper idiosyncrasies of character which
an analysis of the mode of expression adopted by distinguished or
undistinguished authors may reveal. The meaning now attached
to the famous phrase is purely personal, and the proposition now
laid down is that one may trace, very much more frequently than
is perhaps generally supposed, a strong likeness between books
and their authors – that the ring of the printed sentence often
echoes in the writer's voice; that his or her casual conversation
reflects the published periods, whether long or short; that the
letter-press is an extension of the presence; and that as the poet,
humorist, or historian is on paper, so is he for the most part in
society. ... I have never yet been told that Dickens lacked, at
Gad's Hill or in London, or wherever else he happened to be, the
animal spirits which suffuse every page of his writings; or that
Charles Lever, across the walnuts and the wine, was not precisely
the man in whom one would expect to recognise the creator of
Charles O'Malley and Harry Lorrequer. I have never yet found
Professor J. S. Blackie less exuberant in his conversation than in
his printed prelections on modern Greek, modern education
generally, and in his 'Lays of the Highlands and Islands'. It seems
to me that the gifted author of *Piccadilly* talks and acts in private
life very much as one would expect the profound believer in the
virtues of episcopacy, which he is known to be, to act and talk.[1]

This list of such instances might be materially lengthened from
the resources of even a limited experience, but it will be enough to
crown it with one crucial illustration. If the identity between the
Mr Anthony Trollope of private life and the Mr Anthony Trollope
who has enriched English literature with novels that will yet rank
as nineteenth–century classics is not immediately perceived, it
can only be because the observer is destitute of the faculty of

perception. 'The style is the man'; the popular and successful author is the straightforward unreserved friend; the courageous, candid, plain-speaking companion. As it is with the dialogue of Mr Trollope's literary heroes and heroines, so is it with the conversation of Mr Trollope himself. In each there is the same definiteness and directness; the same Anglo-Saxon simplicity which can only not be called studied, because in all things it is Mr Trollope's characteristic to be spontaneous. As a writer – I do not of course speak of the elaboration of his plots – Mr Trollope is precisely what he is as a talker, and what he is, or used to be, as a rider across country.[2] He sees the exact place at which he wants to arrive. He makes for it; and he determines to reach it as directly as possible. There may be obstacles, but he surmounts them. Sometimes, indeed, they prove for the moment serious impediments. Perhaps they actually place him *hors de combat*, like a post and rails that cannot be negotiated, or a ditch of impracticable dimensions. It does not matter. He picks himself up, pulls himself together, and presses on as before. The sympathy which is the invariable accompaniment of a broad and manly imagination, Mr Trollope has in abundance. But an opinion rapidly crystalises with him into a conviction, and a conviction is, in his estimation, a thing for which to live or die. He does not exclude from his consideration all that conflicts with this view, but he has for it only a theoretical toleration. One is almost reminded in his case of the nearly instantaneous luxuriance displayed in the growth of tropical vegetation – a phenomenon, by the by, which was never described better than by Mr Trollope himself in his book on the *West Indies and the Spanish Main*. The impression seems hardly to have been formed when it blossoms forth into an article of faith. The climate may be uncongenial to the development; so much the worse for the climate; the facts may be stubbornly opposed to it; but is man, then, a slave, that he should bow to facts?

One could scarcely have a better illustration of this generous and most chivalrous tendency on the part of Mr Trollope, as it may be witnessed in his writings, than is to be seen in his recently published little work on Thackeray.[3] The view here taken of Thackeray's character is, if I may be pardoned for saying so, the conventional one – that the immortal author of *Vanity Fair* had nothing in the veins of his moral nature but the pure unadulterated milk of human kindness; that he was superior to petty animosities and literary jealousies; that he had nothing about him

which was not great and almost godlike; that it is as prepost-
erously unrighteous to hint at the presence of the cynic in his
writings as to suppose that envy, malice, or any other form of
uncharitableness has a home in the Elysian fields. This is
hero-worship with a vengeance. ...

In this temper may be seen evidence of the intensity of
enthusiasm with which Mr Trollope's nature is charged. Never
certainly was there an enthusiast who had about him so little that
is dreamy and so much that is absolutely impracticable. The
ordinary enthusiast meditates largely, perpetually cultivates a
fine sort of inspired frenzy, and does nothing. He builds castles in
the air, and he never thinks of inhabiting them. He piles
imaginary towers upon fictitious foundations, and the whole
fabric topples over because the lessons of experience have been
disregarded by the architect. Now Mr Trollope, enthusiast and
castle-builder though he is and has always been, is practical as
well. He may have his fantasies and chimeras and crotchets and
hobbies; yet for all this the world in which he lives is no visionary
one, but one in which close attention to facts and details is a
paramount necessity. Enthusiasm – it may be impetuosity – is
only one of the accidental modes of development assumed by Mr
Trollope's imagination. It has become a species of necessary
condition of his thought; and just as great athletes find it desirable
frequently to exercise their muscles and sinews by wielding
dumb-bells, brandishing Indian clubs, and other feats of strength,
so does Mr Trollope keep his mental elasticity fresh and vigorous
by tilting against windmills and by defending paradoxes. This is
part of the charm of the man, or at least of the secret of his charm.
As with his writings, so with his social converse. In Mr Trollope's
nature extremes may be said to balance extremes. The most
enthusiastic of men, he is of all men also the most practical. The
qualities which he has consistently displayed in the exercise of his
art as novelist are those which, applied to any other department of
intellectual industry, would have secured him success, and
probably eminence. His energy has been untiring; his productive
powers have neither flagged nor paused. ...

Unless I am mistaken, the golden harvest which *The Warden*
yielded was not ingathered till its author had not merely reached,
but passed, Thackeray's age of wisdom, and was the wrong side of
the Rubicon of 'forty year'.

The publication of this novel was the first great era in Anthony Trollope's literary life. It placed a career manifestly within his reach; it gave him a name; it opened up to him large opportunities of future and most remunerative toil. The chief historical and general interest of the book arises from the fact that it was the earliest venture made by Mr Trollope in that department of socio-ecclesiastical fiction which he may be said to have created for his own special delectation and profit. It is natural to ask what were the circumstances which first led Mr Trollope to seek the materials of his fictions in the doings of ecclesiastical circles, and what were the special opportunities of observing these which he had enjoyed. The son of a barrister, his mother being an authoress of great power and sprightliness, Anthony Trollope was at two public schools – Winchester first and Harrow afterwards. He did not go to Oxford; and before he was twenty got an appointment in the Post Office. He kept up his Classics; and he did more than this, he perpetually cultivated his faculties of observation. He was always recording the experiences of his everyday life on the tables of his memory, always planning something, always devising situations, and mentally enquiring what action on the part of individuals, of a certain variety of temperament, placed in certain circumstances, would follow a particular set of motives. This is the true education of the brain, and, indeed, of the pen, of the novelist, or of any artist who determines to make mankind his theme. Ever observant, ever vigilant, Mr Trollope gradually acquired a fund of knowledge, gathered first-hand, and relating to a hundred different phases of existence, which was certain, sooner or later, to fructify. It was natural that accident should for the most part decide the line in which he was to make his début as a successful novelist. Accident did decide it, and an accident of a character which shows the enthusiastic quality of his mind. Rather less than twenty-five years ago there appeared in *The Times* a correspondence raising the issue whether a beneficed clergyman was morally justified in being a systematic absentee from the congregation for whose spiritual welfare he was responsible.[4] The unfortunate ecclesiastic who had placed himself in this position was vehemently attacked. He or his friends advanced on his behalf the best defence possible; and so, after an empty bout of controversy, the matter ended. But with Mr Anthony Trollope it had only just begun. Perhaps no man has, in his broad views of life, less of the casuist about him; in minor matters few have the same fondness for the arguing of nicely casuistical questions.[5] Here was a *casus conscientiae* after his own heart. It set him thinking. His quick imagination and social experience opened up a vista of characters and situation, and *The Warden* was the result.

But what is to be said of the originals of the characters of *The Warden* – Bishop Proudie, Mrs Proudie, and the rest of them? Probably Mr Trollope might tell us that, after all, in clerical nature, masculine or feminine, there is a great deal of human nature; that though the outer garb of humanity may vary much, its inward heart varies astonishingly little; that prelates with aprons, gaiters, shovel-hats, and other clerical trappings, are amenable to the same laws and considerations as any other middle-aged gentleman clad in black, or in whatever other hue may be affected.[6] Be this as it may, it is quite certain that Mr Trollope took to writing novels of clerical life with no special knowledge of clerical character; and that he certainly knew not a tithe of what was known by George Eliot of the gossip and scandals of cathedral precincts, when he made Barchester Towers and all their chief personages thoroughly familiar to the English public. In the town of Barchester one will in vain search for any evidence of identity with Winchester. Here and there a touch of Salisbury may be detected, but for the most part it is the general idea of a cathedral town that is depicted, and not any particular city.[7] Knowledge of the world, based upon great and varied experience, increased by study, fortified and enlarged by culture – these are the data out of which Mr Trollope has manufactured what it is only natural to consider his extraordinary knowledge of, and insight into, clerical life. And is this not, it may be asked, the way in which genius usually works? The facts genius itself cannot create; but the facts once given are capable of any number of combinations; and facts, when they are placed in juxtaposition, have a tendency to create new facts. ...[8]

Practice, skill, literary ability, would not have enabled him to do all that he has done. It was necessary that these should be informed and quickened, as in Mr Trollope's case they have been, by that enthusiasm which is itself a certain mood of genius – an enthusiasm intimately allied, in the case of Anthony Trollope, with the spirit of honour, loyalty and integrity. Had he been less chivalrous, he might, from a purely worldly point of view, have been even more successful. He has had, and he has never abandoned, his views of the uses and objects of fiction; and he has endeavoured consistently to act up to them, writing nothing which shame could ever prompt him to blot, and nothing which has not a practical bearing upon human life. So industriously and so successfully has he done this, that he has won, in a quarter of a century, nearly the most conspicuous place in the first rank of novelists of the day. Of the charm which his novels have to the contemporary reader, this only need be said – that they charm him for the same reason that they will be invaluable to the future historian of social England in the nineteenth century.

NOTES

1. John Stuart Blackie (1809–95), distinguished scholar, first Regius Professor at Aberdeen, 1841–52, and Professor of Greek at Edinburgh, 1852–82. Laurence Oliphant (1829–88), traveller and writer; his novel *Piccadilly* (1870) was a satire on fashionable society. See Anne Taylor, *Laurence Oliphant, 1829–1888* (Oxford, 1982).

2. It is significant that Escott was not perplexed by the contradictions which have been the subject of several reminiscences in this collection.

3. *Thackeray* appeared in May 1879. On what might have been a tender spot Trollope shows no irritation but observes in a kindly manner how relative such judgements are. Both of us have a point, he suggests; it 'only proves how hard it is to put into words all the nebulous ideas as to another man's identity which go to the formation of a man's judgement' (*Letters*, ii, 835–6).

4. For discussions of such sources for *The Warden* see *Commentary*, pp. 155–60; Ralph Arnold, *The Whiston Matter* (1961); G. F. A. Best, 'The Road to Hiram's Hospital', *Victorian Studies*, v (1961) 144–7.

5. For all his notorious inaccuracies Escott had the bones of the matter and knew his man. Recent studies have made much of Trollope's moral relativism and argumentative casuistry. See, for example, Ruth ap Roberts, *Trollope, Artist and Moralist* (1971).

6. He did.

7. E. A. Freeman pressed Trollope on this point. See p. 225 below.

8. In a passage omitted, Escott claims that his best novels are of character rather than of incident, judging *Orley Farm* as probably his finest work. There are few attempts to write about Trollope the man in his lifetime, for obvious reasons, but several assessments of his work are worth looking into. They include, apart from the James item already noted: E. S. Dallas, *The Times* (23 May 1859) 12; unsigned review of *Orley Farm*, *National Review*, xvi (Jan 1863) 27–40; R. H. Hutton (?), the *Spectator* (11 Oct 1862) 1136–8; unsigned article, 'The Novels of Mr Anthony Trollope', *Dublin Review*, lxxi (Oct 1872) 393–430; Alexander Innes Shand, 'Mr Anthony Trollope's Novels', *Edinburgh Review*, clxxvi (Oct

1877) 455–8. See also David Skilton, *Trollope and his Contemporaries: A Study in the Theory and Conventions of Mid-Victorian Fiction* (1972).

As Obstinate as a Pig

H. RIDER HAGGARD AND FRANK COLENSO

Trollope's travels through South Africa, July to Dec 1877, were his most arduous, but once again resulted in a successful book, *South Africa* (1878). Sadleir quotes with approval the comments of Sarah Gertrude Millin that the novelist toured its provinces with characteristic thoroughness: 'He dined with governors, slept in Boer farmhouses, inspected mission-schools, chatted with Kaffirs, with Hottentots, with poor whites, with Dutchmen, with Englishmen' (*The South Africans* (1926) cited *Commentary*, p. 315). One unimpressed Englishman was Henry Rider Haggard, at the time on the staff of Sir Theophilus Shepstone, administrator of the Transvaal, 1877–9. (see *Letters*, II, 738–9; and *South Africa*, II, iii). Another encounter, with Bishop Colenso of Natal, was more satisfactory. Trollope was one of his supporters. For the punishing itinerary of his journey see *South Africa*, ed. J. H. Davidson (Cape Town, 1973) Appendix D, pp. 488–90. Trollope writes home in Aug 1877: 'I own I look forward with dread to some of the journeys I shall have to make on post cars. Five hundred miles at a stretch, – with four five or six hours allowed at night according to the fancies of the black drivers' (*Letters*, II, 734). By Oct he is writing 'I do so long to get home. South Africa is so dirty. But I shall not do so before first week in Jan. Not all the books in Xendom shall make me later than that' (MS Parrish Collection, cited *Letters*, II, 740n). Trollope, as usual, took great care to be informed and accurate. Before sailing he was present at the Royal Colonial Institute on 7 June 1877, when Donald Currie, founder of the Castle Steamship Co., lectured on the country. While he travelled, moreover, he wrote at white heat, having agreed with the publisher, Nicholas Trübner, to supply fifteen travel letters for the Press. (1) from Sir Henry Rider Haggard, *The Days of My Life, An Autobiography* (1920) I, 136–7. Henry Rider Haggard (1856–1925), appointed to the staff of Sir Henry Bulwer, Lieutenant Governor of Natal in 1875, rapidly distinguished himself in colonial affairs; attached to Sir Theophilus Shepstone's administration he became Master and Registrar of the High Court of the Transvaal in May 1877. He was thus twenty-one when he encountered Trollope that year in late Sep or early Oct; (2) from Lilias Rider Haggard, *The Cloak That I Left: A Biography of the Author, Henry Rider Haggard, KBE* (1951) p. 73; (3) from Frances Sarah Colenso, *Letters from Natal*, ed. Wyn Rees (Pietermaritzburg, 1958) pp. 337–8. John William Colenso (1814–83), Bishop of Natal, whose *Commentary on St Paul's Epistle to the Romans* (1801) and examination of the Pentateuch brought calls for his resignation; the Bishop of Capetown passed a sentence of deposition in Dec

1863, but Colenso fought back with much laity support (see Peter Hinchcliff, *John William Colenso: Bishop of Natal* (1964) p. 140).

(1) Another noted man who visited us was Mr Anthony Trollope, who rushed through South Africa in a post-cart, and, as a result, published his impressions of that country. My first introduction to him was amusing. I had been sent away on some mission, I think it was to Rustenberg, and returned to Government House late one night.[1] On going into my room where I was then sleeping I began to search for matches, and was surprised to hear a gruff voice, proceeding from the bed, asking who the deuce I was. I gave my name and asked who the deuce the speaker might be. 'Anthony Trollope,' replied the gruff voice, 'Anthony Trollope'.

Mr Trollope was a man who concealed a kind heart under a somewhat rough manner, such as does not add to the comfort of colonial travelling.

[Letter to his mother, Oct 1877.] I have been travelling hard – in the veldt for eight or ten days and then a spurt of work in the Pretoria Office and then more veldt. Do you know one quite gets to like this sort of life. It is a savage kind of existence but it certainly has attractions, shooting your own dinner and cooking it – I can hardly sleep in a house now, it seems to stifle one. ...

(2) Anthony Trollope has been out here. The first I saw of that distinguished author was one morning when I met him in a towering rage (at a roadside inn) because he could not get any breakfast. He stopped in the country about twelve days, and now is going home to write a book about it – in which, no doubt, he will express his opinions with a certainty that an old resident would hesitate to adopt. I talked with him a good deal, he has the most peculiar ideas and is as obstinate as a pig. I call such a proceeding downright dishonesty: making use of a great name to misrepresent a country.

(3) [Letter from Frank Colenso, 5 Sep 1877.] Nothing definite has been settled as yet about Mr Trollope's visit [to Maritzburg]. We are almost afraid lest he should fall completely into the hands of the officials and be hoodwinked.[2] And yet, I imagine, he will prove too keen an observer for them to deceive him. It will be a

great triumph if we can supply him with really trustworthy facts about Zululand. Tomorrow the Mayor gives a dinner to him at which Father will be a guest, and it will be the first occasion of his appearing in public, since the Langalibalele matter.[3] He has a way of winning men's hearts be they never so shallow, worldly and incapable of appreciating noble motives. Father is a great admirer of Trollope. The *Barchester Towers* series gives him immense enjoyment.

NOTES

1. Soon after arriving in Pietermaritzburg from Durban, Trollope heard Colenso preach (2 Sep); he accompanied Bulwer on a Vice-regal tour of Natal Midlands (8–11 Sep), leaving Pietermaritzburg for Pretoria (13 Sep). See Davidson, *South Africa*, Appendix D, 488–9.

2. Writing to Mrs Katherine Lyell from Natal, 15 July 1878, Frances, wife of Bishop Colenso, wrote: 'If you see Anthony Trollope's book on South Africa, please to remember that he "looks through a pair of government spectacles", this is my Harry's [Harriette, their eldest child] expression. She took great pains to clear his vision, and to show him things as they are, but in vain' (*Letters from Natal*, p. 337). Similarly, Sir Henry Barkly, experienced Governor of the Cape Colony, wanted Trollope to get correct information and was a little anxious about what he would report. See Davidson, *South Africa*, p. 38.

3. Colenso had been a staunch supporter of the native people in the case of Cetawayo and Chief Langalibalele, the latter's tribe having been harassed sorely over possession of guns.

'Please Leave My Coat Alone'

THOMAS HARDY AND OTHERS

Trollope's public interests have only recently come under scrutiny. Curiosity about social, political and religious issues of his day, fed by his own journalism and club associations, became not merely background for fiction or topics for dinner-table discourse, but part of his active round. As a result of his Post Office connections, he had taken part in a variety of public functions. Later, literary eminence ensured that he served on the Royal Commission on International Copyright to which he was named in Apr 1876, and which sat through 1877, delivering its report on 24 May 1878. In Feb of that year John Blackwood wrote to his nephew: 'Anthony has come back in great force: Lord John [Manners] says he is like to drive them all mad at the weary Copyright Commission, going over all the ground that has been discussed in his absence' (Mrs Gerald Porter, *Annals of a Publishing House*, p. 317). On another occasion he observed drily: 'Trollope too is rather in the speech-making line' (Porter, *Annals of a Publishing House*, p. 409; cited *Letters*, II, 759n). See *Report of The Royal Commission on Copyright* (1878). Trollope also worked hard for the Royal Literary Fund for over twenty years, serving on its General Committee from 1864, examining cases of need, arranging stewards and speakers for annual dinners, serving as Treasurer and producing the Literary Fund Report, and frequently speaking in public. See R. H. Super, 'Trollope at the Royal Literary Fund', *Nineteenth-Century Fiction*, 37 (3 Dec 1982) 316–28. He also involved himself in lectures for working men and women, showing particular concern for self-improvement, reading and free libraries. Active, concerned, with many friends in high places, he kept abreast of current events, formed his own opinions and made them known with characteristic vehemence. Younger men in branches of public life often came to him for advice. (1) from *Chapters from My Official Life*, ed. Everilda MacAlister (1916) p. 241. Sir Charles Rivers Wilson (1831–1916), longtime Civil Servant, served as Private Secretary to Disraeli as Chancellor of the Exchequer, 1867–8; spent part of his service in Egypt particularly in administration of the Suez Canal Company; a member of the Garrick Club for nearly 60 years; (2) from *With Anthony Trollope in New Zealand*, ed. Reed, p. 50–1; (3) from *Dublin Review*, IX (Apr 1883) 316–17, 324; (4) from Florence Emily Hardy, *The Life of Thomas Hardy, 1840–1928* (1962) pp. 112–13.

(1)   On the reconstruction of the Government of Jamaica in 1866, after the rebellion in the suppression of which Governor Eyre received so much undeserved obloquy from Exeter Hall and the philanthropic extremists, Mr Cardwell, the Secretary of State for the Colonies, offered me the Financial Membership of the new Council.[1] The post was well remunerated and was not without attractions. Before making up my mind I consulted Anthony Trollope, who, in his capacity of Inspector of the Post Office, had recently visited the West Indies, and had written a very entertaining book full of information on the various islands.[2] He advised dead against my acceptance, speaking with much disdain of social and official life in Jamaica, which he described as something inferior indeed to 'beer and skittles'. He confirmed me in my inclination to decline Mr Cardwell's kind offer, which would have shifted me into a colonial career, and removed me from the opportunities and advantages connected with HM's Treasury.

(2)   [Henry Johnston, Secretary of the Glasgow Athenaeum, invited the novelist to lecture at Glasgow.] I met with Anthony Trollope by appointment at the Athenaeum Club, Pall Mall, on 15

July 1869. I had a white card and a free hand to engage as many eminent lecturers for the following winter course at the Glasgow Athenaeum as I could secure, but was seriously handicapped by the extremely limited amount of money placed at my disposal for that purpose. It was therefore with some trepidation that I kept my appointment with such a popular and successful *littérateur* as Anthony Trollope. On entering the Club I found waiting for me a tall, breezy, sun-tanned, farmer-like man with a hearty manner and an encouraging handshake. I had carefully intimated beforehand the object of my visit. He had evidently thought the matter well over, and after some enquiry regarding the Institution, he frankly acceded to my request. I was, of course, much gratified, but the delicate part of the negotiations had yet to come – his terms. This question I approached delicately without betraying the poverty of the Institution I represented, but he waved the matter brusquely aside. 'Do not speak of terms,' he said; 'when a man has something to say, and a suitable place and opportunity are offered to him for saying it, that should be sufficient for him.' I thanked him and said he would at least allow us to pay his travelling expenses. 'I'll come,' he said at last, 'but say no more about money.' What he had to say was about 'Prose Fiction as a Rational Amusement.' The lecture was one of the most successful of a brilliant course.[3] ...

(3)   All are agreed that Trollope was a warm and generous, if occasionally a dictatorial, friend; and that his rough manner disguised kind and genial feelings, whilst his conduct would often show true consideration for others. This will surprise none who are acquainted with his books. No one who was himself without refinement and delicacy of feeling could have drawn so skilfully the Quixotic self-sacrifice of that gentlest of men, Septimus Harding. No one, not himself gifted with sensitiveness, could have pictured after so lifelike a fashion Mr Crawley's painful and obstinate pride, and his soreness at the kindly attempts of his friends to aid him in his constantly recurring troubles, and in his ever present distress. But this side of Mr Trollope was not the prominent one; and we believe that many who had been for long delighting in the delicate touches of humour, and the true pictures of the subtler side of our feelings with which his books abound, experienced some disappointment on first making his acquaintance. We remember this being the case ourselves. We had long

and anxiously looked forward to a meeting, and at length found ourselves dining in his company. It was at the time of the Danish and Prussian war, and Trollope was a hot partisan of the Germans, the unpopular side.[4] Unluckily there happened to be at the table a gentleman fresh from the Danish camp, who, if more moderate in the expression of his feelings – which were entirely antagonistic to Trollope's – was equally keen in experiencing them. The result was not fortunate. Mr Trollope's loud voice and domineering manner, although they did not carry conviction, somewhat marred the pleasure of the argument. We can believe the anecdote lately told of him by a friend. Indeed, if it be not literally true, it is *ben trovato*, and so characteristic as to deserve mention. Trollope and a party of congenial friends were dining together on a summer's evening at Henley. At the further end of the room from that in which Trollope was engaged in conversation someone ventured to give an opinion: 'I differ from you entirely,' he exclaimed in his loud, sonorous voice: 'I differ from you entirely! *What was it you said?*'[5]

Trollope's temperament was one which undoubtedly shone better as a host than as a guest. His nature forced him to take the lead in everything, and his exuberant spirit rarely cared to follow. He was naturally, therefore, seen to greater advantage in his own house, where his love of generous hospitality could have full play and where his prominence in conversation was simply fitting. Where he is said to have been pre-eminently delightful was in a tête-à-tête, particularly if his companion was younger than himself and was not indisposed to listen. He would then talk freely, and the less he was interrupted the better worth hearing he would be. The result was not unlike listening to an interesting chapter of one of his books. That Trollope was a kind husband and an affectionate father, all agree in stating. We learn, too, from a short notice in the *Guardian* newspaper, written apparently by a friend living near his last home in Sussex, that he was truly benevolent to his poor and sick neighbours, whom he would visit personally, and cheer by his kind and genial manner; that he was active in all matters connected with the education of the people; that he never missed the services of his parish church on Sunday, and that he joined in the Anglican Communion office. These few particulars of Mr Trollope's life are all that have been, so far, given to the public, beyond the mapping out of his day, which was as regular as a clock. The work by which he was best known was done very early in the morning. He rose at five o'clock, and wrote his novels until called to a late breakfast. When summoned he obeyed at once, however critical might be the point in his story he had reached, or however doubtful the position in which he was obliged to leave his characters. He apparently felt confident that he could take up the thread exactly as he had left it. The result justifies this confidence; for we can recall no untoward breaks or wants of smoothness in any of his scenes, and nothing that suggests an interruption. Every episode is worked out to its legitimate ending, and finishes naturally with the chapter. He treated novel-writing as a craft. To use his own words, he sat down to write 'as a cobbler sits down to make shoes'. That he could do better one day than another, or that his skill would fail him if he forced his inspirations at an unwilling moment, seemed to him impossible. The rest of Mr Trollope's day was divided between official work, riding, and when in London a visit to his club, the Athenaeum. ...

If we look back at our own lives for the last five and twenty years, is not this very much what we have actually experienced? Acquaintances going and coming, though our friends remain: chance meetings leading to real friendships, and again, chance circumstances changing friends into comparative strangers? We think Mr Trollope not alone has created his character and plots, but that he must have lived a real, though imaginary, life with them all; that he felt a genuine love for his pleasing characters, and a genuine hatred for his unpleasant ones. We ourselves recollect shortly after the completion of *The Small House at Allington*, that finding ourselves in Trollope's company, we expressed to him the warm interest which the character and story of Lily Dale, perhaps the most graceful of his women, had aroused in our mind. We can well remember the evident gratification with which he answered, 'You can have no idea how pleased I am to hear you say that: I am so fond of her myself.' Perhaps he was specially glad to hear that Lily Dale was appreciated; for if the reader of *The Small House at Allington* found himself unable to sympathise with her, the whole book was a failure. ...

Space fails us to mention any more; and we believe no one knows exactly the number of novels Trollope has written. A lady once asked him the question point blank. 'I know, but I shall not tell you', was the answer. [There were 47 novels including the unfinished tale *The Landleaguers* (1883).]

Whilst Trollope's books are light and pleasant reading to the careless and unintelligent devourer of novels, who is sure to be entertained and amused by them, they are of serious value to the student of human nature. The story runs amusingly along, and can easily be mastered by the general reader. But beyond this wide circle he appealed to real critics by revelations of life, and touches of fine humour and keen knowledge of men and women, which may have been overlooked by many. He was fortunate in pleasing at the same time both the popular and the critical taste, and those who have unfairly designated him 'the Tupper of fiction', must either have ignored or have been simply unable to appreciate the more subtle side of his genius. We are glad to be able to add that his labours were well rewarded; and if, as is calculated by one reviewer, his profits from literature amounted to nearly £100,000, he must have been amongst the best remunerated authors of the age. But, in any case, being once asked to contribute a novel, as a friend, to a new literary venture, he replied: 'You might as well ask me to give you a thousand pounds.'

(4)   During a visit to London in December, Hardy attended a Conference on the Eastern Question[6] at St James's Hall, and heard speak Mr Gladstone, Lord Shaftesbury, Hon. E. Ashley, Anthony Trollope and the Duke of Westminster.[7] Trollope outran the five or seven minutes allowed for each speech, and the Duke, who was chairman, after various soundings of the bell, and other hints that he must stop, tugged at Trollope's coat-tails in desperation. Trollope turned round, exclaimed parenthetically, 'Please leave my coat alone', and went on speaking.[8]

NOTES

1. Exeter Hall, London, was the meeting place favoured by many of England's religious and charitable societies. Trollope was once asked to attend for the *Pall Mall Gazette*. He wrote to George Smith: 'I will tomorrow morning write you an article ("A Zulu at a May meeting"), for which the materials arranged themselves not unhappily; but I *can do no more*. Suicide would intervene after the third or fourth ...' (*Letters*, I, 301). The article appeared as 'The Zulu in London', *Pall Mall Gazette* (10 May 1865) 3–4. The Eyre controversy blew up in Oct 1865 when disorder was brutally suppressed in Jamaica under martial law. Public indignation at home led to the recall of the Governor, Edward John Eyre, and led to changes in the government of the island.

2. *The West Indies and the Spanish Main* (1859).

3. The lecture was delivered at Glasgow, 27 Jan 1870 (*Letters*, I, 483).

4. The Danish and Prussian War, 1864. Whether the topic was world affairs, politics or religion, Trollope could be relied upon to strike a combative posture. As Bradford Booth said: 'The give-and-take of dialectics in defence of one's prejudice he found exhilarating, but he scarcely cared on what side of a question chance threw him. Some observers did not see that his fondness for argument arose not from the vanity of sour opposition, but from pleasure in the cultivation of intellectual agility' (*Anthony Trollope*, p. 12). His old friend Sir Henry James was a favourite opponent. Writing to John Blackwood in Mar 1877, Joseph Langford spoke of 'a great scene between Trollope and James. Trollope raging and roaring with immense vehemence against the system of cross examination as practised and James defending it with calmness and good nature' (MS National Library of Scotland, cited *Letters*, II, 950). Early in 1874, when Thomas Hughes was seeking nomination as Liberal candidate for Parliament against Daniel Grant, Trollope put his case to James, then Gladstone's Attorney-General, with vehement debate until one-thirty the following morning (E. C. Mack and W. H. G. Armytage, *Thomas Hughes: The Life of the Author of Tom Brown's Schooldays* (1952) pp. 206–7).

5. Edmund Yates ascribed this retort to a meeting of Surveyors (p. 51 above).

6. See p. 170 above for a fuller account of the meeting.

7. The Duke of Westminster, Hugh Lupus Grosvenor (1825–99), took his seat in the House of Lords as 3rd Marquis of Westminster (1870). He adhered to Gladstone throughout the prolonged controversy.

8. Although they were not close, Hardy did consult Trollope on publishing affairs in Mar 1877 (*Letters*, II, 715). James Milne once told Hardy of reading in a George Eliot letter the novelist described as the 'insusceptible Trollope'. Hardy laughed and said the phrase was exactly right 'because Trollope, in conversation, just went on, indifferent to attention and to other people' (*The Memoirs of a Bookman* (1934) p. 135).

He Talked as Well and as Heartily as Usual

E. A. FREEMAN

From 'Anthony Trollope', *Macmillan's Magazine*, XLVII (Jan 1883) 236–40. Edward Augustus Freeman (1823–92), distinguished historian and regular contributor to *Saturday Review*, 1855–78, Regius Professor of Modern History at Oxford, 1884–92. His historical studies included *History of the Norman Conquest* (1867–79), *Growth of the English Constitution* (1872) and *Historical Geography of*

Europe (1881–2). Without losing sight of the crusty, disputatious Trollope, Freeman manages to suggest a mellowing (so eloquently present in the letters of the last years). Escott, too, noted his cordiality to those guests invited to converse in the book-lined nook which adjoined the double drawing-room at South Harting. He spoke of Trollope as peacemaker between Edward Pigott and Edward Dicey who had hardly spoken for a generation. His way of bringing them together 'reminded both men of a sixth-form boy who, separating two juniors engaged in fisticuffs, bids them, with a gentle kick, go about their business' (*Anthony Trollope*, p. 307). This occurred some eighteen months before he died.

Mr Anthony Trollope is dead. There is no need for me either to write his life or to criticise his writings. That has been done plentifully already by others.[1] But as it happened that it was my lot to see very nearly the last of him before the seizure which took him from us, I feel a kind of call to put on record a few remembrances of him during the present and last years. He was not an old friend of mine, though, but for the chances of an examination, he easily might have been. He was eight years older than I; so it must have been about the year 1833 that he stood for a scholarship at Trinity.[2] He was not elected, and Mr Arthur Kensington, who was tutor in my earliest days, was. Mr Kensington, if he be still alive, is lost to the world. But he was a fine scholar and a man whom everybody was fond of. Still I think we should have been well pleased to reckon either the creator of Barchester or the champion of Cicero among the scholars and fellows of Sir Thomas Pope.

This little fact in his early life was told me by Mr Trollope last year. It was then that I made his personal acquaintance at Rome. I saw him there for the first time on 29 March 1881. I had long wished to see him. Some may remember that, about a dozen years before that time, I had controversy with him on the question of the 'Morality of Field Sports'. Mr Trollope answered an article of mine which appeared under that heading in the *Fortnightly Review*.[3] I cannot say that Mr Trollope's article at all converted me to an approval of his favourite amusement; but it gave me the very best personal impression of at least one of its votaries. I need not say that before that I was familiar with a good many of Mr Trollope's novels, especially the inimitable *Warden* and *Barchester Towers*. Those tales always spoke specially home to one whose life has somehow been cast a good deal among bishops, deans and canons, though I must very positively add that it has never been my lot to come across Mrs Proudie in real life. But I never saw Mr Trollope himself till that day at Rome. There I met him, and one who was by described the meeting – 'They took to one another in a moment.' I certainly took to Mr Trollope, and I have every reason to think that Mr Trollope took to me. He told me afterwards that before that time he had hated me for two reasons. One was that in the controversy about field sports I had, with special reference to the last moments of the fox, asked the question which Cicero asks about the *venationes* of his time: '*Quae potest homini polito esse delectatio?*'[4] I was a little proud of this ground of hatred, as I took it for a sign that I might fairly cry '*Habet*'. The other ground I thought was less reasonable. When one of the last meetings on South-Eastern affairs was held, as late as 1878, while I was away at Palermo, I was asked, as I could not be there, to write something, and what I wrote was read at the meeting.[5] Mr Trollope hated me because time was spent in reading my letter, which would have been better spent in hearing a living speech – perhaps from Mr Trollope. I have no doubt that Mr Trollope was quite right in so thinking; but he should surely have hated those who asked me to write, not me who simply did what I was asked. But these, I fancy, were feelings of a past time. As I certainly never hated Mr Trollope at any time, neither do I think that Mr Trollope hated me after that pleasant 29 March. ... With Mr Trollope I did not go much about in Rome, but I went with him to the most fitting of all places to go with him, to the hill where once stood the white streets of Tusculum. On the whole, my head was most full of Octavius Mamilius and his of Marcus Tullius Cicero; still we found much kindred matter to think of and talk of. We climbed the *arx* together, and from that Ebal we cursed a common enemy who shall be nameless. And may I tell both Mr J. C. Morison and his critic in the *Spectator* that, on the slope of that *arx*, hard by the tomb of some praetor or dictator of old Tusculum, I repeated, and Mr Trollope was well pleased to listen to, the soul-stirring lines which begin:

> Fast, fast, with heels wild spurning,
> The dark-grey charger fled. ...

A writer in the *Pall Mall Gazette* said the other day of Mr Trollope, that 'it was honourable to his taste for literature that he should have maintained through one of the busiest lives of our generation his taste for the classics; but his books on Caesar and

Cicero are worthless'. Now when one hears about 'the classics', one knows at once what the argument is worth. When a man opposes 'the classics' to something of our own day, say to a 'busy life', one knows at once that his 'classics' are something apart from the run of real human affairs, scraps perhaps from Horace and Virgil, according to the old 'scholar and gentleman' doctrine. Now Mr Trollope's interest in Roman history was something much higher than this. He took it as something which was a part of the real course of human affairs. I must speak with diffidence as to details; for, though I have talked a good deal with Mr Trollope about such matters, I have not read his books on Caesar and Cicero. To confess the truth, I mean to read them, but I have not yet got to them; if they had dealt with Gaius Licinius and Appius the Blind, I should doubtless have mastered them before now. But I can bear witness that two very eminent historical scholars, one English and one German, think quite differently of Mr Trollope's Roman studies from the writer in the *Pall Mall Gazette*. My English friend held that, notwithstanding some slips in minute scholarship – which might have been avoided if Mr Trollope had been elected at Trinity – he had the root of the matter in him, that he thoroughly understood the real life of his period and his characters. My German friend – whose remarks I showed to Mr Trollope to his extreme delight – took the exactly opposite line to the *Pall Mall* writer; he held that it was just Mr Trollope's own busy life which enabled him really to enter into the true life of Cicero and his contemporaries. This is indeed hitting the nail on the head; it was because Mr Trollope had seen a good deal of men and things in England and Ireland and other parts of the world that he was able to understand men and things at Rome also. I know not how it may sound either at Balliol or at Berlin; but nothing is more certain than that Arnold and Grote, simply because they were active citizens of a free state, understood ten thousand things in Greek and Roman history which Mommsen and Curtius, with all their fresh lights in other ways, fail to understand. And, though I have not read Mr Trollope's Roman books, I have talked enough with him on Roman matters to see that he had read not a little, and that he had made good use of his reading. I dare say he has made slips in detail, but he certainly understood the general state of the case.[6] There was no fear of his thinking that, if a patrician noble married or was adopted into the house of a plebeian noble, he thereby went down into the gutter or

mixed himself up with the *'canaille'*. Mr Trollope had written
stories enough to know that, in England also, there is nothing
miraculous in a duke marrying the daughter of a baronet or
esquire, or in a baronet or esquire marrying the daughter of a
duke. For Cicero Mr Trollope had a genuine enthusiasm; one
might have thought that his life had been given to Cicero and
nothing else. It was a subject on which he would harangue, and
harangue very well. It was the moral side of Cicero's character, or
at any rate of Cicero's writings, that most struck him. Here, he
said, was a Christian before Christianity. And certainly that man
would be no bad practical Christian who should live according to
Cicero's standard of moral duty. I once ventured to whisper, with
less knowledge of the subject certainly than Mr Trollope's, that
there was something not quite pretty about the divorce of
Terentia and the second marriage with Publilia. But Mr Trollope
did not forsake his friend at a pinch. Terentia had behaved badly
about money-matters during her husband's banishment, and to
divorce her was quite the right thing.

Mr Trollope paid me a visit the week before his seizure.[7] I was
delighted to have him with me for many reasons, not the least
because I wanted to put him on in the geography of Barset and
Barchester. I used to chuckle over the names, thinking how lucky
the novelist was who had made his shire and his city fit so neatly,
as if there really had been *Barsoetan*, as well as *Dorsoetan* and
Sumorsoetan. (So Macaulay's 'Brussex rhine', – which I strongly
suspect is simply the rhine of Mr Busick, – always suggests an
anotherwise unrecorded tribe of Saxons, *Butseseaxe* or *Boet-Sax-
ons*, most fitting indwellers for that marshy land.) It was perhaps
fitting that, in the short time that Mr Trollope was with me, the
only people we had a chance of introducing him to were two
bishops, of different branches of the vineyard. In company with
one of them, Bishop Clifford of Clifton, I took him over part of the
range of hills between Wells and Wedmore, that he might look out
on the land of Barset, if Barset it was to be. It is a land that Mr
Trollope knew well in his Post Office days; but he was well pleased
to take a bird's-eye view of it again. He enjoyed our scenery; but
he did not enjoy either our mud or our stiles, and it was pleasant to
see the way in which the Bishop, more active than I was, helped
him over all difficulties. For then, and even at Rome, Mr Trollope
was clearly not in his full strength, though there was no sign that
serious sickness was at all near. This was on 25 October; the next

day he was shown Wells and Glastonbury in due order. He allowed Barset to be Somerset, though certainly Gatherum Castle has been brought to us from some other land. But he denied that Barchester was Wells. Barchester was Winchester, where he was at school, and the notion of Hiram's Hospital was taken from Saint Cross.[8] But I argued with him that, if Barchester was not Wells, at any rate Wells, perhaps along with other places, had helped to supply ideas for Barchester. The constitution of the church of Barchester, not exactly like either an old or a new foundation, and where the precentor has the singular duty of chanting the litany, seemed to imply that ideas from more than one place were mixed together. The little church over the gate could not come from Wells; but it might come from Canterbury as well as from Winchester, or even from Langport within the bounds of Barset. And was it not *Barchester Towers*? and towers are a feature much more conspicuous at Wells than at Winchester. And if the general ideas of Hiram's Hospital came from Saint Cross, the particular notion of woolcombers must have come from Wells, where a foundation for woolcombers with a becoming inscription is still to be seen. But no; Barset was Somerset, but Barchester was Winchester, not Wells. He had not even taken any ideas from Wells; he had never heard of the Wells woolcombers. Still I cleave to the belief that Mr Trollope, when he went to and fro in Somerset on behalf of Her Majesty's Post Office, had picked up some local ideas, and had forgotten where he found them.[9]

We had also talk about other matters, among them, as was not unnatural, about Lord Palmerston. On that subject I could see that Mr Trollope's Liberalism, though very thorough, was more traditional and conventional than mine, and that we looked at things somewhat differently, if only because he was eight years older than I was. I could see that Mr Trollope felt towards Lord Palmerston as a head of the Liberal party, while to me he was simply the long-abiding deceiver of the Liberal party. Mr Trollope, I could see, measured things by the remembrances of an older time than I did. Mr Trollope had much to say about English interests in Syria, about getting the better of Louis Philippe, and such like, which he clearly knew more about than I did. Only I had a vision that, in this case – perhaps not in this case only – English interests meant, when there was a choice between two despots, putting down the less bad despot to set up the worse. But he seemed little amazed when I told him that to me Lord Palmerston was simply the consistent enemy of freedom abroad and of reform at home, the abettor of Bonaparte and the Turk, the man who never failed to find some struggling people to bully and some overbearing despot to cringe to. If I was a little dim about Louis Philippe, Mr Trollope seemed a little dim about those Greek, Roman and other Southern-Eastern questions, in which Mr Gladstone already stood forth as the champion of good, while Lord Palmerston showed himself no less distinctly the champion of evil than Lord Beaconsfield did afterwards. It was a curious discussion; it was not so much that Mr Trollope and I differed about any fact, or in our estimate of any fact, as that each looked at the question from a side which to the other seemed to have very little meaning.

Mr Trollope left me on 27 October. On 2 November he dined at Mr Macmillan's at Tooting, where I was staying. He talked as well and heartily as usual. We all knew, as I had known the week before, that he was not in strong health, and that he needed to take some care of himself. But there was nothing to put it into anyone's head that the end was so near. The next day came his seizure, and from that day onwards the newspapers told his tale.

NOTES

1. For the range of tributes after his death see Terry, *Anthony Trollope: The Artist in Hiding*, pp. 50–1, 269.

2. Trollope himself records two attempts for a sizarship at Clare Hall and one for Trinity before the idea of a university career was abandoned (*Auto.*, i).

3. *Fortnightly Review* (Oct 1869) 353–85. Trollope responded with 'Mr Freeman on the Morality of Hunting', Dec 1869; a further article 'A Few Words on Mr Trollope's Defence of Hunting', signed Helen Taylor, appeared Jan 1870, pp. 63–8. The *Saturday Review*, 11 Dec 1869, and the *Daily Telegraph*, 18 and 19 Dec 1869, also took up the debate. See also *Auto.*, x.

4. 'What pleasure can it possibly be to a man of culture' ['when either a puny human being is mangled by a most powerful beast, or a splendid beast is transfixed with a hunting spear?] (Cicero, *Letters to His Friends*, trans. W. Glynn Williams, Loeb Classical Library (1965) II, 1). According to William Ballantine, a fellow Garrick member, Trollope declared 'that the fox ought to be deeply obliged to the sportsman, as through his instrumentality it led a comfortable life during a great portion of the year, living in luxury upon the poultry of the surrounding farmer' (*The Old World and the New* (1884) p. 207).

5. To Mrs Katherine Bronson Trollope wrote in Dec 1876: 'Here we are all

agog about the Turks and the Russians, and are so hot that everybody is ready to cut everybody's throat' (*Letters*, II, 700).

6. A timely tribute to the non-university man who had laboured assiduously in his study, it offsets the pedantry his classical efforts had met with in some quarters; note the graceless comment of Dean Merivale (see p. 165 above).

7. Trollope's acceptance of the invitation to Freeman's home, 'Somerlease' near Wells, Somerset, gives clear indication of his ill health: 'I can, with due time, walk up anything, – only I can't sleep, walking or not walking. I can't write, as you see, because my hand is paralysed. I can't sit easily because of a huge truss I wear, and now has come this damnable asthma! But still I am very good to look at; and as I am not afraid to die, I am as happy as other people' (*Letters*, II, 990).

8. The case of the hospital of St Cross, Winchester, often mentioned in the papers during the early 1850s.

9. Trollope does, of course, refer to the germ of *The Warden* from his wanderings in another area while on postal duties: 'In the course of this job I visited Salisbury, and whilst wandering there on a mid-summer evening round the purlieus of the cathedral I conceived the idea of *The Warden* from whence came that series of novels of which Barchester, with its bishops, deans and archdeacon, was the central site' (*Auto.*, v).

How Simple, How Straightforward, How Sincere He Was

CECILIA MEETKERKE

From 'Last Reminiscences of Anthony Trollope', *Temple Bar*, LXX (Jan 1884) 130–4; 'Anthony Trollope', *Blackwood's Magazine*, 133 (Feb 1883) 316–20. Cecilia Elizabeth Meetkerke (1823?–1903) was granddaughter of the second Earl of Arran and daughter of the Hon. Edward Gore. Her friendship with the novelist has an irony which returns us neatly to the starting point of this volume: her husband was the son of that very Adolphus Meetkerke (1753–1840) whose marriage and begetting of an heir had ended those expectations of wealth which had precipitated the downfall of Trollope's own father. Cecilia benefited over the years from Trollope's tips about writing (see *Letters*, I, 212–14; II, 848) and went on to enjoy modest success in periodicals and as a writer for children. Her book *The Guests of the Flowers; A Botanical Sketch for Children* (1880) was followed by *The Guests at Home* (1881). The first tribute was for many years wrongly attributed to Alfred Austin. The second article, from a year earlier, contains the fullest account of the writing out of Mrs Proudie from *The Last Chronicle of Barset*.

Seven years ago, before he had been threatened with any symptom of decay, in the midst of full contentment and success, Anthony Trollope finished the last words of his *Autobiography*; so closing the record of his literary life, when it was in truth by no means finished. *The Duke's Children, Ayala's Angel, [Why] Frau Frohmann [Raised Her Prices: And Other Stories], The Fixed Period, [Life of] Thackeray, [The Life of] Cicero, An Eye for an Eye*, and some other stories, had not been published, nor had his imagination begun to fail, or his routine been in any way altered.[1] He wrote that year, of himself; 'I observe when people of my age are spoken of, they are described as effete and moribund, just burning down the last half inch of the candle in the socket. I feel as though I should still like to make a "flare up" with my half inch. In spirit I could trundle a hoop about the streets, and could fall in love with a young woman just as readily as ever; as she doesn't want me, I don't – but I could.'[2]

The time left unrecorded was of no less interest than that earlier one; it was still full of profit and pleasure, and was possibly richer in the means of judging fairly of the failures and the successes of authorship. If he expected a little less of himself, if he exacted less, he still performed certain methodical tasks. The punctual and deliberate habits of years were only slightly modified in strictness, and there was certainly no idle moment of his day.

But still the record was closed. It must be a matter of regret that it was so, and the critic who best understood him [Escott] does not hesitate to express his surprise that the popular author should have chosen to cut his own written life short, and consider it rounded and completed at this particular date, but the reason is doubtless to be found in the painful affection [*sic*] of the hand from which he had begun to suffer, and which is called the writer's cramp, although by no means solely confined to authors.

It becomes difficult to hold a pen, and though the difficulty may, at first, be overcome by a vigorous effort, it is soon found that no amount of effort will prevail. In such cases there is no remedy but rest. The novels and most of the correspondence had to be written from dictation, although he still kept a few friends as the recipients of what he himself described as the illegible scrawl regarded by him as his own letters to his own special correspondents, 'and which', he added, 'they tell me afterwards they can't make out a word of'.

He found in his niece, who was to him the tenderest and most devoted of daughters, an untiring and reliable secretary; but still, the record of daily personal impressions could not be carried on with the same spontaneous ease as heretofore, so it was brought to an end, and the farewell spoken, as if already from the further shore.[3]

But still the old accustomed method of literary industry was pursued. No one ever acted up more fully to his own convictions or followed more conscientiously himself the advice he gave to others; insisting constantly that the author wants a habit of industry as well as every other workman. ...

During their residence in Montagu Square some hours of writing were accomplished before the midday breakfast, leaving the rest of the day more free for other business, and for the enjoyments which were no less energetically pursued.

To this partly foreign and wholly substantial meal, any intimate friend was welcome, and those who came for counsel, or sympathy, might count on both, and solid information and assistance too, which always might be had for asking.

A not too hurried interview might be obtained in the quaint and quiet book-room, where his five thousand volumes had been carefully stored; and after a search upon the chimneypiece amongst a whole army of spectacles for the exact pair which should enable him to read the face of his guest, he would take his own armchair: not however occupying it for long, but jumping up violently, and taking up his usual position on the hearthrug, too impetuous even for the appearance of ease. It was here, as Mr Escott graphically describes, the identity of the man and the author was immediately perceived. ...

He used to complain that one had to apologise nowadays for all eagerness. 'We are all so very smooth', he writes, 'in our usual intercourse that any urgency takes the guise of violence. I own I like a good contradictory conversation in which for the moment the usual subserviency of coat and trousers to bodies, skirts and petticoats, may be – well – not forgotten – but for the moment put on one side.'[4]

The writer of these lines was once emboldened to request from him an introductory letter to the editor of the *Fortnightly*, and was asked, with look and manner well characterised by Wilkie Collins as the embodiment of a gale of wind, 'But why the *Fortnightly*? The learned editor is so indefatigable, that every word you write down will be weighed to the last pronoun. Perhaps you wish to be so weighed – but you are ignorant! ignorant! *not of what you ought to know – but of what you ought not to know!*'[5] I.e. the characteristics of editors and the different requirements of magazines. This was explained with an inimitable force and facility of diction; an enormous amount of information was hurled about, and then the storm subsided, the article in question was glanced at, and the letter written. A gust was raised on mention being made of a highly eulogistic article on his personal and literary merits, from the pen of a partial writer. He was sensitively alive to anything of that kind of praise seeming to be the product rather of personal love than of enquiry or judgement, and in a letter alluding to the article, he said, 'I don't like such notices, particularly when they are written by friends. I would much rather be left to the mercies of the real critics. Sydney Smith used to say, speaking of practical jokes, that it was impossible to say how much melted butter a gentleman would bear to have poured into his dress-coat pocket; I dislike it almost as much when it is poured down my back.'[6]

This sensitiveness as to the personal details of private life was doubtless very strong in him, but like some other of his strongly expressed opinions, may be practically exaggerated. It has been so forcibly present to his relations and friends that his true and most uncommon character has hardly been so well defined for the sake of those who shall come after him, as it has every right to be, and it would be very regrettable should the delicacy of the living man be seriously allowed to rob his memory of that which is his due.

There is certainly such a thing as a misleading reticence, and in the preface to the *Autobiography* some honest tribute seems to be missing.

The book will live as the exact and faithful portrait of the man, and might well have been supplemented by a few more finished touches telling, as his own words could not so fully do, how simple, how straightforward, how sincere he was, with what a tender heart, and what an open hand. Had this been not withheld, there would have been less room for offhand ignorant criticism such as lately found a place in a prominent review, where an impression is produced, at least as false as it is ignorant, that Anthony Trollope's vehemence was roughness, and his manner coarse.[7] ... [Reference follows to Trollope's meeting with J. S. Mill, described earlier.]

In the summer of 1880 the Trollopes left London and went to live at Harting, a village on the confines of Hampshire, chosen because they found there a house to suit them, and the end of that year Anthony Trollope wrote: 'Yes, we have changed our mode of life altogether. We have got a little cottage here, just big enough (or nearly so) to hold my books, with five acres and a cow and a dog and a cock and a hen. I have got seventeen years' lease, and therefore I hope to lay my bones here. Nevertheless I am busy as would be one thirty years younger, in cutting out dead boughs and putting up a paling here and a little gate there. We go to church and mean to be very good, and have maids to wait on us. The reason for all this I will explain when I see you, although, as far as I see at present, there is no good reason other than that we were tired of London.'[8]

The life at Harting was very happy; the Rector of his little village has described it in a few brief sentences written with the regard Trollope always won at first sight from all who were in any way brought near him.[9]

'Though he rigidly maintained his lifelong habits of industry, he was no recluse, and his genial frankness soon made him the honoured friend of us all. The sick poor in particular found him a staunch benefactor. To the last he was never weary of generous deeds, generally done on the spur of the moment. A labourer of looting propensities and unable to obtain farm work, employed at Mr Trollope's fences, was seen by the gardener to take some fallen apples. The master was informed and the gardener suggested the policeman. Mr Trollope, apparently in thunder, left his sanctum, and found the culprit eating his dinner under a tree, a piece of bread in one hand and an apple in the other.

'"Who allowed you to take my apples?" said the thunder.

'"I had nothing but bread, and it's better with an apple", quothed Ishmael.

'Mr Trollope walked indoors, cut some slices of ham and cheese from the luncheon table, took them out and threw them into the man's lap, saying: "Eat and *be better*."'

With characteristic tenderness of conscience he afterwards doubted if he had done rightly, or the tale of his mercy would never have been told.

But alas! the happy time at Harting had to be brought to a close. The health which had been so strong was evidently failing, and he often spoke more seriously than in jest of his own novelette *The Fixed Period*, then coming out in *Blackwood's Magazine*, declaring it to be his own unaffected opinion that it would be well if England were to adopt the laws of Britannula, and abolish the miseries, weakness and *fainéant* imbecility of old age by the pre-arranged ceasing to live of those who would otherwise become old.

It was at the close of a lively morning-visit that he first told one of his greatest friends that his life was in danger, saying in the most common conversational tone, 'I have had a terrible verdict pronounced against me since I saw you last. They say I have got angina pectoris. I am to eat and drink, and get up and sit down at my peril, and may drop down dead at any moment.' He subsequently consulted Dr Murrell, the well-known authority on angina pectoris, who did not endorse the verdict, but found that his heart was weak, and that hard work had made an old man of him.[10]

For more than a year he remained under the same medical care, and got comparatively well. He was enabled to resume his favourite exercise, and his usual animated life, being, however, fairly warned, and that impressively, that he must neither overwork nor over-exert himself. The injunction was perfectly vain. He was extraordinarily impatient and reckless of his own condition; would still dash out of railway carriages before the stopping of the train, would hurry in and out of cabs, and give way in all things to his usual impetuosity.[11] The end was grievous as it was sudden, and is briefly described in the preface:

'On the evening of 3 November 1882, he was seized with paralysis of the right side, accompanied by loss of speech. His mind also had failed, though at intervals his thoughts would return to him. After the first three weeks these lucid intervals became rarer, but it was always very difficult to tell how far his mind was sound or how far astray.'

He was moved from the rooms in Suffolk Street, which he had taken as soon as it was decided that he could not live at Harting, and where the doors were besieged with anxiously enquiring visitors, to a quiet house in Welbeck Street, where he died nearly five weeks from the night of his attack.

The wish he had expressed so strongly in his days of health and strength was granted.[12] The power of work was over, and he was taken from the world in which, according to his own view, there could be no longer any joy.

[Cecilia Meetkerke's second tribute begins by noting Trollope's distaste for eulogy.] There was no kindlier or more genial man than

Anthony Trollope, no one more hospitable and easy of access. Address him with a friendly word, and after a keen glance through his spectacles, under his heavy brows, you would have of his best in return. He had no idea of keeping his pearls for a chosen companion, but would lavish them freely for the entertainment of the hour and his chance companionships.

He had travelled much, and met with all sorts and conditions of men. He liked to know of what sort of metal they were made. If a man were only true, that was all he wanted of him: from a woman he would put up with something less – having, by means of that faculty which has no other name than genius, become more thoroughly acquainted with the ins and outs of the feminine mind than almost any other author. From, probably, the last letter he ever wrote with his own hand, may be quoted one of those subtle touches of which so many are to be found in his novels.[13] His correspondent had reproached him for some imaginary neglect, in the words 'a worm will turn'. And he replied: 'A woman will turn, – so will a worm, or a fox, or a politician, but, like the politician, has often no honest ground for turning: the truth is, a woman delights to have the opportunity of turning, so that she may make herself out to be injured.'

One of the chief characteristics of his conversation was the vehement enthusiasm he was able to get up with a suddenness which was even startling. He would maintain his own opinion almost with violence; yet no one more thoroughly enjoyed an argument, or put up more delightedly with flat contradiction – so fully able to enter into the right side of the question, that, in the genuine joy and hurry of the fight, he would sometimes forget which was his own. It was seldom that he constituted himself the hero of his own story; but on one occasion the merits of his novels coming under discussion, and he giving his own verdict decidedly in favour of *The Last Chronicle of Barset*, one of his friends remarked that, contrary to his usual smooth-going style, he had actually fallen into tragedy whilst describing the death of Mrs Proudie. 'Ah, that was not altogether my doing', he replied, jumping up from his chair and putting himself on the hearth-rug, in the attitude which will be so readily recalled by all who knew him.

'This was how it happened. I was writing a note at a table in the Athenaeum, when two men came in and settled themselves at each side of the fireplace; one had a number of *The Last Chronicle of Barset* in his hand, and they began discussing the story. "Trollope gets awfully prosy,' said one of the critics; "he does nothing but repeat himself, – Mrs Proudie – Mrs Proudie – Mrs Proudie, – chapter after chapter." "I quite agree with you," replied the other, "it is Mrs Proudie *ad nauseam*; I am sick to death of Mrs Proudie." Of course they did not know me, so I jumped up and stood between them. "Gentlemen," I said, "I am the culprit – I am Mr Trollope – and I will go home this instant and *kill* Mrs Proudie."'

In the very next page, accordingly, the weak and persecuted bishop is made actually to pray for the removal of the masterful partner who has brought so much grief and humiliation upon him; and hardly has the tragic prayer been uttered than he is made aware of its fulfilment. ...

It would be a work of supererogation to say that not a shadow of envy or jealousy was ever noticed in Mr Trollope's literary career. He was gratified as much by the success of a friend as by his own. But his views of literary probity were no less strict than those he applied to every other transaction; and what he most thoroughly objected to was any attempt at what he called 'underhand approaches': that is to say, private recommendations to editors or influential friends. His advice when applied to for such assistance was invariably the same: 'Stand fast on your own honest ground, and care for nothing beyond, let what will come of it.' On one occasion his applicant had the audacity to remark that standing on one's own honest ground was all very well, and a finely sounding phrase, but that 'A. T.' on a paper enclosing a manuscript from an unknown author would certainly have some weight with an editor. The following letter was received by return of post:

MY DEAR FRIEND, The verses, which are very pretty, I have sent on, withdrawing your note and substituting one from myself. They may not improbably print and publish them; I do not think they will pay for them. But A. T. will neither in one case nor the other have done either good or harm in the matter. If you don't believe in one's own honest ground, what should you believe in? As for favour, you should not condescend to accept it; but there is not much favour in it – though perhaps a little. The owner of the magazine wants to make money, and would sooner have the worst verses a man could put together with Tennyson's name to them, then the most charming poetry from you, because Tennyson's work would sell the periodical. But for you, as for me formerly,

there is nothing but honest ground that will do any good and no
good coming from anything else is worth having. – Your most
affectionate friend and mentor. A. T.[14]

NOTES

1. The other books were *South Africa* (1878), *Is He Popenjoy?* (1878), *How the
Mastiffs Went to Iceland* (1878), *John Caldigate* (1879), *Cousin Henry* (1879), *Dr
Wortle's School* (1881), *Marion Fay* (1882), *Kept in the Dark* (1882), *Mr Scarborough's
Family* (1883), *An Old Man's Love* (1883) and *The Landleaguers* (unfinished, 1883).

2. *Letters*, II, 702. Trollope seems determined at this time of reappraisal to
keep active: 'No, I certainly do not like idleness – what the Italians say *fare vita
beata*, – i.e. at the end of life to live on your means with nothing to do, would be
miserable to me', he wrote to G. W. Rusden in Oct 1876 (*Letters*, II, 696).

3. Florence Nightingale Bland (b. 1855) was the daughter of Rose Trollope's
sister who had married a Joseph Bland. When both her parents were dead she
came to the Trollopes at Waltham in 1863. Acting as the novelist's amanuensis
she took *Cousin Henry* (begun in Oct 1878) from his dictation and large portions of
all later manuscripts are in her hand. He rode with her, liked showing her off,
and came increasingly to see her as the daughter he and Rose had not had (see
Letters, II, 978–9). It was something of a family joke that if she dared interrupt the
flow Trollope threw a tantrum. A letter to Millais of 25 June 1881 records his dire
anxiety when she became seriously ill (*Letters*, II, 911). Trollope said of her:
'However early the hour, however dull and depressing the dawn, we soon warm
to our work and get so excited with those we are writing about, that I don't know
whether she or I is most surprised when the time comes to leave off for breakfast'
(Escott, *Anthony Trollope*, p. 300).

4. *Letters*, II, 998.

5. Not quite the text of the letter of 10 Apr 1876, but close (*Letters*, II, 684). The
irony in John Morley's direction is clear.

6. Probably written in the 1870s (*Letters*, II, 997).

7. John Morley and Mrs Humphry Ward, 'Anthony Trollope', *Macmillan's
Magazine*, XLIV (Nov 1883) 53–6.

8. *Letters*, II, 887–8.

9. Revd H. D. Gordon. See pp. 236–7 below.

10. He wrote in similar terms to Tom in mid-1881: 'They tell me my heart is
worn out having been worked too hard. I cannot among them, understand
anything of it, and do not' (*Letters*, II, 912). *The Times* obituary notice also
recorded that overwork had contributed to his sudden collapse. Medical opinion
was sought from Sir William Jenner, Physician in Ordinary to the Queen, and
Trollope's old friend Sir Richard Quain.

11. It has to be remembered that besides a holiday in Rome and Florence in
1881, Trollope undertook two exhausting journeys to Ireland, May–June and
Aug–Sep 1882, for his novel *The Landleaguers*. See also his frenetic social and club
schedule in Jan 1882 (*Letters*, II, 936–7).

12. What he had dreaded – enforced immobility – was not to be his fate.
As he wrote to G. W. Rusden in June 1876: 'As the time for passing away comes

near me I have no fear as to the future – I am ready to go. I dread nothing but physical inability and that mental lethargy which is apt to accompany it' (*Letters*, II, 691).

13. Among letters of uncertain date (*Letters*, II, 1004). Not necessarily his last letter, but perhaps a reference to the fact that the handwriting was his own and not Florence Bland's.

14. The applicant for advice was, of course, Cecilia Meetkerke; the exchange occurred in Nov 1879 (*Letters*, II, 848).

The Last Days

H. D. GORDON AND OTHERS

In early July 1880, Trollope gave up his residence in central London and moved to the Sussex/Hampshire border, where he took a lease on a house called North End at South Harting, near Petersfield. He fussed over having bins made for his precious wine and getting his own and Henry Merivale's books down, writing at last to his son on 8 July 1880: 'Here we are on our journey down to Harting. Indeed we have been hard at work at Harting all day and have retired here for our mutton chop at night' (*Letters*, II, 875). The establishment included two horses, a brougham and a pony carriage. Still with an eye for equine niceties, he observed, 'The pony is a nice little beast but rather old.' Next the neighbours came to mind: 'We like the neighbours as far as we have seen them as yet' (*Letters*, II, 877); that the new resident quickly made his presence felt among them the following tribute makes clear. But he was going downhill, and asthma aggravated by damp country conditions plagued him sorely until the onset of the stroke announced in the third item below. (1) from Revd Henry Doddridge Gordon, *Publishers' Circular*, xxv (18 Dec 1882) 1515–16. Vicar of Harting and one of those unfussy clergymen Trollope warmed to, Gordon also published *The History of Harting* (1877) and *Among the Birds of Harting* (1886); (2) from Sir John Tilley, *London to Tokyo* (1942) p. 8. John Tilley (1869–1952) was Trollope's godson. John Tilley, Trollope's brother-in-law, whose wife had died in 1880, was at home on the occasion described with his daughter Edith; (3) from J. B. Atkins, *The Life of Sir William Howard Russell*, 2 vols (1911) II, 316–17; Sir William Howard Russell (1820–1907), 'Billy' to his Garrick friends and a stalwart of Trollope's club circle; (4) from 'Trollope's Last Illness and Death', *Letters*, II, Appendix D, 1035–9.

(1)   In the Sussex village which he made his last earthly home, though he rigidly maintained his lifelong habits of industry, he was no recluse, and his genial frankness soon made him the honoured friend of us all.[1] The sick poor in particular found in him a staunch benefactor, and he would find a few minutes in his daily ride to visit

them and say a few cheery words. He was the life of our school manager meetings, and a generous patron of the education of the poor.[2] He sympathised with the farmers in their troubles, and was always a promoter of the union of the classes. Though a strong Liberal, he was against disestablishment; his ardent wish was that the Church of England should be stronger, and he believed that as a fact she was growing stronger day by day.[3] He rarely, even when his health was failing, missed Sunday morning service, always punctual to the minute – an alert and reverent and audible worshipper, and a steady communicant.

(2) My father joined the Post Office Service in 1829 on the nomination of Sir Francis Freeling, the then Secretary, who was a friend of his mother's. He had to pass some form of qualifying examination, which was conducted by Sir Francis himself in the presence of his daughters. In 1839 my father was made Surveyor of the North of England, and in that year married Cecilia Trollope. He settled at Penrith, and as his district included Northumberland, Cumberland and Yorkshire, a great part of his life at that time was spent on coaches. My father's great friend while he lived in Cumberland, and indeed afterwards, was Sir George Musgrave of Edenhall. Sir George was decidedly of the old school. When my father went to congratulate him on his son's engagement he was very angry. 'Congratulate me because my son is going to marry a pawnbroker's daughter.' 'Surely not,' said my father. 'I understood the father was a stockbroker.' 'What, pray, is the difference?' asked Sir George.

My father and his wife brought their families with them, for old Mrs Tilley and old Mrs Trollope both came to live in the neighbourhood, though the latter was not very happy there. She once took my father to call on Wordsworth, but he insisted on waiting outside, and when she came out she said he had done well, for the poet was most disagreeable.

In 1849 my father became Assistant Secretary of the Post Office, and Secretary in 1864, having married my mother in 1861. Anthony Trollope was my godfather, and I remember him very well, with his somewhat shaggy appearance and boisterous laugh. On one occasion he wrote to say that he would look in next day for lunch: anything would do for him; a crust of bread and a scrap of cheese. My half-sister (his niece) and I arranged in a small back-room a table covered with a grubby kitchen cloth, smeared with grease and mustard; and on this we set the tail end of a stale loaf, some mouldy bits of cheese and a jug of water. When Uncle Tony arrived my sister led him to the feast, explaining that as she knew he would be in a hurry she had everything ready. He looked at the table with loathing, but when my sister said: 'Well, that is what you asked for, but if you have changed your mind there is some more lunch in the dining-room', he fairly roared and hugged her like a bear. A little later, while I was away at school, he came to dinner one night; after dinner my sister read *Vice Versa* aloud to him and my father, also a great laugher. Uncle Tony roared as usual; suddenly my father and sister noticed that while they were laughing he was silent: he had had a stroke from which he never recovered. I do not think he ever heard me say my catechism, but I once wrote to him from my private school to tell him, with an eye to the main chance, that I had won second prize in a spelling bee, a form of entertainment then rather popular. He replied, sending me half a sovereign, but alleging, I still believe untruly, that in my letter to him I had spelt night with a k.

(3)   [Hearing of Trollope's illness, Russell wrote home for information and received this letter from Millais, dated 5 Dec 1882.] My Sweet William, – I was quite delighted to hear from you, and receive your admirable artistic performance. I regret to say that dear old Trollope is in a *very critical state*, and I believe there is little hope. I have called frequently and know that he is rarely conscious and has only been able to utter one word since the attack – 'No.' In case you are ignorant of the particulars, I may tell you shortly that he was struck down suddenly while dining.[4] The whole of one side was paralysed and his speech gone. He was removed to his old lodgings in Suffolk Street.[5] The last few days they have difficulty to feed him. Need I say more to prove how hopeless his condition is, and is there one word necessary from me to say what I think of the man we have both lost? 'Fill up the ranks and march on' – as Dickens said when he heard of Thackeray's death – is the spirit in which I pass on to other subjects.

(4)   [After the blow fell Trollope was taken to a nursing home in Welbeck Street. No less than 13 bulletins in *The Times* followed his gradual decline until he died on 6 Dec 1882. The obituary notice next day paid tribute to 'the most methodical romance writer of whom we have ever heard', remarkable both for his 'five o'clock in

the morning genius' and the 'wonderful uniformity of quality in each of his novels'. Trollope, said *The Times*, 'has enriched our English fiction with characters destined to survive'. He would be missed by many friends 'to whom he was endeared by his kindly nature and his genial manners' (*The Times*, 7 Dec 1882, p. 6). His brother, Thomas Adolphus, had been telegraphed in Rome immediately after the stroke, and some of his comments in letters to Henry Merivale Trollope conclude this account.]

[4 or 5 Nov 1882, Rome.] ... We are very anxious to hear whether and how far he has recovered the use of his mind. I have indeed very little doubt now of his recovery from the seizure. But I would give much to know that his mind returns. You [tell] me – no doubt judiciously – not to come. And indeed it would have been difficult for me to do so. But if it could have been of any comfort to him I would willingly have done so. I fully trust now that long before I could reach him he will be out of any such condition as should require my coming. I agree with you that the varying intonation of his voice must be taken to shew that he is in possession of his reason. The mischief is, I take it, physical in its nature, and consists in inability to say the words he wants to say. This is not an uncommon thing in many cases of illness far from serious. ...

[2 Dec 1882.] Thanks for your carefully written letter. It is not a reassuring one. I am distressed at the instances you mention of his *unreasonable* actions – such as wanting to undress in the dining room. It seems to me that such things can with difficulty be explained by 'obstinacy' and 'irritation'. Does Murrell know of these things? And does he think that they can be attributed to effects of a paralytic attack from which recovery may be hoped? You say he will 'never be the same man again'. But this is a very elastic phrase. It may mean that he will never be able to write another book, or it may mean much worse. ...

[9 Dec 1882.] I can't say how great a consolation it is to me that I came to England and saw what may be pretty well considered the last of him, while he was still the man I have known – man and boy – for 60 years! ...

[10 Dec 1882.] … The *Standard* does not say nearly enough of his official services; – nor probably will any of the others; because his official life is altogether overshadowed by his literary position, and because the men of your generation have forgotten or never heard anything about it.

Very few men would or *could* have done what he did in establishing the house-to-house delivery throughout several counties, walking himself over *every* footman's walk to ascertain the proper time and best arrangement of delivery.

[12 Dec 1882.] … Yes! my dear Harry no man as you say ever had a better father; and he was a very loving brother too. And as you also truly say he had a heart capable of loving much. Yes! I have *no* doubt, that he is happy; and I trust to meet him again.

I have this morning letters from Charles Wortley and from Austin giving me a few word[s] of account of the funeral.[6] Austin says there were but few persons present. I am *very* glad that you are all of opinion, that I was right not to think of coming – that is – *I did think* of it; but decided against it. I would have given much to see him once again in his right mind; but I care little for funeral attendances, and would not wish any human being to cross the street to come to mine.

NOTES

1. 'North End or, as it is today known, The Grange, lies in Harting parish, some twelve miles from Chichester and four from Petersfield. At one time two farmhouses, but now joined together, it is among the best and prettiest buildings in the district. Surrounded by an estate of nearly seventy acres, its long line of windows and doors opens on a delightful lawn, with a background of copse, studded with Scotch firs and larches. Under these a long walk, worthy of Windsor or Kensington, starting from the garden gate, leads through fields up to a South Down hill. On the lawn itself might have been seen, even since Trollope's day, at one end, the greenhouse, whose flowers he used to tend' (Escott, *Anthony Trollope*, pp. 299–300). The gardens were said to have inspired Alfred Austin's poem 'The Garden That I Love'.

2. 'Penny Readings were in those days still popular. Trollope not only patronised and assisted them, but delighted his rural neighbours by securing on the platform, or in the body of the room, some of his well-known London visitors, notably Sir Henry James and J. E. Millais' (Escott, *Anthony Trollope*, p. 300).

3. Trollope's political hue – as the advanced but still Conservative Liberal he termed himself (*Auto.*, xvi) – took a bluer tinge as he grew older. He was sorely disappointed in Gladstone's conduct of foreign affairs and disgusted by the turn

of events in Ireland. He wrote to W. Lucas Collins in Sep 1882: 'I for one cannot forgive him the injustice which he has done in Ireland at the behest of Mr Bright' (*Letters*, II, 984).

4. Sadleir's account suggests a build-up of tension on the fateful day of 3 Nov 1882. Trollope had been disturbed in the afternoon by a German band playing under his hotel window and routed the musicians with his customary vocal powers.

5. Garlant's Hotel (later Garland's) Suffolk Street, Pall Mall, a favourite haunt since 1860. In 1868 he recommended it to Longfellow for a London stop-over: 'a place much frequented by country Bishops and Archdeacons, and highly respectable', noted Longfellow (*The Letters of Henry Wadsworth Longfellow*, ed. Andrew Hilen (Cambridge, Mass., 1982) v, 235).

6. Trollope was buried on 9 Dec in Kensal Green, not far from the grave of his adored Thackeray. Among the mourners were Robert Browning, J. E. Millais, Alfred Austin, Frederic Chapman and G. W. Rusden.

Such a Very Thorough Gentleman

MURIEL TROLLOPE

From 'What I Was Told', *Trollopian*, II (Mar 1948) 223–35.

And this brings me to my dear Grandfather Anthony. As I said, he was, above all, a very thorough Englishman. That is why his chief stories of country life seldom go beyond his own country of Barsetshire, 'a little bit of England which I have created myself'. His characters were varied pictures of human nature, and I do not think that many of them were taken from actual life. My father always maintained that Mrs Proudie, that most detestable old lady, was merely a domineering woman such as can be met with in any age, anywhere. She was so skilfully drawn that many originals were found for her. A gentleman wrote to me years ago that his friends had assured him that Mrs Proudie was, in sober truth, the wife of an Essex parson. 'I did not answer, as I considered it useless.' He also told me that Dean Stanley, a famous Dean of Westminster, was supposed to be the chief character in *Tom Brown's Schooldays*. Arthur Stanley had left Rugby and had taken his degree at Oxford before Tom Hughes entered the school. In such manner does rumour distort fact.

Mr Michael Sadleir's *Commentary* and the late Sir Hugh Walpole's *Life* revived Anthony Trollope to a forgetting world. People were so accustomed to the beautiful old cathedrals, cloisters and closes in their midst that they took them all for granted. When I was a girl I met many people abroad who told me they had been brought up on my grandfather's books, but the later generation had not realised how faithful were the pictures that he drew of cathedral and country life till Mr Sadleir's and Sir Hugh Walpole's book appeared.[1]

I think this is why some of you in your United States, many of you of pure old English descent, are so fond of my grandfather's books. For all your independence and emancipation, your justified pride in the great country of your achievement, which so many races have combined to create, you have retained a deep affection for the little country from which some of you originally sprang and 'love of her mellow landscape and green sequestered vales' is always with you.

I was brought up in Switzerland, among the great mountains of the Bernese Oberland and in Florence, the home of beauty. I did not return to England till I was grown up. I do feel that my own dear American friends' love of England opened my eyes to her gentle loveliness. I will not, however, talk about my grandfather's books, for you all know them as well as I do.

All their lives, my grandparents retained their love for Ireland. When at ninety-five my grandmother was told that I was going to work in a Red Cross Hospital, in the First World War, she asked at once: 'Will there be any Irish soldiers there?'[2]

My mother greatly enjoyed her visits at Montagu Square before she married my father. She had been at school at Aix-la-Chapelle (Aachen) in Germany with Florence Bland, my grandmother's niece. My mother and Anthony got on capitally together. He declared they must be 'first cousins fifty times removed'! With a young girl's audacity she asked him one morning at breakfast whether he would ride in the Park with her? The hour suggested was one of his sacred working hours! 'Do you want to see me begging my bread?' he jested. However, he consented. 'Can you hold a horse?' he asked. 'Oh yes, of course', replied mamma gaily. So off they started. Somehow her whip tickled her horse's head, and he suddenly bolted down Rotten Row in Hyde Park with all the vigour he could muster. Mercifully my grandfather caught her up and stopped the animal. The result might have been very much worse than a lesson – never to dangle a whip near a horse's ears again. I never heard that the ride was repeated!

She was taken to many interesting gatherings, among them a soirée of the Royal Society of Literature, where she beheld Charlotte Brontë being lionised. The old London City Companies also entertained sumptuously in those days. Before their marriage, my mother and father attended a ball given by the Fishmongers' Company. The flowers which decorated the rooms and the roses for the ladies' dresses cost £1000. My grandfather was made an honorary member of the Grocers' Company, and either before or after that he became a Freemason.[3] ...

There are those who have been grossly unfair to my grandfather. Remarks have been repeated which were made by men who never really knew him, nor understood him, for they only met him but once or a few times. How could they be an indication of his real character or reveal the whole man? Such judgements are purely ephemeral. In fact, many things have been said which can only have been intended to be derogatory to his memory and to disparage it. As his only surviving grandchild in England, I feel this misrepresentation very keenly. My father was in the habit of saying, 'Rarer than diamonds or pearls is the spirit of discernment.' Discernment is decidedly a necessary qualification for a biography. Mr Michael Sadleir has it in fullest measure. His *Commentary*, besides being a mine of information, is an eminently trustworthy and reliable one because he looked beneath the surface. No one wishes to see bad qualities glossed over in a biography, but deliberately to refuse any compensating good ones is to taint oneself with injustice and even worse. Mr Sadleir never minimised Anthony Trollope's 'tempestuousness', in fact he wrote about it fully, but he showed the man's sterling qualities, his honesty and integrity with deep and sympathetic insight. Others have denied him these. Not only did my grandfather buy his old friend's library (at a just price) because he feared his widow was in financial difficulties; there were probably other kindnesses beyond talking or sending chicken and grapes to someone ill, of which few knew.[4] When I left my old home here some years ago, I gave away three quite good still-life pictures, painted by a young German artist in London. Someone told my grandfather the young fellow had fallen on evil days. He promptly sought him out and paid him £50 for the pictures.

My grandfather may have been somewhat irritable occasionally: my father told me as much. That was partly the result of
heredity and of his early years. Later on, the hard relentless life he
led must have made itself felt. He must have nearly worn himself
out unknowingly, and he may have had a 'tired heart' for years.
Few can work as he did, rising at 5.30, writing regularly so many
hours a day (he said three hours should be the most a man should
set himself to write), hunting three days a week in the country and
later on from London, and leading the busy social life he did,
without affecting their health. He went out enormously and
entertained in his own house. I used to think he must have had a
physique of iron, but now, knowing how overwork and strain can
affect a heart (and consequently a temper!) – and his doctor told
him of angina – I understand my grandfather much better.

He was a good judge of wine, especially of claret. He laid down
twenty-four dozen Leoville and told my Father they would be
ready for use in a few years' time and that he was to consider them
as his own at his death, adding: 'You will pardon the intrusion if I
take a few bottles for my own use.'[5]

All his letters to his wife and son are studiously polite and
affectionate. Likewise, in *What I Remember*, Uncle Tom stated that
the tenderest friendship existed between his mother and her son
Anthony.

As a proof that Anthony Trollope could be genial in trying heat
is the fact that he made a lifelong friend somewhere in the West
Indies – if I am not mistaken. He had to see a British official on
business, and on seeking admission he heard the words: 'Oh, tell
Mr Trollope to go to the devil. It's much too hot to see anyone!'

William Follett Synge was the man.[6] Instead of taking
umbrage, my grandfather and Mr Synge became fast friends. It
was a friendship of sixty years between the two families. Mr
Synge's boys spent their holidays at Waltham House. My
grandfather was greatly amused when the eldest son, Bob, offered
a banana at dinner, refused it with the remark, 'At school that's
the cheapest grub we can buy!'. ...

My grandparents made several trips abroad to Italy, France
and Switzerland. My grandmother told me she had been four
times over the St Gotthard: by diligence, by sleigh, by train and on
foot. Abroad she could be a tireless walker, though my
grandfather observed that in London she could not walk a mile!
Uncle Tom thought nothing of hurrying off to London at short

notice. On one occasion his luggage consisted solely of a toothbrush! (*Se non e vero almen e ben trovato!*) On my grandfather's return from Australia in 1871 a full-page cartoon showed Mr Punch bidding 'Mr Trollope, welcome Home.'[7]

As to Anthony Trollope's *Autobiography*, a working-man who had requested that I should lend it to him, returned it with the words: 'Every young man should read it! Your grandfather always made the best of everything.' Sir Hugh Walpole deemed it 'one of the most honest, sincere and noble-minded books in the English language'.

Those of you who enjoyed Mr Sadleir's *Commentary* will remember his speaking of a friend of my grandfather's, the Revd W. Lucas Collins. I should like to quote from a letter of his to my father:

> I have read through my dear old friend's record with a very painful interest. Every word reveals to me the man himself – his warm heart, sterling honesty, abhorrence of meanness and injustice. Even his prejudices (which he had) I can regard with affection.

The Blackwoods were likewise devoted to him. '*You* can have no idea', said John Blackwood's daughter, Mrs Gerald Blackwood Porter, to me as late as 1926, 'of the hold your grandfather had on those who knew him. To know him was to love him. My dear Muriel, he was such a very thorough gentleman.'

'Your grandfather's character is depicted in every line he wrote', has been written and said to me on more than one occasion. ...

NOTES

1. Sadleir's *Trollope: A Commentary* (1927) is still much respected by Trollopians; Hugh Walpole's *Anthony Trollope* (1928) is impressionistic and unreliable.

2. Muriel Trollope's own note records that two Irish servants remained with them over thirty years. 'Barney Fitzpatrick the groom, put my father and uncle on a horse before they could walk, and he ended by taking my grandfather's hunters from London to the country three days a week. Though he could neither read nor write, he was never a penny out in his accounts. When my Father's Irish mare, "Miss Vesey", was prancing on her hind legs in the stable yard, Barney

would say, "Shure, Master Harry, she's as quiet as lamb"' ('What I Was Told', p. 230).

3. Trollope wrote to the Master and Wardens of the Grocers' Company on 20 Nov 1875, expressing his very high sense of the honour (*Letters*, II, 870). The resolution, at a meeting on 15 Dec, recognised 'the great pleasure afforded to many thousands in their hours of relaxation by his admirable works of fiction; and of the valuable information imparted in the accounts of his travels'. Lord Cockburn (similarly honoured) and Trollope attended a Special Court on 12 Jan 1876 when they were made Freemen (MSS Guildhall Library, cited *Letters*, II, 870n). I have found no reference to Trollope becoming a Freemason.

4. The friend was Robert Bell (1800–67), journalist, contributor to the *Cornhill*; recruited Trollope to the Royal Literary Fund, 1861; proposed Trollope for membership of Garrick Club, Apr 1862 (Thackeray seconded). When Chapman & Hall were considering launching a new periodical under Trollope's editorship, Bell was in line for a job in Sep 1863 (*Letters*, I, 230–1) but the idea came to nothing. Trollope organised the Literary Fund's memorial for his widow and it was his library that Trollope purchased.

5. This was in Jan 1882. The Leoville had cost him 72 shillings a dozen; a similar number of Beycheville had cost 54 shillings: 'It is 1874 wine and will not be fit for use until 1884 at the earliest' (*Letters*, II, 938).

6. Synge was appointed secretary to Sir William Gore Ouseley's mission to Central America. Trollope ran across him at San José, Costa Rica, and describes the meeting in *The West Indies and Spanish Main* (p. 275). For more on Synge see p. 70 above.

7. I have been unable to trace such a cartoon.

Suggestions for Further Reading

Several helpful articles are referred to in the text. Readers may also be interested in the following selected list of books.

Indispensable guides to Trollope and his work are Michael Sadleir, *Trollope: A Commentary* (1927, rev. edn 1945) and *Trollope: A Bibliography* (1928, rep. 1964); *The Letters of Anthony Trollope*, ed. N. John Hall with the assistance of Nina Burgis, 2 vols (Stanford, 1983); surveys of criticism in *Anthony Trollope: The Critical Heritage*, ed. Donald Smalley (1969) and by Ruth ap Roberts in *Victorian Fiction: A Second Guide to Research*, ed. George H. Ford (New York, 1978) pp. 143–71, in which she notes that the challenge is still 'to define the very qualities of the man, both as writer and personality' (p. 143); J. C. Olmsted and J. E. Welch, *The Reputation of Trollope: An Annotated Bibliography, 1925–75* (New York, 1978). Also helpful are David Skilton, *Anthony Trollope and His Contemporaries: A Study in the Theory and Conventions of Mid-Victorian Fiction* (1972); J. A. Sutherland, *Victorian Novelists and Publishers* (Chicago, 1976); J. Hillis Miller, *The Form of Victorian Fiction: Thackeray, Dickens, Trollope, George Eliot, Meredith and Hardy* (Indiana, 1968).

The burgeoning of studies over the past twenty years culminating in the centenary of 1982 has produced many valuable works of which only a selection may be offered here. They include: A. O. J. Cockshut, *Anthony Trollope: A Critical Study* (1955); Robert Polhemus, *The Changing World of Anthony Trollope* (Berkeley, Cal., 1968); Gordon N. Ray, 'Trollope at Full Length', *Huntington Library Quarterly*, 31 (1968) 313–40; Ruth ap Roberts, *Trollope: Artist and Moralist* (1971), publ. in US as *The Moral Trollope* (Athens, Ohio, 1971); John W. Clark, *The Language and Style of Anthony Trollope* (1975); P. D. Edwards, *Anthony Trollope: His Art and Scope* (Queensland, 1977); John Halperin, *Trollope and Politics: A Study of the Pallisers and Others* (1977); James R. Kincaid, *The Novels of Anthony Trollope* (Oxford, 1977); R. C. Terry, *Anthony*

Trollope: The Artist in Hiding (1977); Arthur Pollard, *Anthony Trollope* (1978); Robert Tracy, *Trollope's Later Novels* (Berkeley, Cal., 1978); *Anthony Trollope*, ed. Tony Bareham (1980); Geoffrey Harvey, *The Art of Anthony Trollope* (1980); Walter M. Kendrick, *The Novel-Machine: The Theory and Fiction of Anthony Trollope* (Baltimore, Md., 1980); Coral Lansbury, *The Reasonable Man, Trollope's Legal Finction* (Princeton, NJ., 1981); *The Trollope Critics*, ed. N. John Hall (1981); *Trollope Centenary Essays*, ed. John Halperin (1982); W. J. Overton, *The Unofficial Trollope* (Brighton, 1982); Andrew Wright, *Anthony Trollope: Dream and Art* (1983).

Index

Characters